HARD LESSONS

Hard Lessons

Reflections on Governance and Crime Control in Late Modernity

Edited by

RICHARD HIL and GORDON TAIT

ASHGATE

Published by
Ashgate Publishing Limited
Gower House
Croft Road
Aldershot
Hants GU11 3HR
England

Ashgate Publishing Company
Suite 420
101 Cherry Street
Burlington, VT 05401-4405
USA

Ashgate website: http://www.ashgate.com

British Library Cataloguing in Publication Data
Hard lessons : reflections on governance and crime control
   in late modernity. - (Advances in criminology)
   1. Corrections - Evaluation 2. Criminology 3. Criminal
   justice, Administration of 4. Crime prevention
   I. Hil, Richard II. Tait, Gordon
   364.6

Library of Congress Cataloging-in-Publication Data
Hard lessons : reflections on governance and crime control in late modernity / edited by
   Richard Hil and Gordon Tait.
      p. cm. -- (Advances in criminology)
   Includes bibliographical references.
   ISBN 0-7546-2216-9
      1. Crime prevention. 2. Criminal justice, Administration of. 3. Social control. 4.
   Criminal behaviour--Prevention. I. Hil, Richard, 1953- II. Tait, Gordon, 1960- III. Series.

   HV7431.H376 2004
   364.4--dc21
                                                                                    2003052122

   ISBN 0 7546 2216 9

Printed and bound by Athenaeum Press, Ltd.,
Gateshead, Tyne & Wear.

Contents

List of Contributors

Judith Bessant is a Reader at the Australian Catholic University in Melbourne. Her areas of research and teaching include Sociology, Social Theory, Youth Studies and Social Policy.

Belinda Carpenter is a Senior Lecturer in the School of Justice Studies, Faculty of Law, Queensland University of Technology, Brisbane. She lectures in Criminology, and Criminal and Social Justice, and researches in the areas of Prostitution, Domestic Violence and Higher Education.

Associate Professor *Chris Cunneen* teaches in Criminology at the University of Sydney Law School. He is also the Director of the Institute of Criminology at the University of Sydney. He has published a number of books, including *Conflict, Politics and Crime* (2001), *Indigenous People and Law in Australia*, which is co-authored with Terry Libesman (1995), *Juvenile Justice: an Australian Perspective*, co-authored with Rob White (1995) and edited, with David Fraser and Stephen Tomsen, *Faces of Hate: Hate Crime in Australia* (1997).

Richard Hil is Senior Lecturer in Human Services at the Southern Cross University's Coffs Harbour campus, in northern New South Wales. Richard has published in areas of Youth Justice, Child and Family Welfare and Criminology. His current research interests include an empirical study of the application and use of the concept of 'risk' in youth justice and a study of institutional abuses of children and young people in Queensland.

Barbara Ann Hocking is Assistant Dean of Research at the Queensland University of Technology, Faculty of Law, Brisbane.

Murray Lee is a Lecturer in Criminology at the University of Western Sydney where he teaches in Criminological Theory and Drugs and Criminalisation. He has published a number of articles on the 'fear of crime' and 'law and order' politics and has co-produced a documentary video – 'Crime, Rurality and Politics'.

Associate Professor *Hamish McCallum* is with the Department of Zoology and Entomology at The University of Queensland, Brisbane. His research interests are in the applications of mathematics and statistics to biological problems. He has taught biostatistics and ecology at The University of Queensland since 1985.

Anthony McMahon is Head of the School of Social Work and Community Welfare, James Cook University, Townsville, Queensland, Australia. He has published books and articles on child welfare, youth justice and social welfare history. His current research is on wellbeing indicators for indigenous children in care.

Greg Newbold is Senior Lecturer in Sociology at the University of Canterbury, Christchurch, New Zealand. A former prison inmate who served a seven and a half year sentence for selling drugs in the 1970s, Greg has written six books in the fields of Crime, Criminal Justice and Social History. He is well known locally as a social commentator, has published numerous articles in both academic and public media and is often consulted by New Zealand government agencies in relation to crime control policy.

John Pitts is Professor and Director of the University of Luton's Vauxhall centre for the Study of Crime. He has published extensively in the areas of criminology, youth justice, and child abuse and neglect.

Gordon Tait is a Senior Lecturer in the School of Cultural and Language Studies in Education at the Queensland University of Technology, Kelvin Grove campus, Brisbane. His research interests include Youth, Sexuality, Criminal Justice and Education … and Humour.

Introduction

The title of this book, *Hard Lessons: Reflections on Governance and Crime Control in Late Modernity*, contains a number of clues about its general theoretical direction. It is a book concerned, first and foremost, with the vagaries of crime control in western neo-liberal, English speaking countries. More specifically, *Hard Lessons* draws attention to a number of examples in which discrete populations – those who have in one way or another offended against the criminal law – have become the subjects of various forms of state intervention, regulation, surveillance and control. We are concerned most of all with the ways in which recent criminal justice policies and practices have resulted in what are variously described as unintended consequences, unforeseen outcomes, unanticipated results, counter-productive effects or negative side-effects. At their simplest, such terms refer to the apparent gulf between intention and outcome. Evidence of policy-practice disjuncture of this sort often form the basis of policy reappraisal, soul searching and even nihilistic despair among the mandarins of crime control.

Unintended consequences can, of course, be both positive and negative. Occasionally, crime control measures may result in beneficial outcomes, such as the use of DNA to acquit wrongly convicted prisoners. Generally, however, unforeseen effects tend to be negative and even entirely counterproductive, and/or directly opposite to what may have been originally intended. All this, of course, presupposes some sort of rational, well meaning and transparent policymaking process so beloved by liberal social policy theorists. Yet, as Judith Bessant points out in her chapter, this view of policy formulation tends to obscure the often covert, regulatory and downright malevolent intentions contained in many government policies and practices. Indeed, history is replete with examples of governments seeking to mask their real aims and intentions from a prying public eye. Denials, cover-ups, obfuscationism and the use of various sorts of 'techniques of neutralisation' serve to conceal the real or 'underlying' aims of the powerful (Cohen 2000). The latest crop of 'spin doctors' and 'official spokespersons' have helped to ensure that the process of governmental obfuscation, distortion and concealment remains deeply embedded in neo-liberal forms of governance.

There is little that is new or surprising in this; nor should we be shocked when things 'go wrong' in the domain of crime control since many unintended consequences are, more often than not, quite predictable. Prison riots, high rates of recidivism and breaches of supervision orders, expansion rather than contraction of control systems, laws that create the opposite of what was intended – all these are normative features of western crime control. Indeed, without the deep fault lines running between policy and outcome it would be hard to imagine what many policy makers, administrators and practitioners would do: their day-to-day work practices (and incomes) are directly dependent upon emergent 'negative outcome' and 'service delivery' problems. Despite recurrent howls of official anguish and occasional despondency it is apparent that those inVolved in the propping up the apparatus of crime control have a vested interest in ensuring that polices and practices remain in an enduring state of review and reform.

The sad story of unintended consequences has been well and truly raked over in Cohen's rightly celebrated study, *Visions of Social Control* (1985). Additionally, there now exists a significant body of literature that deals in considerable analytical depth with contradictory and self-sustaining processes of government in western societies. Following Foucault (1977), this body of work has concerned itself with the intricate and over-arching processes of state control and self-regulation that constitute the foundations of governmental power in western systems of crime control. These studies are less interested in how 'effective' a particular measure, strategy, system or scheme might be than with the discourses, justifications and legitimations that underpin particular regimes of regulation and control. The examples we cite in this book – prostitution laws in Australia, parental restitution, drug laws in New Zealand, the emergence of genetic technologies, boot camps, fear of crime campaigns, youth justice policies in the UK – all tell a familiar tale of good intentions turning sour, of policies going wrong, of unexpected/unanticipated/negative costs, results, outcomes and research findings.

This is a tale accompanied by a litany of responses used to guide the next phase of policy implementation, or indeed, of the abandonment of policy altogether. In his summation of governmental responses to the discovery of serious (and occasionally terminal) policy-outcome disjuncture – in this case the much vaunted shift from exclusionary institutional control to an supposedly more benign and inclusive form of 'community control' – Cohen notes that the rapid process of disillusionment (presaged by news of ineffective outcomes, repressive local practices, punitive regimes and the emergence of a culture of surveillance) led to three dominant responses:

1. *evangelical*, in which we are told that this or that project has achieved a breakthrough in reducing recidivism, in involving the community or whatever (and that further research is needed to confirm this result);
2. *fudgy*, in which under the heading of evaluation words such as process, control group, feedback, flowchart, objectives goals, inputs, and system are arranged in random order (and more research is called for);
3. *nihilistic*, in which it is shown that nothing, after all, works, everything costs the same (and more research is probably needed) (Cohen 1985:7).

The policy loop of hope, good intentions, despair, disillusionment and then hope and good intentions again is integral to the history of penal 'reform' movements over the past two centuries or so. Typically, such on-going angst has been underpinned by a steadfast belief in the modernist imperative of 'progress' through which, it was believed, new systems and practices could be converted into permanent and axiomatic pillars of regulation and control. Unfortunately, as we know all too well, the development of systems of crime control in particular has been characterised by a seemingly endless process of fluidity, revision and reform. New initiatives soon become discredited or outmoded, old ideas are reintegrated back into systemic practices, and of course, the search for alternatives continues unabated, as does the process of evaluative research and policy deliberation. While some aspects of contemporary crime control are certainly preferable to the brutalisations of previous eras, other aspects are recycled form earlier times and moulded into the latest fashion statement (Young 1999). Indeed, the path of criminal justice policy has never been smooth or based on a trajectory of enlightened and upwardly spiralling progress. The realities of government in western countries are too complex for that. As Paul Rock (1995: 16) points out: '(Criminal justice policy) would be an otherwise smooth metamorphosis was it not for the sudden lurches and opportunities imposed by uncontrollable problems of timing and context'.

We have chosen in this book to focus on some of these lurches and opportunities to illustrate once again the familiar story of things going wrong in the domain of criminal justice. But more than this, we consider why it is that the particular style, trajectory and pace of change takes the form it does. Indeed, it would be futile in the extreme to merely record yet another round of unintended consequences without attempting to explain this in some sort of coherent and theoretically meaningful way. It is in this regard that we draw from Foucault's notion of governmentality as a means of explaining the strategies, discourses, technologies and myriad justifications and legitmations that underpin the exercise of power in neo-liberal democratic states. The concept of power (allied to the process of knowledge construction) is central to our understanding of why criminal justice policies take the shape they do. As noted by Stephen Box (1983:211):

> Power as a central instrument of regulation and control of one agency over another is demonstrated graphically in the arena of western crime control, not simply in the imposition of discredited, outmoded and absolutely counterproductive measures, but also, and most significantly, in the ability to impose measures in the face of informed opinion.

The latter is particularly evident in a range of penal measures adopted in western countries over recent years. Despite claims to the contrary (Farrington 2000) the general reluctance of governments to listen to 'informed opinion', or to listen only to certain sorts of opinion, is a feature of contemporary criminal justice policy formulation (Pratt 2000). The emergence of what has been called the 'new punitiveness' (Simon and Feeley) in the context of the 'new regulatory state' (Braithwaite 2000), with its emphasis on 'tough' law and order measures and underpinned by a new strain of moral individualism, certainly flies in the face of not only academic opinion but also the views of those charged with administering crime control on a day-to-day basis. Part of the reason for this seemingly bizarre situation is what might be termed the 'culture of appearance' brought about through the self-referenced pursuit of political legitimacy

(Pitts 1998). Quite simply, there are votes in being 'tough on crime'. Thus it is hardly surprising that faced with what appears to be a culture of 'high crime' (Garland 1996), western governments have sought to impose all manner of punitive measures ranging from longer sentences, mandatory ('three strikes') penalty, parental restitution, 'zero tolerance', curfews and punitive by-laws and so forth (Hogg and Brown 1998; Garland 2000; Hurst 2000). Such measures are of course predicated upon the idea that criminal justice measures can in themselves tackle the 'problem of crime'. Leaving aside the tremendous difficulties and perverse actuarial logic associated with any conception of a 'crime problem' (Young 1996), the use of crime control measures to tackle this problem appeals mainly to those political parties who wish to placate a 'public opinion'. As Rutherford (1996: 11) points out: 'Policy simply as an instrument to combat crime has immediate appeal, and it has become especially seductive in recent times because of its populist simplicity'. In a similar vein the former (and highly disgruntled) US Deputy Attorney General, Phillip Hayman (cited in Rutherford 1996: 11) remarked in his resignation speech that:

> ... it has been too easy to pretend that we're going to solve the problem of crime with a set of measures that look good for about the first fifteen seconds and look worse as you get to the half minute... The problem here is that the whole area is so much a matter of political debate that there is no room for reasoned debate.

Garland (2000) points out that the politicisation of crime is a relatively recent phenomenon and that its presence in the process of policy formulation has led to all manner of ill-judged measures. Yet while the pursuit of political legitimacy has proven a powerful force in shaping criminal justice policies, especially in the post war era, it would be misleading to see this as the primary influence on such matters. In our view it is important to see the development of criminal justice policies as reflective of local, regional and national issues and imperatives, and as integral to the management and control of certain so-called 'problem populations'. Two points need to be made in this regard: first, crime control policies and practises need to be seen alongside other 'devolutionary' and 'responsibilised' initiatives that have occurred across a range of policy arenas. This is important insofar as it signals a move away from centralised state control to various sites in the 'social body' (see

Jordan 2000; Garland 2001; Crawford 1999. Although for a critique of this position, see Stenson and Sullivan 2001).

Criminal justice polices of the sort analysed in this book belong largely to that area of governmental power characterised by the targeted implementation of particular measures in relation to specific populations. These populations are, each in their own way, regarded as a threat to normative social order. Rendered as 'the other' they are either subject to inclusionary strategies aimed at 'reintegrating' them back into the 'community' or excluded on permanent or semi-permanent basis from the rest of the 'law abiding' population.

Secondly, offending behaviour is once again explained under a revitalised form of moral individualism, in which aberrant and 'anti social' behaviours are seen in terms of personal failure and 'social suicide' (Bauman 2000: 25). Against this background, the usual suspects – the urban and rural poor, the disadvantaged, marginalized and disaffected – find themselves enmeshed further in the control apparatus of the state and subject to longer, harsher and more extensive penalties (Hudson 1996). The 'progressive minimalism' (Currie 1986) of the 1970s has thus been replaced gradually by new regimes, systems and technologies aimed at operationalising a reinvigorated penal ethos of 'toughness'. 'Risk' and a pervasive sense of 'ontological insecurity' shape the terrain upon which punitive penal measures have been formulated (Young 1999). What in the post war era was seen as the fruitful hopes of a new world order have now been replaced by cultures of fear, insecurity, risk and danger (Lupton 1999). Crime, like other domains of the market economy, becomes a commodifed and actuarial feature of everyday life, requiring continuous surveillance and state/private-corporate intervention and control (Taylor 1999). In this context the governmental task is to preside over the implementation of crime control measures that appear 'tough on crime' and, to a lesser degree, its 'causes' – the latter is often given short shrift since it would inevitably raise the awkward spectre of institutional change (Downes and Morgan 1997).

The emergence over recent years of a culture of 'new punitiveness' in western countries must be seen in the context of a range of transformations linked to what has been called 'late modernity'; hence the inclusion of the latter term in the title of this book. Although we have some doubts over its temporal optimism ('late' seems to suggest some imminent process of transformation), 'late modernity' is taken to refer to a wide range of changes linked to the most recent phase of social, economic, political and cultural organisation under the umbrella of corporatised market capitalism (Giddens 1998). Specific changes in this era are said to include transformations to the 'dynamics of capitalist production and exchange', 'secular' age and gender alterations in the organisation and structure of family life; social ecological and demographic changes brought about through technologically-driven, time-space compression; the 'democratisation' of social and cultural life through the 'desubordination' of social groups and shifts in state and civil power and authority relations (Garland and Sparks 2001: 15). It is in the context of such transformations that contemporary crime control needs to be understood. Particularly important are the changes occurring as a result of 'globalisation' and its consequences upon government in neo-liberal democratic states, and the changing relationship between state and civil society. Such changes are complex, often confused and ambiguous. Given the deepening divides brought about by 'turbo capitalism' and particularly the emergence of growing numbers of poor people and other groups of the 'new marginalised' (Taylor 1999), governments find themselves confronted with the presence of what are euphemistically referred to as 'excluded' populations.

In Australia – often referred to quaintly (and misleadingly) as the 'Lucky Country' – this problem has led to a number of governmental policy shifts in which 'welfare to work' programmes, 'mutual obligation' and more monitoring and surveillance of 'dole bludgers' has ushered in a new era of punitive regulation of the poor and marginalised. At the same time State and Territory governments have introduced a range of tough law and order measures similar to those of many other western countries (Hogg and Brown 1998). Such changes are reflective to a significant degree of the transformations occurring across various domains of contemporary 'western' government (Jordan 2000). The emergence of new and recycled modalities of discipline, regulation and punishment signal the application of forms of governmental power aimed at the control of certain problem populations. Discourses of 'risk management' and cultures of deVolutionary self-regulation have contributed to contemporary expressions of crime control aimed at the more intense management and control of troublesome and irksome social groups (Rose 2000).

Yet while the actuarial vision of crime has given rise to a complex range of strategies, practices and techniques that befit the contemporary era, it is likely that new stories of unfulfilled promises and enlightened hope will emerge. Indeed, the litany of hard lessons in crime control remains both the point of despair as well as the driving force of changes that arise in any given era. Influenced by political ideologies, populist sentiment and economic considerations, cultures of crime control remain ever vulnerable to recycled wisdoms, effervescent hope and crass expediency. The fact is that the hard lessons of crime control in western countries are an integral and endemic feature of all those systems, practices and technologies designed to regulate and control the behaviours of certain problem populations. The next cluster of changes (and the next round of disappointments) will occur in a context governed increasingly by the divisive nature of capitalist globalisation. Yet, the more things change, the more they remain the same especially since those who find themselves ensnared in systems of crime control will undoubtedly be the usual suspects: those from the 'lower' ranks of the socio-economic (dis)order.

However, just as we appear to have confidently and safely described the main features of contemporary western crime control as 'punitive' and 'tough' so we learn that policies are once again undergoing a process of doubt, review and change. Worried by the cost of imprisonment (currently amounting to about $30 billion per annum in the United States) and by the operational problems and differential excesses of 'zero tolerance', mandatory sentencing and 'three strikes' measures, US state governments are now embarking upon a process of 'creeping liberalisation' with a return to talk of diversion, community alternatives and treatment. Execution rates have also dropped with even Texas (the state once presided over by the governor, George W. Bush) now experiencing a significant downturn. Once ultra-punitive states like Louisiana are beginning to review their sentencing practices with calls to do away with mandatory penalties (perhaps the major factor contributing to escalating prison numbers). As noted in British broadsheet, "The Observer": 'A 20-year trend towards ever-tougher sentences is apparently in reverse. There is evidence the states with the toughest penal policies have been no more successful in fighting crime than those with more humane regimes' (Beaumont 2000).

While it is likely that the new wave of liberalisation in the United States will result in the recycling of old ideas, and the creation of new or reworked approaches, it is possible (given the recent history of crime control) to foreshadow yet more changes aimed at displacing the latest round of reform. Perhaps the real question here is not whether systems change but rather how and, more importantly, why? To answer these questions we need to take our analysis well beyond the narrow confines of crime control to other areas of government upon which the process of endless reform is contingent. That said, this book will restrict its attention to a number of different sites of governmental intervention and regulation, as pertaining to the control of crime.

In Chapter One, *Modernity and the 'Failure' of Crime Control*, Gordon Tait seeks to chart some aspects of the conceptual terrain of late modernity – the theoretical foundation upon which the ensuing case studies are built. Rather than understanding the recurrent failure of various attempts at crime control as unfortunate and undesirable aberrations, all too familiar glitches in an otherwise uninterrupted teleological march to a better society, such failures are instead positioned as part of the fabric of late modernity itself. That is, society changes not according to a predetermined logic along neatly defined and clearly reasoned tracks, rather it hurtles from crisis to crisis, from failure to failure, and it is the regulation of that failure which produces new initiatives and new forms of governance. Utilising the example of the modern prison, Tait contends that too great an emphasis upon this institution's 'failure' results not only in a neglect of the many other functions that it serves in the regulation of difference, but also, and more generally, it results in an underestimation of the importance of failure in providing new impetus for social transformation.

In Chapter Two, *Governing 'Fear of Crime'*, Murray Lee applies elements of this logic to investigate the social and governmental consequences of the fear of crime within 'the community'. At first glance, it might appear as if the level of concern and apprehension help by the general population about criminal conduct would correlate directly with the degree to which the government fails to provide protection from its more unruly elements. However, Lee argues that the situation is considerably more complex, and that 'fear of crime' can equally well be understood as an effective and versatile tactic of social regulation. This tactic works in a number of ways; it promotes a particular kind of governance, governance-through-fear, which operates by more actively recruiting citizens into practices of crime prevention; it provides the engine for neo-liberal arguments about the increasing importance of private policing; and it acts as a locus for a variety of discourses and expertise, from the political to the criminological, all of which relate, in one way or another, to the governance of the social body.

Simple explanations of complex problems are also the target of Greg Newbold's chapter: *The Control of Drugs in New Zealand*. In terms of issues within criminal justice, few have as high a profile as the 'drug problem', and few failures have been as spectacular or as widely commented-upon as that associated with 'the war on drugs'. Prohibition has, to date, failed to achieve its aim of stamping out the flow of illegal narcotics into the community, not only in New Zealand, but also the evidence would suggest, in all western industrial countries. Indeed, far from solving the problem, it would appear as if, at best, it has had little or no effect on patterns of drug use, and at worst, it has spawned a range of problems of its own, such as an exploding prison population, the fostering of organised crime, and in some countries, endemic official corruption.

Chapter Four, *Korrectional Karaoke: New Labour and the Zombification of Youth Justice*, by John Pitts, addresses British initiatives into the 'youth crime problem'. In terms of critical analysis, Pitts rightly notes that it is not necessarily helpful or enlightening to record the 'success' or 'failure' of any given program – some may have 'worked', to some degree, with some population cohorts (as have some of the programs they replaced!). Rather, it is to note that there has been a significant contraction in the operation of youth justice and a corresponding quantum shift in direction in criminal justice policy over recent years. A largely conservative and populist 'correctionalist' agenda on criminal justice on the part of the New Labour government has had the counter-productive effect of drastically increasing incarceration rates, largely by reducing the number of possible alternatives for dealing with young offenders. That is, by decreasing the complexity of possible responses to what is arguably an incredibly difficult, multi-layered and persistent set of social problems, far from making the situation better, and in spite of overwhelming evidence of deleterious social and personal costs, young people are finding themselves behind bars in record numbers.

In Chapter Five, *Expect the Unexpected: DNA, Guilt, and Innocence*, by Barbara Ann Hocking and Hamish McCallum, a new element in the State's arsenal against crime is examined and assessed. DNA testing has long been touted as the ultimate modernist solution to the crime, providing incontrovertible, hard-scientific proof of the guilt of transgressors. Whenever circumstances would allow, and in particular in the severest of cases with blood and assorted bodily fluids involved, the outcome of the case would no longer come down to dodgy eye-witnesses, circumstantial evidence, or a contest between the relative skills of the opposing barristers. Rather, the facts would speak for themselves, and the guilty would not be able to wheedle their way off the hook. However, the unforeseen flip-side of this new technique of investigation involves not the filling of gaols with the guilty, but the emptying of gaols of the innocent. This is a significant problem in itself, given that the judicial system is not renowned for admitting its mistakes, and neither is the general public likely to be too happy that a potentially large number of unpunished criminals are still at large. Still, as the authors note, the implications of DNA technology, both for guilt and innocence, still have to work their way through the system.

Chapter Six, *Parental Restitution: Soft Target for Rough Justice*, by Anthony McMahon examines a relatively new tactic within the state's overall vocabulary of approaches to crime control. In addition to the familiar set of policies that police and punish the conduct of young people, a number of countries are now beginning to hold parents responsible for the conduct of their children. Capitalising upon moral panics concerning the 'wilful neglect' of some parents, neglect deemed to result directly in the criminal behaviour of their children, countries such as Australia, Britain and the United States are now punishing parents for their wayward offspring. The evidence suggests that far from deterring criminal behaviour among young people, this kind of individuating approach is likely to have no effect on crime rates at all, or even make the situation worse. That is, given the socio-economic strata that the majority of juvenile offenders are drawn from, punishing already impoverished parents could result in anything from increased youth homelessness to catapulting entire families into further poverty.

Richard Hil *In Pursuit of the Responsibilised Self: Boot Camps, Crime and Punishment*, examines a recurrent call to 'get tough' on young offenders. This has taken a number of forms, but the focus here falls upon a set of approaches which all have the same underpinning logic: the subjection of young people to the 'short, sharp shock' of a period of severe and intense carceral discipline. As in the preceding chapter, the emphasis here is upon an individuating, moralising approach to crime control that seeks to locate social problems within given individuals, as opposed to any notion that effects of wider forces and structural issue might be at play.

'Boot Camps', and their various equivalents, aim to regulate the conduct of young people by introducing them to traditional values and forms of conduct most frequently associated with military life; that is, those of discipline, obedience, marching, early mornings and cold showers. While striking the usual populist chord of a return to the 'good old days', the stated goals of the program – crime prevention and a reduction in adult prison populations – have not materialised. Instead, the outcomes are likely to be predicable, one among others being the production of a set of brutalised young people who will eventually fit in only too well into prison life.

Chapter Eight, *The Political Resonance of Crime Control Strategies: Zero Tolerance Policing* by Chris Cunneen, addresses probably the mostly timely and visible of all contemporary strategies of crime control. Following the example of New York, a large number of cities and governments have now adopted the 'broken windows' thesis, a policing mantra arguing that the neglect of trivial issues, such as immediately replacing broken windows, inevitably results in the creation of a social atmosphere wherein more serious crimes will flourish. The most convincing evidence supposedly supporting the 'zero tolerance' position has come from New York itself, where large decreases in serious crime figures have been reported. However, Cunneen argues that all is not necessarily as it appears, in that the fall in the crime rate may well have little to do with the 'zero tolerance' policy, instead the result being broader trends within the fabric of American society. Furthermore, the practices of zero tolerance policing point to a drastic rise in police misconduct, a reduction in the acceptance of social diversity, and the shifting of crime to adjacent municipalities, rather than its genuine reduction. Thus, the unintended consequences of zero tolerance policing seem very high indeed.

Belinda Carpenter in *Good Prostitutes and Bad Prostitutes: Some Unintended Consequences of Governmental Regulation*, examines attempts to bring aspects of the sex industry, in particular prostitution, into the domain of the governable. Prostitution has long been the subject of moral concern, and its position outside the legal mainstream renders it vulnerable to any number of undesirable influences and contingencies, leaving aside debates about its innate undesirability. These concerns would include the spread of venereal disease, the intrusion of organised crime, public nuisance issues, and so on. Therefore, the decision to legalise prostitution seems, on the face of it, to be a wise, and socially innovative policy decision. However, it too brings with it unforeseen and unintended consequences. The regulation of prostitution has resulted in a two-tier system of sex workers: those who work within the law, and who are generally younger, more 'attractive' and able to gain employment within licensed brothels, and those who are older, or less attractive and hence unemployable, who remain outside the law, and who are therefore now more vulnerable than ever to both criminal control and police harassment.

Judith Bessant's chapter offers a useful corrective to the idea that the removal 'neglected' or 'at risk' children has resulted in unanticipated outcomes is perhaps a misleading interpretation of the motives of those who legitimated such actions in the first place. The proposition of 'good intentions turning sour' is an integral part of governmental discourse and an explanatory gloss that is often placed on the deleterious actions of the powerful. For, as Bessant highlights, whatever else the policies and practices of those who promoted racial hygiene strategies might have been, the reality was that they were part and parcel of 'civilizing' processes aimed at placing the interests of the 'dominant' culture to the very forefront of everyday life.

In summary, the chapters in this book are intended to provide a series of case studies supporting the contentions that not only is government in late modernity a continually failing operation, but also that various attempts to regulate the social body have generally brought with them sets of unintended, and largely unforeseeable, consequences. Using issues as diverse as boot camps, prostitution, DNA testing, and drugs, this evidence suggests that the process of regulating criminal activity is, and will remain, far more complex, contingent and arbitrary than dominant public discourses on crime control would have us believe.

Perhaps the major, on-going challenge for critical criminology (that branch of the discipline most keenly aware of the fads and foibles of crime control) is not only to identify the peculiar idiosyncrasies of government in late modernity but also to highlight the differential ways in which crime control polices and practices continue to apply to particular social groups. Despite all the recycled, new and planned measures designed to deal with the 'crime problem' the fact remains that those who end up in the human warehouses (prisons) and extended 'nets' of social control (such as 'community based' programmes), and who are regularly gazed upon in families, schools and the neighbourhood, are most often among the most powerless and vulnerable sections of society. And while the rich and powerful secure themselves in insular estates far removed from the badlands of the poor and marginalized the state continues to turn its regulatory eye upon those who are seen as troublesome, difficult and recalcitrant. It is worth noting that all the talk of crime control, prevention and reduction takes place in a narrow discursive context not all that far removed from the governmental discourses of the nineteenth century.

Thus, while crime control mandarins and liberal theoreticians may indulge in endless processes of reflexive review, rethinking and occasional despair the fact remains that new policy formulas and poling practices will be directed towards those populations that have always offended the 'respectable classes'. The divisive processes associated with globalisation (deeper and more extensive socio-economic and political divisions) and the associated reconfigurations of neo-liberal governance may well spawn new forms of crime control dedicated to the maintenance of a certain sort of 'social order'. It is likely that by the year 2025 (if not sooner) a book similar to this one will be required in order to catalogue the latest round of unintended consequences in crime control.

A Final Word

Ultimately, to say that the criminal justice system, or any other social system for that matter, produces unintended consequence is rather like saying that cars produce noise. Indeed, as David Nelken commented in relation to an earlier version of this Introduction: '… all social action has unexpected consequences. For some, sociology is defined as the study of these!'. Quite. Given this, it would be entirely unhelpful to take the view that because the criminal justice system is characterised by good intentions going wrong – indeed, that is one of *its* defining characteristics, that all initiatives in this domain are either inevitably doomed to failure, or not worth pursuing in the first place.

Clearly, as essays in this Volume on drug control policies in New Zealand and the use of DNA in Australia and elsewhere demonstrate, good outcomes can and do result from new crime control initiatives. Further, there are numerous examples of crime control measures that have produced some good and justice (Crime Prevention Consortium 1999, Gilling 1997, Homel 2000, Hughes 1998, Sutton 1996). These are surely worth retaining and developing. Indeed, many crime prevention policies may not have prevented crime but they may have brought about an improved quality of life for some people in disadvantaged communities. Situational and environmental crime prevention/reduction measures have undoubtedly made some dangerous places a lot safer, and few would deny that for all their shortcomings, family group conferences are preferable to the excessively punitive and stigmatising consequences of a court appearance.

Measures that offer alternative to crude expressions of punishment are surely better than not trying anything at all. Indeed, although the record on 'effectiveness' in western crime control is (to say the least) patchy, and despite the recurrent lurch towards punitive measures in western countries, it is also the case that there are instances where more progressive and humanitarian practices occur. At times, crime control mandarins and politicians may come to peek over the parapet of the criminal justice system and acknowledge the structural conditions and regulatory practices that contribute to crime, criminality and criminalisation. Indeed, Judges, Magistrates, Probation Officers, Correction Officers, Social Workers and others make frequent public pronouncements in this regard.

However, as noted earlier, it would be misleading to see current crime control policies and practices as heading down the roads of progress and rationality. The repeated failures, recycling of old ideas, false dawns, dashed hopes as well as the achievements, victories and goal attainments make any such assessment highly suspect. At the same time, it would be myopic in the extreme to ignore the fact that criminal justice policies and practices are shaped to a considerable extent not simply by the fads and fashions of current theory and 'best practice', but also by the political environment within which they occur. Indeed, over the past few decades, and especially since the late 1970s, developments in crime control in western countries have been linked to a range of factors, including the political articulation of how particular 'solutions', 'treatments', 'interventions' and 'cures' might be broached. Again, however, the picture in western countries is patchy, with some exhibiting (temporary and longer term) signs of progressive thought, while others appear permanently immersed in reactive conservatism.

Most systems of criminal justice are in fact a collage of reactive, progressive and pragmatic institutional practices. Rarely, however, are penal measures introduced in some sort of vacuum. Indeed, it is apparent that wider historical, social, economic and other considerations set the contexts within which debates over crime are conducted. In our view, it is not possible to make sense of crime control measures without locating them in these wider contexts, and without taking stock of how governmental practices are to some extent contingent upon them. Without consideration of these contexts there is always the danger of slipping into the assumption that the system has a few faults, but ultimately, we should all keep trying to improve it, or at least learn to live with the consequences of repeated failure.

Progressive policy makers, practitioners and others do of course take both routes. Indeed, acceptance, compromise and pragmatism may be useful techniques of survival in such situations. And at the end of the working day, when the mortgage or rent has to be paid, perhaps we can only do our best and seek (and celebrate) small victories.

References

Bauman, Z. (2000), 'The Social Use of Law and Order', in Garland, D. and Sparks, R. (eds.) *Criminology and Social Theory*, Clarendon Press: London.

Beaumont, P. (2001), 'America Loses Taste for Zero Tolerance', *The Observer*, 9 September.

Box, S. (1983) *Power, Crime and Mystification*, Routledge: London.

Braithwaite, J. (2000), 'The New Regulatory State and the Transformation of Criminology', in Garland, D. and Sparks, R. (eds.) *Criminology and Social Theory*, Clarendon Press: London.

Cohen, S. (1985), *Visions of Social Control*, Polity Press: Cambridge.

Crime Prevention Consortium (1999), *Pathways to Prevention*, Canberra: Anti-Crime Strategy.

Currie E. (1986), *Confronting Crime: An American Challenge*, Pantheon: New York.

Downes, D. and Morgan, R. (1997), 'Dumping the Hostages to Fortune? The Politics of Law and Order in Post War Britain', in Maguire, M., Morgan, R. and Reiner, R. (eds.) *The Oxford Handbook of Criminology*, Oxford University Press: Oxford.

Farrington, D. (2000), 'Explaining and Preventing Crime: The Globalisation of Knowledge', *Criminology*, Vol. 38, No. 1 February 1-24.

Foucault, M. (1977), *Discipline and Punish*, Penguin: Harmondsworth.

Garland, D. (1996), 'The Limits of the Sovereign State', *British Journal of Criminology*, Vol. 36, No. 4.

Garland, D. and Sparks, R. (2000), 'Criminology, Social Theory and the Challenge of Our Times', in Garland, D. and Sparks, R. (eds.) *Criminology and Social Theory*, Clarendon Press: London.

Gilling, D. (1997), *Crime Prevention: Theory, Policy and Politics*, London: University College of London Press.

Hogg, R. and Brown, D. (1998), *Rethinking Law and Order*, Pluto: Armadale.

Homel, R. (2000), 'Blazing the Development Path', *Youth Studies Australia*, Vol. 46, No. 1: pp. 44-52.

Hudson, B. (1996), *Understanding Justice*, Open University Press: Buckingham.

Hughes, G. (1998), *Understanding Crime Prevention: Social Control Risk and Late Modernity*, Buckingham: Open University Press.

Lupton, D. (1999), *Risk*, Routledge: London.

Pitts, J. (1988), *The Politics of Juvenile Crime*, Sage: London.

Pratt J. (2000), 'The Return of the Wheelbarrow Men: or, the Arrival of Post-modern Penalty?', in *The British Journal of Criminology*, Vol. 40, No. 1, Winter, pp. 127-45.

Rock, P. (1995), 'Opening Stages of Criminal Justice Policy', *British Journal of Criminology*, Vol. 35, No. 16.

Rutherford, A. (1996), *Transforming Criminal Justice Policy*, Waterstone Press: Winchester.

Stenson, K. and Sullivan, R. (2001) (eds.) *Crime, Risk and Justice*, Wiilan Publishing: Cullompoton.

Sutton, A. (1996), *Crime Prevention: Promise or Threat*, Australian and New Zealand Journal of Criminology.

Taylor, I. (1999), *Crime in Context: A Critical Criminology of Market Societies*, Polity Press: Cambridge.

Young, A. (1996), *Imagining Crime*, Sage: London.

Young, J. (1999), *The Exclusive Society*, Sage: London.

Chapter 1

Modernity and the 'Failure' of Crime Control

GORDON TAIT

Introduction: Modernity and Social Governance

Modernity is a very resilient creature. As Clare O'Farrell (1999) observes, since it was first pronounced dead in the 1960s, modernity has, like some operatic diva, not stopped dying since. However, irrespective of the number of texts variously eager to deny its existence (Latour, 1993), reinterpret it (Bauman, 1991), rework it (Beck, 1992), or to change it into something else altogether (Lyotard, 1984) the logic of modernity seems as strong as ever – certainly, at least, when it comes to the management of crime. For those whose memories need jogging, modernity is generally regarded as arriving around the time of the Enlightenment in the 17th century, and is most frequently characterised as an era dominated by the underpinning belief that, through the use of reason, it would be possible to solve all the problems of humanity. Not only were we now to be responsible for our own collective destinies, free finally of the religious dictates that had previously determined our fates, it would now also be possible, if we only tried long and hard enough, to construct any kind of society we wanted. Social problems, political problems, natural problems … all would eventually circum to the relentless march of reason. With its mantra of truth, objectivity and progress, modernity had arrived, the dark ages had ended, and humanity had come of age.

This was, of course, a lovely, optimistic story, and a story taken up in many different sectors of society. Probably the greatest advocate, and exemplar, of modernist thinking is science. With the exception of a few notable heretics (Popper, 1959; Feyerabend, 1975), science has long been its own best publicist, cordoning off the rights to the production of truth, and anointing itself as the vanguard of society's inexorable journey into a better future. However, science was not alone in its embrace of modernity. Social governance also came to be shaped as a modernist project. That is, through the judicious management of the conditions of existence of the population, it was now regarded as possible to endlessly improve the wellbeing of the social body in its entirety. Within this system, given social problems are to be identified, addressed and, ultimately, solved. Indeed, Nikolas Rose and Peter Miller (1992) argue that government is, first and foremost, a problematising activity. They suggest that the history of government could be written solely in terms of a history of the problematisations that it seeks to address. Thus, various sites of failure are identified, and these provide the focus for the countless programs of intervention characteristic of contemporary government: '…government reports, white papers, green papers, papers from business, trade unions, financiers, political parties, charities, academics proposing this or that scheme for dealing with this or that problem' (Miller and Rose, 1990: 4). The most important issue here is that the entire modernist governmental project is premised upon the fundamental assumption that reality is actually programmable, and that it is a domain subject to rules, norms and processes that can be acted upon and improved by authorities. However, as Rose and Miller (1992: 191) point out:

> Whilst we inhabit a world of programmes, that world is not itself programmed. We do not live in a governed world so much as a world traversed by the 'will to govern', fuelled by the constant registration of 'failure', the discrepancy between ambition and outcome, and the constant injunction to do better next time.

But surely if modernity were to have any purchase at all, there would exist evidence not only of the possibility of a viable (although not necessarily utopian) end-point, a time when the most important questions of social management had been asked and answered, but also of evidence that the social body responded in precisely the way that the social planners had envisaged. Perhaps, in order to address these issues, it would be wise to examine the work of some of modernity's more interesting critics – such as Michel Foucault, Anthony Giddens and Ulrich Beck – and see where their arguments leave our understandings of social governance, and in particular, our understandings of the dominant model of crime control, and its apparent ongoing failure.

Foucault and the Rise of Normalising Detention

In contrast to the seamless, teleological logic of modernity, Foucault makes no attempt to weave his theories into a single all-encompassing account of society. His understanding of the social world is not based upon a totalised theory, operating within an unbroken model of progress, rather his work describes societies characterised by a fragmented and discontinuous series of transformations, supported and augmented by a multiplicity of different knowledge, practices, and truths. Contrary to the position adopted by most social theorists, he suggests that power is not a coercive entity, exerting a global and homogeneous influence across all the elements of social life. Instead, power also acts in diverse ways in different locations, exercised through the practices and technologies of government. These technologies of government institute and arrange new ways of understanding and new codes of behaviour. Power does not constrain and compel, primarily it brings things into being – new practices, new identities and new forms of social management.

Foucault (1977) applies all these arguments in his most famous text, an analysis of the greatest of all modernist systems of crime control: Discipline and Punish: the Birth of the Prison. He famously begins this text with a gruesome description of the execution of Damiens, the regicide in 1757, which he then contrasts with the timetable for the running of a prison from some eighty years later. There were a number of purposes behind this juxtaposition, but the main point of interest here is how Foucault sets out the central features of three different regimes of punishment, and how one in particular – normalising detention – came to be regarded as the only appropriate and effective way of dealing with wrongdoers. By the mid-eighteenth century, the practice which had long been the centrepiece of European systems of punishment – symbolic public torture/execution in the name of the sovereign – was coming under challenge. It is at this point that teleological arguments about human progress are normally introduced: of course it was just a matter of time before the barbarity of this regime would be rejected, of course more human methods of punishment would prevail, and so on. In fact, the evidence suggests the reasons for the shift are far more complex, and are mostly based around much broader changes in the way society was to be governed. Foucault (1991) argues that until the early eighteenth century, government remained yoked to the imperatives and interests of sovereignty, and it was only when the notion of 'the population' eventually became the new raison d'etre of government, involving the emergence of governmental apparatus and the development of new techniques for amassing knowledge about the state, that alternative methods of dealing with social transgression became thinkable.

This is not to say that humanism had no role to play in the eventual demise of the model of sovereign torture. Indeed, a second paradigm of punishment was championed by a number of humanist reformers who, around the time of the French Revolution (ironically, given the form and function of the subsequent Reign of Terror), sought to reduce the possibility of the excessive and arbitrary exercise of sovereign power. Not only were punishments to be fixed, measured and transparent in their application, but also the logic behind the punishment was no longer to be the symbolic reinforcement of the power of the king. Rather, as Dreyfus and Rabinow (1982: 148) neatly summarise:

> The chief theoretical justification lay in the theory of the social contract, that society is made up of individuals who have come together and through a contractual arrangement formed a society. Crime became not an attack on the body of the sovereign but a breach of contract in which society as a whole was the victim. Society therefore had the right to redress this wrong, and punishment became the obligation of society.

The central mechanism of punishment was to be public works – road gangs, treadmill operators, field labourers – where criminals were seen to pay their dues to the community at large, both physically and symbolically, a fact Foucault (1977: 109) notes when he states that 'the convict pays twice, by the labour he provides and by the sign he produces'. In the final analysis however, this 'semio-technic' regime of punishment ultimately failed, as sovereign torture had before it, not because it fell victim to the inevitable march of reason and the humanist, trans-historical superiority of incarceration, but for an aggregation of reasons to do with the exercise of power in the wider society, as well as political and social contingencies of late eighteenth century life, such as the rise of Napoleon and the refusal of criminals to play their publicly penitent roles properly.

All aspects of this model were not to be lost to history. Some elements, such as the belief in the possibility of reforming the criminal came to constitute one of the domain assumptions of the third paradigm: normalising incarceration. As previously mentioned, it is this model of punishment that we all take so much for granted. However, as Foucault points out, imprisoning offenders is a far more complex and governmentally significant process than the simple removal of the socially undesirable from public circulation for fixed periods of time. Foucault's (1977) arguments here are now well known. He contends that architectural and organisational changes within prisons resulted in a series of new possibilities regarding the role such institutions could play in the modification of human conduct, in that it was now thought to be possible to enlist prisoners in the process of their own reformation. Intrinsic to the success of this disciplinary mechanism was to be the dual strategies of individuation and normalisation. Each prisoner was now to be allocated their own cell, each knowing their own space and, in turn, being known. Likewise, such disciplinary societies were also to be characterised by the taking charge of the time of individual existences, not simply extending to the rigorous demarcation of the working day, but also organisation of time into successive or parallel segments. Within these temporal and special frameworks, and in association with new administrative techniques such as the keeping of extensive individual records, criminals could not only have their characteristics and conduct tightly monitored, but also, in theory, they could be normalised in ways which were previously inconceivable.

What the Contemporary Prison says about Modernity

Foucault raises three important points here, all of which are relevant to traditional arguments concerning modernity. The first is that the final model outlined above does not constitute an inevitable teleological advancement in both social governance in general, or in the regulation of criminals in particular. In many ways, *Discipline and Punish* acts as an effective counterpoint to what is arguably the dominant, modernist position on prisons: that they are the logical historical endpoint of the humane punishment of wrongdoers. After all, we no longer expect punishments which inflict pain on the body, or which are carried out in public, or which permit members of the public to join in. As John Pratt (2000; 184) points out: 'Punishments targeted at the human body, no matter how meticulous the level of surgical skill that they involved, progressively faded from the legitimate array of sanctions in modernity'. Punishments are now to be carceral, out of the public gaze, and administered by trained professionals, and whether or not this shift is an example of Norbert Elias' 'civilising process', as Pratt concludes, or whether its origins lie elsewhere, one thing that does seem certain: it all could have been very different. That is, we have not ended up at this point due to the inexorable and inevitable logic that prisons are the best way of dealing with significant forms of social transgression. Rather, all the evidence suggests that the modern prison is simply an historical contingency, the product of a set of political, cultural, technical and administrative accidents and alterations that, over a period of two hundred years, resulted in the institution we now take so readily for granted as a natural part of our social landscape.

The second point is that this new form of governance had implications far beyond the boundaries of the prison. In piecemeal ways, it became the model for a number of other important social institutions. For example, schools also soon adopted this system of organisation, with it quickly becoming the norm for all classrooms. Placed within an identical special and temporal grid, and the focus of similarly extensive record-keeping, pupils can readily have their particular characteristics, skills, capacities and weaknesses identified and be immediately subjected to intervention and normalisation. This form of governance then spread out of institutions such as the prison, the school and the hospital, and once again, in a piecemeal and contingent manner, gradually came to be the dominant mechanism and rationale of governance for our entire society. To reiterate: these were largely unintended and unforeseeable outcomes that sprang from an initially unrelated set of changes occurring elsewhere in the social body.

The third point is that this paradigm of crime control now represents, at least in theory, probably the most perfect of all modernist systems. After all, here is an institution which purports to tackle arguably the most significant problem within the social body: dealing with those who break the rules. In what Hacking (1982) referred to as 'an avalanche of printed numbers', more and more statistical information was being gathered as the 19th century progressed about almost every conceivable aspect of existence, information which succeeded in fleshing out the 'inherent' characteristics, features and categories of the population. No longer was crime control to consist of a simple dichotomy between those who obeyed the law and those who did not, with transgressors facing generally the most severe and terminal of punishments. Instead, incarceration could be used as a vehicle for complex and integrated forms of social management, based largely upon various new taxonomies of crime, the various components of which could be addressed and managed in their own way, most frequently by varying lengths of time in prison. Furthermore, not only did incarceration promise the finely-graded governance of criminal conduct, it also held out the promise of the reformation of the criminals themselves – a true modernist, utopian vision. However, this wondrous dream has little to do with the reality of the form and function of contemporary prisons. As Foucault (1977: 271-2) notes:

> If the law is supposed to define offences, if the function of the penal apparatus is to reduce them and if the prison is the instrument of this repression, then failure has to be admitted. Or rather – for in order to establish it in historical terms, one must be able to measure the effects of the penalty of detention on the overall level of criminality – one should be surprised that for the past 150 years the proclamation of the failure of the prison has always been accompanied by its maintenance.

Many writers would not be the least bit surprised by the apparent failure of one of modernity's premier institutions. Foucault aside, probably the most common response to arguments about modernity is to assert that it has been eclipsed by a new form of social and intellectual (dis)order: that of post-modernity. By rejecting the grand narratives of modernism, post-modernism and its champions – most significantly Jean-Francois Lyotard (1984) and Jean Baudrillard (1993) – sought to describe a world now characterised not by truth and progress, but instead by the production of many different truths, and by the belief that history lacks the directionality, or unity, to speak of progress, when really all that can be claimed is change. The post-modern universe is one of floating signifiers and radical uncertainty, and within this conceptual framework, the logic of a singular, centralised system of crime control becomes, at very best, an anachronism, or at worst, an illusion and a pointless waste of time.

Needless to say, this position has been the subject of considerable criticism, including from within the literature on crime control. Criminologists such as Garland (1995) and Simon (1995) have tentatively pointed to the emergence of a post-modern penality, characterised by 'the disarticulation of the prison from the modernist social and institutional relations, and its re-articulation with what could be seen as post-modern relations and conditions' (O'Malley, 2000: 156). While remaining unconvinced by the possibilities of such a penality, Pat O'Malley points instead to a cluster of work premised around the notion of a 'risk society', work most frequently associated with a development in, rather than the ending of, modernity: that is, the period of late modernity.

Giddens and the Juggernaut of Late Modernity

According to Anthony Giddens (1990, 1991), it is somewhat premature to speak of the end of modernity. That is, most of the central features of modernity are still firmly in place, and apparent fragility of many of its supposed certainties – the pre-eminence of reason, the inevitability of progress, the stability of structure – are not the heralds of a new order, but simply evidence of the radicalisation of an old one. He draws the analogy of modernity being a carefully controlled and well-driven motor car, and argues that while the comfortable image of the car may have gone, it has not been replaced with random post-modern bits of a car, or even no car at all (in the sense of the Lyotardian claim that there are no longer any viable ways of sustaining knowledge claims), rather it has been replaced by a careering juggernaut, a lumbering leviathan over which we have only the most rudimentary control. So, continuing the automotive metaphor, rather than the modernist, utopian model of social governance permitting neat left-hand turns, controlled overtaking and gentle parallel parking, in reality the governance of late modernity more closely resembles a hurtling road-train, without brakes and with almost no steering. That said, ineffective, slow to respond, and often counter-productive though the steering is, Giddens (1990: 154) rightly contends that '… none of this means that we should, or that we can, give up in our attempts to steer the juggernaut. The minimising of high-consequence risks transcends all values and all exclusionary divisions of power'.

According to Giddens, late modernity has a number of specific features that mark it out from previous epochs, four of which are worthy of mention here. First, he argues that there has grown a widespread scepticism about the potential of reason to solve our problems (Giddens, 1991: 27). As one of the foundational assumptions of modernity, it was deemed to be the power and pre-eminence of reason that most clearly signalled our break from the past, a past based upon superstition and fear of the unknown, and it would be reason that charted our path to the future. It has become increasingly apparent, for example, that our scientific and technological institutions, the shibboleths of modernity, are incapable of controlling the side-effects of their advances. That is, the technical reasoning which produced industrialisation, space travel and antibiotics, also produced global pollution, intercontinental nuclear missiles and thalidomide. The same scepticism applies for the possibilities of effective social governance. Modern prisons – widely deemed the humanitarian terminus to a long and brutal history punishment, as well as the cornerstone of a complex, integrated and reformist system of crime control – are now popularly depicted as holding pens for the socially undesirable and training grounds for future professional criminals.

A second feature of late modernity is that it appears to be in a perpetual state of flux/crisis (Giddens, 1991: 184), most certainly the case when considering social management issues concerning law and order. However, the rejection of established categories is nothing new to modernity. Indeed it could be argued that modernity's underpinning teleology is based upon its ongoing rejection of old truths and its replacement with new and more convincing ones. Where late modernity breaks with this approach is that this state of epistemological flux becomes a permanent component of the social fabric, a state of affairs that dominant forms of knowledge actually contribute to. This realisation does not inexorably lead to post-modernity, rather Giddens argues that while knowledge may no longer be stable, it is possible to produce all manner of viable epistemologies that can be reflexively adapted as necessary.

This reflexivity constitutes the third significant feature of late modernity. Giddens contends that knowledge about the circumstances of the social world is employed as a fundamental element in its ongoing organisation and transformation. More specifically, 'the reflexivity of modern social life consists in the fact that social practices are constantly examined and reformed in the light of incoming information about those very practices, thus constitutively altering their character' (Giddens, 1990: 38). This reflexivity has a number of implications, not only for crime control, but also for the discipline of criminology – of which this chapter loosely constitutes a part – after all, as Giddens notes, late modernity presumes wholesale reflexivity, including reflection on the nature of reflection itself. For example:

How does reflexive modernisation affect the practice of criminology? It does so in three ways. First, criminology as a science is demystified or at least its status as an authoritative source of truth is undermined as a result of further scientisation. Second, users of criminological research have become 'co-producers' of criminological knowledge and shoppers in the supermarket of ideas and arguments. Third, new forms of law and order politics begin to emerge which defy old political categories (Chan, 2000: 126).

The final aspect of late modernity pertinent to this chapter concerns the notion of risk, and its centrality to contemporary social governance. While Giddens has a number of things to say about this topic, another proponent of the notion of late modernity, and one who wrote extensively on the notion of risk, was Ulrick Beck. Unpacking some elements of his work might be more profitable at this juncture.

Late Modernity and Risk

In his influential book, *Risk Society: Towards a New Modernity*, Beck (1992) catalogues numerous important changes that have occurred within contemporary society. The most important of these changes, he argues, is that the conflicts and social positions characteristic of a wealth-distributing society, are slowly being displaced by those of a risk-distributing society. So, whereas until recently the analytical focus fell continually upon the unequal disbursement of social resources, Beck suggests that, since the early 1970s, a new set of variables has become increasingly important – those related to the notion of a society based around risk. Although he concentrates primarily upon what he sees as the by-products of modernisation – pollution, deforestation, radio-active fallout – Beck also notes that risk now occupies a far broader and more pervasive discursive position, arguing that it has become central to the way in which we become located within the social fabric. Therefore, Beck contends, in late modernity there is the need to focus on the varying relations of risk, that is, although some risks are evenly distributed ('poverty is hierarchic, smog is democratic'), many others cluster in ways peculiar to themselves. As such, social risk positions arise wherein some people are more at-risk than others of a given outcome-such as, for example, becoming involved in crime, or being sent to prison.

Although Beck undoubtedly raises some interesting points regarding the evident currency of the concept of risk rather than adopt his meta-narrative of a totalised risk society replacing an equally totalised class society, it is possible simply to ask how and why, in late modernity, the notion of risk is deployed so extensively within contemporary forms of government, particularly those concerning crime control. Some clues as to the reasons behind its popularity are given by Robert Castel (1991) in his influential article 'From Dangerousness to Risk'. Although he writes primarily about the issue of mental medicine, his arguments are equally applicable to the problem of crime control. Castel suggests that the original justification for intervention was always around the notion of dangerousness – detecting, diagnosing, confining, and treating dangerous people. Dangerousness was thus viewed as a quality inherent to a given individual who was deemed capable of dangerous actions. However, an approach founded upon inherent dangerousness had significant problems associated with it, in that it limited any possibility of establishing and maintaining an effective policy of prevention. After all, 'One could only hope to prevent violent acts committed by those whom one had already diagnosed as dangerous', furthermore, 'harmless today, they may be dangerous tomorrow' (Castel, 1991: 284).

Castel argues that this new approach to social problems, signalled by the shift from dangerousness to risk, has two important implications for the government of populations. First, the preventative policies associated with risk are constituted in terms of factors rather than individuals. One result of this shift is that the factors themselves constitute the object of intervention, and not the concrete individual. Future dangers are now to be found, not hiding within the subject themselves, but within recognisable constellations of relevant risk factors. For example, a child/youth no longer possesses a seed of delinquency, visible to the competent expert; rather, delinquency lies within any number of statistically validated risk factors, such as poverty, abuse, homelessness, and addiction. Second, risk legitimates increased governmental intervention. Whereas more traditional forms of surveillance (such as those associated with disciplinary institutions such as the prison) require the spatial arrangement of the target population under a central, watchful, panoptic gaze, this new strategy almost entirely avoids the need for such direct scrutiny, given that the focus falls not upon a given subject but upon a set of abstract factors determined by diverse governmental information gathering techniques. Consequently,

Castel contends that the deployment of risk in this manner permits a virtually limitless augmentation of the possibilities of government, based primarily upon unlimited suspicion.

'Prevention' in effect promotes suspicion to the dignified scientific rank of a calculus of probability. To be suspected, it is no longer necessary to manifest symptoms of dangerousness or abnormality, it is enough to display whatever characteristics the specialists responsible for the definition of preventative policy have constituted as risk factors (Castel, 1991: 288).

Beck was correct in his premise that it is possible for certain social categories to be more at-risk than others. For example, various manifestations of the 'at-risk youth' now dominate the theoretical landscape across the disciplines and departments dealing with youth issues. The at-risk youth appears at the intersection of various knowledges/problematisations, within law enforcement, the labour market, youth welfare, health, education, and family management. Importantly, this final domain has become especially important, as not only is criminal conduct among the young most often explained in terms of the failed family, but also so are most other problems associated with youth – delinquency, suicide, violence, drug abuse, stealing, and so on (Tait, 1999). Indeed, governmental programs aimed at these concerns have been directed both at the problem youth itself, and in equal measure, domains such as the family (and the school). Currently, the incarceration of young offenders remains secondary to the concerted attempts made to reform potential problem youth while still within the bounds of the family. This focus on families has resulted in the formation of a new network of experts (welfare officers, guidance officers, teachers, health visitors) – a network that has attempted to align the practices and aspirations of the family to a broad range of wider governmental imperatives, while simultaneously observing the liberal dictum that demands a high level of family autonomy from state interference.

Kerry Carrington (1993: 89), in *Offending Girls*, makes some similar observations. For the vast majority of the population, parents become willing recruits in various governmental programs aimed at avoiding the production of problem youth. While families are at liberty to enjoy what Donzelot (1979: 47) refers to as supervised freedom, this liberty is premised upon the assumption that parents will meet certain basic social expectations. When parents fail in the management of their children, the family is then subject to a number of graded interventions, with care/incarceration as the final option. Carrington (1993: 90–1) argues that in her particular study of problem youth – largely dealing with aboriginal and working-class girls – the evidence suggests that the balance between successful government at a distance of the family, and direct intervention has been askew.

Conclusion: Reinterpreting the Failure of Crime Control

This kind of disagreement over precisely how and where to set governmental limits has been a recurrent feature of contemporary government, particularly in relation to the family. Furthermore, far from being a problem, Gary Wickham (1993: 9) argues that perpetual dissatisfaction with government is actually essential to its continued operation. While not decrying the many mundane achievements of contemporary government, he suggests that government is necessarily never complete, never totally successful. Indeed, if it did not continue to fail, there would be no government, as it is through the continually disappointed reassessment of governmental outcomes that more effective programs are introduced, in time only to be replaced themselves by newer and even more effective programs.

Wickham is not alone in his assessment. Rose and Miller (1992: 190) also consider government to be a congenitally failing operation. They note that the very nature of governmental programs often makes them ambiguous, contradictory, partial, and inexact, and that this heterogeneity ultimately results in the targets of government 'refusing to respond according to the programmatic logic that seeks to govern them'. Furthermore:

> Unplanned outcomes emerge from the intersection of one technology with another, or from the unexpected consequences of putting a technique to work. Contrariwise, techniques invented for one purpose may find their governmental role in another, and the unplanned conjunction of techniques and conditions arising from the very different aspirations may allow something to work without or despite its explicit rationale (Rose and Miller, 1992: 190-1).

As the various chapters in this book amply demonstrate, this appears to be particularly the case when addressing the notion of crime control. Furthermore, these arguments also dovetail neatly with the position outlined earlier regarding the reflexivity, as it is through the constant recursive assessment of the outcomes of various elements of social management – positive and negative, intended and accidental, direct and indirect – that governance operates. And such governance becomes an end in itself. That is, it is arguably the *social process* of crime control within modernity which is ultimately of the greatest significance, and not its success or failure. Foucault sums this up perfectly.

> ... the prison, and no doubt punishment in general, is not intended to eliminate offences, but rather to distinguish them, to distribute them, to use them; that it is not so much that they render docile those who are liable to transgress the law, but that they tend to assimilate the transgression of the laws in a general tactics of subjection ... the 'failure' of prison may be understood on this basis (Foucault, 1977: 272).

References

Baudrillard, J. (1993), *Symbolic Exchange and Death*, Sage: London.

Bauman, Z. (1991), *Modernity and Ambivalence*, Polity: Cambridge.

Beck, U. (1992), *Risk Society: Towards a New Modernity*, Sage: London.

Burchell, G. (1991), 'Peculiar Interests: Civil Society and Governing 'The System of Natural Liberty', in G. Burchell, C. Gordon and P. Miller (eds.), *The Foucault Effect: Studies in Governmentality*, Harvester Wheatsheaf: London.

Carrington, K. (1993), *Offending Girls: Sex, Youth and Society*, Allen and Unwin: Sydney.

Castel, R. (1991), 'From Dangerousness to Risk', in G. Burchell, C. Gordon and P. Miller (eds.), *The Foucault Effect: Studies in* Governmentality, Harvester Wheatsheaf: London.

Chan, J. (2000), 'Globalisation, Reflexivity and the Practice of Criminology', in *The Australian and New Zealand Journal of Criminology*, Vol. 33, No. 2, pp: 118-35.

Donzelot, J. (1979), *The Policing of Families*, Pantheon Books: New York.

Dreyfus, H. and Rabinow, P. (1982), *Michel Foucault: Beyond Structuralism and Hermeneutics*, Harvester: London.

Feyerabend, P. (1975), *Against Method*, Verso: Norfolk.

Foucault, M. (1977), *Discipline and Punish: The Birth of the Prison*, Penguin: Harmondsworth.

Foucault, M. (1991), 'Governmentality', in G. Burchell, C. Gordon and P. Miller (eds.), *The Foucault Effect: Studies in Governmentality*, Harvester Wheatsheaf: London.

Garland, D. (1995), 'Penal Modernism and Postmodernism', in S. Cohen and D. Blomberg (eds.) *Punishment and Social Control*, Aldine: New York.

Giddens, A. (1990), *The Consequences of Modernity*, Polity Press: Cambridge.

Giddens, A. (1991), *Modernity and Self Identity: Self and Society in the Late Modern Age*, Polity Press: Cambridge.

Gordon, C. (1991), 'Governmental Rationality: An Introduction', in G. Burchell, C. Gordon and P. Miller (eds.), *The Foucault Effect: Studies in Governmentality*, Harvester Wheatsheaf: London.

Hacking, I. (1982), 'Bio-power and the Avalanche of Printed Numbers', *Humanities in Society*, Vol. 5, pp: 279-95.

Latour, B. (1993), *We Have Never Been Modern*, Harvester Wheatsheaf: Brighton.

Lyotard, J. (1984), *The Postmodern Condition: a Report on Knowledge*, Manchester University Press: Manchester.

McCallum, D. (1993), 'Problem Children and Familial Relations', in D. Meredyth and D. Tyler (eds.), *Child and Citizen: Genealogies of Schooling and Subjectivity*, Institute for Cultural Policy Studies, Griffith University: Brisbane.

Miller, P. and Rose, N. (1990), 'Governing Economic Life', in *Economy and Society*, Vol. 19, No. 1, pp: 1-31.

O'Farrell, C. (1999), 'Post-modernism for the Uninitiated', in D. Meadmore, B. Burnett and P. O'Brien (eds.), *Understanding Education: Contexts and Agendas for the New Millennium*, Prentice: Sydney.

O'Malley, P. (2000), 'Criminologies of Catastrophe? Understanding Criminal Justice on the Edge of the New Millennium', in *The Australian and New Zealand Journal of Criminology*, Vol. 33, No. 2, pp: 153-67.

Popper, K. (1959), *The Logic of Scientific Discovery*, Hutchinson: London.

Pratt, J. (2000), 'Civilisation and Punishment', in *The Australian and New Zealand Journal of Criminology*, Vol. 33, No. 2, pp: 183-201.

Rose, N. (1993), 'Government, Authority and Expertise in Advanced Liberalism' in *Economy and Society*, Vol. 22, No. 3, pp: 283–99.

Rose, N. and Miller, P. (1992), 'Political Power Beyond the State Problematics of Government', in *British Journal of Sociology*, Vol. 43, No. 2, pp: 173–205.

Simon, J. (1995), 'They died with their boots on: the boot camp and the limits of modern penality', in *Social Justice*, Vol. 22, pp: 25-48.

Tait, G. (1999), *Youth, Sex, and Government*, Peter Lang: New York.

Wickham, G. (1993), 'Citizenship, Governance and the Consumption of Sport', Paper presented at the Australian Sociological Association Conference at Macquarie University, Sydney, December.

Chapter 2

Governing 'Fear of Crime'

MURRAY LEE

Generally speaking, researchers and policy makers alike, characterise fear as a destructive force, interfering with full participation in everyday life in civilised society. Many people for example avoid certain sections of the city or a neighbourhood, hesitating to frequent shops, theatres, pubs or sports events because they are anxious about their personal safety. Moreover, worrying about being attacked or having their homes invaded by burglars causes an exceptional amount of stress for certain groups, especially the elderly and women. These people have had crime prevention and fear reduction techniques specially designed for them (Stanko, 1990).

Introduction

Governing 'fear of crime' is big business. The business of governing 'fear of crime', and formulating attempts to govern it, have become major enterprises for criminology, related disciplines, private enterprise, and also for government and various government and non-government agencies. Research into the causes and cures of this late-modern malady has kept many researchers funded, conducting 'fear of crime surveys' and 'community safety studies'. Such matters have also fuelled much academic debate.[1] 'Fear of crime' has concerned all levels of government and has resulted in the formulation of a diverse range of programs, schemes and strategies. Moreover, private interests such as the security and insurance industries are increasingly finding that 'fear of crime' is something that can be invoked in order to sell particular risk reducing products; products aimed at either hardening possible crime targets, insuring prospective targets, policing prospective targets, or all of these. In many Australian suburbs it is impossible to purchase contents insurance without the required target hardening hardware (and increasingly software). Even real estate is sold specifically on its safety credentials.[2] Further, media organisations have increasingly discovered that the public 'fear of crime' can sell newspapers and attract viewers if it is invoked with just the right editorial zeal.

Armed with reams of crime prevention and public safety advice, literature, security devices, private police and insurance, the 'responsible' citizen should, it might be thought, be relatively free of anxiety in relation to crime. Unfortunately, it seems that this is not the case. For despite all these varied and ongoing attempts to curtail 'fear of crime' recent criminological studies suggest that the public are becoming ever more concerned about crime, or more specifically, about becoming a victim of crime or having somebody close to them become a victim of crime[3] (cf. Weatherburn *et al*, 1996; Sherman, 1995/96; Hough, 1994; Maxfield, 1985). This is also reflected in surveys undertaken by various media organizations.[4]

This chapter does not intend to question the notion that, for many people, concern about crime is an everyday reality, nor is it interested in discussing the rationality or irrationality of crime fear, a long running concern within some criminological and governmental bodies of literature (Mugford, 1984; Garofalo and Laub, 1978). Rather, my aim here is to illustrate how 'fear of crime', as an object of governance, is the target of a range of attempts at policy intervention, and why each of these attempts has failed to a greater or lesser extent. Paradoxically, it seems that the more we attempt to govern fear the more fearful we become.

A 'realist' might argue that this is simply because crime rates continue to rise and that the vast 'dark figure' of undetected crime makes crime fear a reality in many people's lives (cf. Jones, MacLean and Young, 1986). It might also be argued that the growth in recorded crime rates over the past thirty years or so has been reflected in a general increase in the 'fear of crime'. Additionally, the attempt by some scholars to unhinge 'fear of crime' from actual risk (cf. Toseland, 1982) seems to lead us down some rather strange policy paths in a way similar to those attempts aimed at reducing fear without actually doing anything at all about actual risk. Nevertheless, many scholars have persuasively argued that crime fear seems to operate independently of actual risk or recorded crime rates (cf. Hough and Mayhew, 1983).

I want to argue that there is something much more complex going on than any of these readings might assume. If we use a more appropriate framework for the analysis of crime fear then the apparent paradox I have identified above does not seem so paradoxical at all. To do this, however, we have to dispense with the dichotomies of imagined/real fears and rational/irrational fears. Rather, we need to think about 'fear of crime' by way of understanding the power embedded in its very discourse; in its name; in its very apparent objectivity. We need to conceptualise 'fear of crime' as an artefact of disciplinary and governmental knowledge, and one that now has its own productive capacities and effects. Moreover, we need to understand these in the context of increasingly neo-liberal forms of government and crime prevention strategies, the imperative to govern 'at a distance' by subjecting the objects of governance to the less direct disciplines of the market economy (cf. Stenson, 1993b; Rose and Miller, 1992). I want to suggest in this chapter that 'fear of crime' is not only an object of governance, something to be controlled, reduced, ameliorated, indeed governed, but that it also operates as a tactic or technology of governance, a strategy or tactic that can be invoked with the aim of encouraging individuals to regulate their own risks. Further, that this governmental interest in the 'fear of crime' renders the actual processes of government highly problematic and liable to failure. This analysis will draw on a number of policy documents, statements and strategies in order to illustrate some of the conflicting discourses of governing 'fear of crime'. Moreover, it will explore how attempts to govern 'fear of crime' almost inevitably result in a number of perhaps unintended consequences.

Fear of Crime as a Contingent Concept

I have argued elsewhere (Lee, 1999, 2001) that 'fear of crime' is a contingent object of inquiry. It is not pre-discursive, self evident, or ahistorical. Indeed, 'fear of crime' has emerged at the intersection of a number of late-modern governmental and disciplinary discourses. Broadly, these could be identified as the growth and sophistication of social scientific statistics, a new democratisation of knowledge using these statistics, the birth of large scale victim surveys, the politics of law and order – often developing around race issues, the growth of disciplines such as criminology which objectify crime fear, and sensational headlines in the media. 'Fear of crime' thus became an object of governance not because it was 'out there' and/or 'waiting to be discovered', but because of a number of accidental or contingent discursive alignments.[5]

To understand the nature and effects of governing 'fear of crime' we need to acknowledge these contingent dimensions.[6] Moreover, we also need to understand that as objects emerge into the realm of governance they become somewhat legitimised, or more to the point, 'normalised'. 'Fear of crime' research is not only now a 'sub-discipline' of criminology, as Hale (1996) has put it, it is now part of the normal language of crime prevention. For example, take the following extract from the Wollongong City Council Crime Prevention Plan (2001): 'Fear of crime and apprehension about safety is a matter of extreme concern to residents in the Wollongong area'. This serves to objectify a phenomenon whose presence in the area is both insidious and pervasive – a constituent and abhorrent part of everyday life.

In modern crime prevention literature 'fear of crime' is as important an object of governance as crime itself (cf. Home Office, 2001; Braithwaite et al, 1982). I will revisit the language of crime prevention below. First, however, I wish to more thoroughly set out a theoretical framework in which we might situate the governance of 'fear of crime' so as to better conceptualise and explain its productive effects and capacities.

Governmentality as Method

Throughout this chapter I will draw on Michel Foucault's (1991) notion of 'governmentality'[7] as a theoretical and analytic framework. Foucault's methods give an insight into a 'micro-physics' of governance and I want to use this in identifying and discussing the governance of 'fear of crime'. In his later work Foucault refers to modes of governance as governmentalities, or mentalities of government. According to Foucault (1991), governmentality is the 'rational' practice of government. It is government through calculated mentalities and reason,[8] which occur via the knowledges and technologies of modernity. He believes that from the sixteenth century onwards, new forms of governance began to develop in addition to the existing governing power of sovereign rule. Foucault (1991) counterposes governmental forms of power to sovereign forms of power. Sovereign power, he suggests, is exercised from above, with the provenance of god over men. Thus, the prince governs with ascribed license over his subjects.[9] Although sovereign power may well have as its aim the 'common good', in its ultimate circularity the common good is 'obedience to the law, hence the good for sovereignty is that people should obey it' (Foucault, 1991: 95). Governmental power is distinguished from sovereign power in that the former relies on tactics and technologies for arranging things, whereby the latter relies largely on formally constituted laws. Governmentality is government through knowledge, primarily knowledge of populations which are rendered the subjects of governmental attention. It is through the knowledge obtained through disciplines like criminology that 'fear of crime' becomes a central part of what is known about the characteristics of particular populations. Thus, the government of 'fear of crime' is intimately entwined with the calculations and assumptions emergent through a multiplicity of disciplines, their practices, research programs and subsequent objectified knowledges. Governmentality is the 'disposing of things' so as to lead, not so much to the common good necessarily, 'but to an end which is convenient for each of the things that are to be governed'. With government it is a question of not imposing law on men (sic), but of "employing tactics rather than laws, and even as using laws themselves as tactics" (Foucault, 1991: 95).

Government, Foucault suggests, is both of art and economy. It is an art in that it requires the development of techniques and technologies that allow the most minute and specific forms of governance to occur. Such forms of government are transformative in nature and seek, through various means and rationalities, to develop new, more sophisticated and perfected modalities of regulation and control – which is not to suggest these can ever be perfect, quite the contrary, for perfection is a normative notion that Foucault would be at pains to avoid. Government is about economy in that its exercise is aimed at securing the greatest possible return from the least investment of power; it must ensure that the greatest quantity of wealth is produced, that people are provided with a sufficient means of subsistence, that the population can multiply and reproduce itself (Foucault, 1991: 95). It must also aim to ensure the safety and security of the population in an economically viable and sustainable manner. Government, or governmentality, emerged by necessity around the problem of population. Population in Europe was progressively accumulating in cities as a result of the industrial revolution. Thus, 'security could no longer be guaranteed through force or conquest – government was no longer about securing territory against external threats – but managing population' (Carrington, Gow, Hogg, and Johnson, 1996: 58) and improving its condition (Foucault, 1991: 100). That is not to suggest that such ends and improvements are always forthcoming. Rather, it suggests that governance should be understood as a set of practices that are not in themselves intrinsically good or evil, positive or negative, oppressive or libertarian.   In this manner governmentality as a form of analysis runs counter to other criticism such as Marxism which conceives power as a largely oppressive force exercised by one group over another. That is not to argue, however, that governmental power may not be exercised in oppressive ways or in manners that make it such for some subjects. Indeed, governmentality as method or critique is largely about identifying the actualities of government and by doing so also identifying other conditions of possibility, silences, and resistances.   It is about how government is brought into being in programmatic form and the particular modalities of language that are invented or deployed to make subjects governable (O'Malley et al 1997:502). In practicing government, as Gordon explains, 'everything is dangerous, with the consequence that things are liable to go wrong, but also that there is the possibility of doing something to prevent this ...' (1991: 46, 47). My interest here is in how things appear to go 'wrong'; that is, the unintended consequences of governing 'fear of crime' and the mentalities of this form governance. In identifying and drawing together the rather fragmented and diffuse sites and strategies of governing 'fear of crime' I wish to open this field to other conditions of possibility.

The Governance of 'Fear of Crime'

Since the early 1980s 'fear of crime' has been the object of a number of different, often overlapping, forms of governmental discourse.   Firstly, there are strategies that specifically target fear through the proliferation of information aimed at its reduction. Secondly, there are more broadly based strategies and programs of crime prevention that seek to reduce both crime and crime fear. I will discuss only briefly examples of the first group of discourses and then develop a more detailed discussion and critique of examples of the second.

Governing Fear From Above

One method of governing fear rather specifically has been to attempt to supply citizenry with knowledge of the relatively low risks of becoming a victim of crime, suggesting instead that one's risk of victimisation is usually overestimated (see Grabosky, 1995: 15). For example, the NSW Bureau of Crime Statistics and Research recently published a well publicised article (Weatherburn et al, 1996) that suggested just this, that 'Australians often greatly exaggerate their risks ... [of being victimised]'. Their findings were given relatively wide publicity through dissemination in most NSW newspapers. Similar strategies have been attempted in the UK with the Home Office constantly disseminating such information. Presently, the Home Office website provides detailed information on crime control measures in the UK as well as advice on personal aspects of crime prevention and risk management. For example:

> The chance that you or a member of your family will be a victim of violent crime is low. Violent crimes are still comparatively rare and account for a very small part of recorded crime. But some people are still frightened that they, or someone close to them, will be the victim of a violent attack (Home Office, 2001).

Such pronouncements tend to reflect forms of sovereign governance. Here, 'experts' proclaim the 'truth' about victimisation to the citizenry in order to reduce 'fear of crime'. This is emblematic of governance from above, 'seeking as its goal the common good', to paraphrase Foucault (1991). This is also in part the reason for the failure of this form of governing crime fear. 'Fear of crime' and concern about victimisation, as discourses, have become so embedded in our everyday knowledges and practices that the voices of 'experts' are likely to offer scant comfort to the potential 'victim'. Rather, governing 'fear of crime' it seems requires a much more precisely targeted set of strategies. Now I want to explore the reasons why many of these strategies also fail.

Governmentality of Fear

The second method of governing fear is primarily through crime prevention strategies. Here, the government of fear is increasingly falling under the auspices of local council and other local agencies, although state government departments take primary responsibility for the coordination of crime prevention strategies. In NSW, for example, this role is carried out by the Attorney General's Department with input from the NSW Police Service and other state based agencies. Knowledge of how to govern fear is supplied by institutions like the NSW Bureau of Crime Statistics and Research or the Australian Institute of Criminology. Publications of these agencies are often cited in council crime prevention plans. State governments formulate and/or organise the technologies and techniques of governing fear, but carry out this governance at a distance. They have, for example, attempted to responsibilise local councils to develop crime prevention plans for local government areas in association with other local agencies and institutions. The NSW Attorney General's Department assists in the development of these plans and provides councils with a clear set of guidelines to facilitate some uniformity in the process:

> Crime, disorder and fear of crime have become major concerns for many communities. Traditionally, we have turned to the police and criminal justice agencies to deal with these problems. In the past, this worked reasonably well because crime levels were low. Today, however, crime levels are higher than they were 20 years ago, society has become more complex and demands on the police have increased substantially... The development of local crime prevention *partnerships* involving organisations such as the police, local councils, government departments (e.g. Department of Community Services, Area Health Service, Department of School Education), local business and community representatives are therefore seen as the best way of tackling local crime problems. To illustrate how this might work in practice, the following example of measures aimed at reducing the incidence of crime in a housing estate is provided... Local government is about more than providing basic services. It is about creating vibrant, lively communities where people can live comfortably and happily. Crime and the fear of crime reduce the quality of life in a community. People enjoy their lives more when they feel safe (NSW Attorney General's Department, 2001).

Likewise, in NSW the State government's Department of Urban Affairs and Planning (DUAP) now takes an active role in the responsibilisation of local councils. A new set of guidelines released by this department (DUAP, 2001) gives local police and councils the power to require that developers provide low risk environments. Unsafe areas are to be 'designed out'. Again the governance of this process, although coordinated at the State level, is devolved to local functionaries.

Local Crime Prevention Plans and Fear Reduction Strategies

We can see the importance of 'fear of crime', as an object of crime prevention strategies, by simply looking in more depth at some examples of NSW local government plans. Hawkesbury City Council suggests that:

> There is a discrepancy between community perceptions of crime and reported incidents of crime... There is a strong... perception that public spaces are unsafe – the fear of crime is most prevalent in public spaces (Hawkesbury City Council, 2001).

Similarly, Newcastle City Council argues that there is 'a perception of unease about the CBD [(Central Business District)]'. The crime prevention plan sets out to 'restore confidence in, and encourage people to use, the CBD' (Newcastle City Council 2001).

The crime prevention plan for Wollongong sets out 'to provide the community with a range of strategies which, when implemented, will enhance peoples feelings of safety and see a reduction in crime in the Wollongong LGA [(Local Government Area)]'. In Wollongong 'fear of crime' and 'concern for safety' were the 'key issues' in the crime prevention plan:

> Fear of crime and apprehension about safety is a matter of extreme concern to residents in the Wollongong area. A recent survey by the Bureau of Crime Statistics revealed that 58% of Illawarra residents perceived a crime or public nuisance problem in their neighbourhood in 1995 and 1996. This compares with a NSW average of 53.4% and 57.3% average for the Sydney region. Illawarra residents have the highest concern about their safety than any other region in NSW. This has also been confirmed by research and surveys that SCAT and its partners have recently undertaken. The Seniors Safety Survey, the Police Safety Survey, the Safe Women Project and the Young People in Public Space Forum all revealed extremely high concerns about safety and anti-social behaviour (Wollongong City Council, 2000).

It is much the same story in the Manly municipality:

> Fear of and incidence of crime stifles the participation of residents in community life and undermines their well being. It can disrupt the effective functioning of the community, damage social harmony and generate tensions which lead to further crime, major costs and significant human suffering amongst victims, perpetrators and their families (Manly City Council, 2001).

The resultant policy response to 'fear of crime' issues from most of these councils has been, in one way or another, to 'increase understanding of crime prevention models and facilitate understanding within communities to address fear of crime' (Wollongong City Council, 2000). In other words, education about the risk of crime and of the strategies being put in place to deal with crime, as well as input from local residents, will result in a drop in 'fear of crime', or so it is assumed.

'Fear of Crime' as a Tactic of Government

All this should seem relatively straightforward and we might be forgiven for thinking that the problem of 'fear of crime' is being well and truly addressed. However, the message being promoted is often ambiguous; reducing crime fear is often not entirely the purpose of crime prevention strategies. Indeed, there is an abundance of evidence to suggest that under some circumstances governments and other agencies believe that particular levels or 'element[s] of fear' – to use the British Home Office language – might actually be desirable in ensuring citizens adequately govern their own safety; fear becomes a governmental tactic or technique for risk reduction. Let us look first at the big picture again. The British Home Office has been explicit about 'fear of crime' being a possible tactic of governance. This is clearly detailed in the following:

> An element of fear can be considered helpful in persuading people to guard against victimisation. Arguably, however, being mentally prepared in this way is better defined as awareness or concern, not fear. Fear itself can slide into hopelessness or terror, either of which can be counter-productive in terms of taking reasonable precautions (British Home Office, 1989: 12).

Without going into the obvious arguments of definition that this passage poses, it neatly encapsulates the dilemma of governing 'fear of crime' and illustrates its utility as governmental tactic. Moreover, this dilemma is not only faced at the level of 'expert' information; this same problem is present throughout the entire web of governance when it comes to crime prevention. Thus, governing 'fear of crime' is indeed an *art*. Government must calculate and balance its policy interventions. But, as noted below, it is also an *economy* and this has serious implications for these interventions, these attempts to govern.

Tactics of Crime Prevention

I have already noted that 'fear of crime' is a major concern of contemporary crime prevention strategies and programs. However, we do not have to delve too deeply to also discover that fear is often used as a tactic of governance in instructing individuals to take preventative measures in order to reduce the risk of crime and victimisation. This process might be termed *governance-through-fear*.

Thus, 'fear of crime' becomes a method of facilitating self-regulation. Individuals are expected to become *fearing subjects* (Lee, 1999, 2001). That is, they are sensitised, through governmental instruction or advice, and constantly expected to evaluate, police, *govern* and insure their body and property against the wrong doings of others. This is government of the self (Foucault, 1991). The *fearing subject* is a responsibilised citizen whose civic duty includes keeping one's self and their belongings safe. This has the effect of minimising active and coercive state intervention in crime prevention but is intervention in itself, albeit of a seemingly much less intrusive kind. There are no curfews in place, no legal restrictions on individuals' movements, yet the *fearing subject* is expected to curfew the self and only venture into areas of low risk. Thus, in the Foucauldian sense *fearing subjects* are not disciplined (Foucault, 1977) as such but *governed*. Indeed, they are governed-at-a-distance.

We can see this process of self governance in the crime prevention literature and advice produced by the NSW police service and distributed from local commands. For example:

> The community needs to be our partner in the fight against crime. We need to be aware of what's happening in your neighbourhood and to

> contact your local police or Crime Stoppers if you notice anything suspicious (sic). We also need to make life more difficult for burglars by increasing the security of NSW homes. Only by working together can we make our homes safe from burglars (NSW Police Service, 1995).

The message is unambiguous. 'We' all have a role to play in policing, and policing 'burglars' also means, to some extent, policing ourselves. We are told, for example, to 'lock all doors and windows', 'don't leave keys sitting in the lock', 'never [put keys] in hiding places', and to 'engrave ... your property' (NSW Police Service, 1995). And if *governance-through-fear* is only implicit in this text then the small drawn images that border the police brochure make the point even more clearly. Images of a pot plant being lifted up by a gloved hand to reveal a hidden key; a lock with a key left hanging tantalisingly in it; a slightly opened window with the pitch black outside, a blackness that could easily hide an intruder. The message is that if you do not self govern you are likely to be victimised.

The more recently updated NSW Police Service website is even more explicit. Indeed, there is advice offered on any number of potentially risky situations. What, for example, to do when visitors call:

> Don't open the door to anyone you don't know and trust. If someone is at the door and you are alone and feel a bit frightened, pretend there is someone else in the house. ... If someone wants to use your telephone for an emergency, don't feel rude about not allowing them in. Offer to make the call for them – if they are a genuine caller they will not mind. ... Be suspicious of people requesting entry to your home to check appliances or equipment. Ask to see their identity card and take time to look at it carefully before letting them in. If you are still unsure, ring their company to check. If in doubt, keep them out (NSW Police Service, 2001).

Suddenly taking visitors sounds like a risky, indeed *fearful*, enterprise. It entails one taking a number of pre-emptive precautions. As does going to the bank:

> Vary the days and times each week that you go to the bank or building society. Varying your routine helps prevent theft. ...Put your money straight into your purse or wallet before moving away from the teller (NSW Police Service, 2001).

Moreover, keeping your home secure is also an ongoing and important process:

> Many burglaries occur during the day. In a large number entry is unforced because people have not locked up properly. Before you go out, double-check all the windows and doors are locked, especially laundry and bathroom windows. ...Lock doors where an intruder might enter, particularly if you have the TV or the vacuum cleaner on and are unlikely to hear someone. ...Never leave keys in 'hiding places' like under the doormat. Leave a spare key with a trusted neighbor or friend (NSW Police Service, 2001).

The point is that all this advice aimed at making us self-governing subjects is potentially, if not explicitly, fear inducing. We are presented with examples of what might happen if we do not regulate our behaviour effectively and 'appropriately' – and for the most part these images and examples are frightening. Paradoxically, much of this information is provided by police, local government, and insurance companies,[10] the same institutions that also attempt to reduce 'fear of crime', the same institutions and agencies that take part in the development of crime prevention plans in part aimed at reducing 'fear of crime'. Local community becomes institutional form for communicating risk management (Stenson 1993a) which may also have the effect of intensifying 'fear of crime' discourse.

We might equate many of the forms of government I have discussed with what has been identified by some scholars (O'Malley, 1991; Stenson, 1993a, 1993b) as a broader shift towards neo-liberalism, policies and practices that emphasise individual responsibility and free choice over broader social and state interventions. Some have argued that neo-liberal government takes the focus off the failures of the police force (O'Malley, 1991); the continued rolling back of the public sector (Stanko, 1998); and structural inequalities, and instead attempts to produce responsibilised individuals that take on many of the burdens once governed by the centralised state. Governmental intervention becomes governance through outsourcing, privatisation, instruction and facilitation rather than direct action. Stanko (1997, 1998) has drawn particular attention to the way in which current regimes of regulation and control have sought to govern women's access to particular public spaces and places. She argues that governmental instructions are misguided and that they ignore the realities of women's risk at the hands of men – particularly men they know. We could well expand this argument to suggest that most of the crime prevention literature and advice available plays down the fact that serious victimisation is most likely to occur at the hands of intimates rather than strangers.

This raises normative issues requiring elaboration. I wish, perhaps in opposition to Stanko, to reject the negative hypothesis regarding *governance-through-fear*. That is not to reject her general conclusions about the body of literature she takes as her object of analysis. Rather, I want to suggest that 'fear of crime', as a tactic or technology of governance – like all knowledge/power (see Foucault, 1978) – should not be conceptualised as an inherently negative regulatory force. Rather we should conceptualise it as a productive force, neither inherently negative nor inherently positive but part of the processes that produce modern liberal subjects. If there is to be some sort of normative evaluation of the effects of *government-through-fear* it should be focused on the performance of specific strategies of governance and their ability to enhance an individual's civic access, sense of ease and worth within their everyday private and social interactions. A thorough evaluation of this, however, is beyond the scope of this chapter. I simply want to emphasise this productive capacity of governmental power rather than painting it as an inherently negative force. By doing this I emphasise the capacities for other possible modes of intervention, other possible governmental strategies.

Thus, we can see that governing 'fear of crime' is complex, paradoxical and multifaceted. Particularly when we identify fear as a tactic of government. However, the task of governing fear becomes even more complicated when we bring other realms of *economy* into the equation.

Privatisation and Governance

Private interests and commercial calculations have become a major part of the neo-liberal governance of fear. The private sector has an economic interest in sensitising populations to representing the social (and/or business) world, in advertisements and other media campaigns, as dangerous; put simply, the fearful buy insurance and security. Indeed, we might think of these private sector institutions as 'servicing' 'fear of crime' amongst other things. One enlists these services for 'peace of mind' – to paraphrase one company's advertising slogan. It (the pursuit of 'peace of mind') is increasingly seen to be the responsible thing to do. Yet, these services come at a cost. For individuals (or companies for that matter) to feel adequately compelled to invest in these services there must exist the notion that financial outlay will be exceeded by the potential savings the service has to offer. This has resulted in a situation whereby some companies engage in the production of advertising and other forms of media that present social life as risky and dangerous; a world so disorganised and untameable that these new service industries are a safety requirement for the self governing subject. Indeed, Shearing and Stenning (1985) argue that with the growth of these services has emerged a whole 'new class of delinquent', the individual or group who does not responsibly take up the preventative services on offer. So, this neo-liberal free market idea dovetails neatly with current governmental tactics.

Thus, extensive and consistent advertising from these industries play on, and often attempt to increase or sensitise us to 'fear of crime'. A 'responsible' *fearing subject* consumes insurance, private security, and security hardware. Moreover, some companies increase their competitiveness by becoming involved with other social institutions and with local communities – the involvement of the NRMA[11] in Neighbourhood Watch schemes being a pertinent example of this strategy.

Governments have been active in encouraging this engagement with the private sector. As Sarre (1997: 67) has pointed out, many governments have actively adopted strategies encouraging specialist forms of social ordering such as the services offered by private policing and security firms. Indeed, he claims they have in recent times been embraced as junior partners in the collaborative production of community safety. This fills the void left by the retreat of the state and is consistent with the neo-liberal ideal of 'governing at a distance' (cf. O'Malley, 1991).

Of course, private policing, insurance companies, and security firms are not new. Private policing dates back to well before the emergence of the public forces and other services we now take for granted. What is new is that with the emergence and quantification of 'fear of crime' (Lee, 1999, 2001) they now have an additional object to service. Fear becomes a target for these companies in the chase for profit. Zielinski (1995: 1) argues that in the North American context, as a result of political rhetoric and fear about crime, the private security industry is 'profitably positioned at the intersection' of the 'right-wing's most cherished crusades: privatisation and law and order'. However, the new wish to have a mix of private and public institutions operating simultaneously is certainly not confined to 'right-wing' governments or politicians. As Sarre (1997: 67) points out, private policing has survived the formation of centralised police forces; it was a crucial component of policing in the past, it is in the present, and still will be in the future. Rather, governments on either side of the political divide have been active in encouraging strategies that could broadly be called neo-liberal even if conservative governments might have been more unrelenting in this pursuit.

Private sector involvement makes the government of 'fear of crime' all the more difficult. With consumer demand in this area given over to the private sector the tenuous balance of governing fear becomes increasingly more fragile. This situation is partially responsible for some of the ambiguities contained in governmental policy on 'fear of crime'.

The neo-liberal shift to smaller government, and to governing at a distance, brings with it the desire for private sector involvement in many areas of social life; including crime prevention. This in turn opens up 'crime fear' to the market economy. Paradoxically, this shift necessitates increased governmental activity – in this case regulation by public authorities – in trying to explain crime fear, 'define it down', and/or declare it 'irrational'; ultimately attempts to counter the sustained campaigns of fear by the private sector.

Fear Reduction and Triumph

There is another interlinked reason that 'fear of crime' has become such an important object of governmental intervention. Put simply, it offers another possibility of a policy or administrative triumph for the police, politicians, criminologists, and an array of other specialists. All of these groups or institutions, in one way or another and often by their own measures, have failed to successfully govern crime (cf. Braithwaite, 1989); crime has not disappeared, recorded crime rates have not fallen dramatically; indeed, some recorded crime has increased. 'Fear or crime' offers another site of possible victory. If policy makers can be seen as doing something about crime fear the constant failure to govern crime can be somewhat obscured.

'Fear of crime' as an object has, developing around it, a new group of specialists dedicated to its government. Requests for more police by police unions and politicians are now often based upon 'fear of crime' rather than crime rates *per-se* (cf. Weatherburn *et al*, 1996). 'Fear of crime' commands the attention of an expanding cohort of criminologists and other researchers who in turn command research funding from governments and private industry. Indeed, entire conferences are held around the problem of crime fear. Fear is increasingly surveyed, calculated and quantified, necessitating the development of more surveys – ever increasing in accuracy and detail.

Conclusion

If the grid of governance I have outlined here is accurate then attempts to govern and regulate 'fear of crime' seem destined to fail to a greater or lesser extent, particularly if we equate successful governance purely with fear reduction. However, if we also conceptualise 'fear of crime' as a tactic of governance, notions of failure or success become quite clouded and subjective; if success in the governance of 'fear of crime' entails obscuring the failures of government agencies and producing citizens who consume services from the private sector, if success means the exercise of government at a distance and the development of self governing *fearing subjects* then perhaps the governance of crime fear is indeed a triumph. It seems, however, that governing 'fear of crime' is a kind of governmental balancing act. There is no doubt that governments and other agencies 'conceptualise fear as a negative force', however, on the other hand, there seems little doubt that many of these same governing bodies also see 'fear of crime' as a tactic to be deployed in the governance of populations. Additionally, private sector involvement complicates this balancing act by feeding fear, which in turn often requires additional input from governments who attempt to keep the balance.

Discourse about 'fear of crime' continues to grow. Even local newspapers now survey crime fear (cf. Gainsford, 1998) at the same time as they present fearful images of crime. As we consume the gruesome stories we can flick the pages and monitor our ever-growing fears as they appear on the pages quantified for us. We can turn to the following page and read a small story telling us that our risk of becoming a victim of crime is relatively low according to such and such a governmental agency. In a sense this constitutes a microcosm of 'fear of crime' in the context of a broader web of governance. Fear has become normalised. It is now a legitimate object of governmental and disciplinary knowledge and as such is not likely to go away. Perhaps then the most insidious unintended consequence of governing 'fear of crime' is 'fear of crime' itself.

Notes

[1]   Debates about; how to measure 'fear of crime'; what groups are most fearful; is fear rational or irrational; is fear of crime different to perceived risk etc.

[2]   One such estate in Western Sydney employed media personality Ita Buttrose as their public advertising face so that the estate could be marketed to an ageing and apparently fearful population.

[3]   For the purpose of this chapter I want to put to one side debates about the accuracy of such studies.

[4]   See Weatherburn et al (1996) for a discussion of a number of these.

[5]   See Lee (2001) for a thorough discussion of the emergence of 'fear of crime'.

[6]   My use of the term in inverted commas is meant to denote and highlight this.

[7]   This concept has fostered a growing body of literature from scholars keen to develop the ideas left in a relatively embryonic stage at the time of Foucault's death. These scholars include Colin Gordon (1991), Ian Hacking (1995), Nicholas Rose (1991, 1999), Jacques Donzelot (1991), and Graham Burchell (1993).

[8]   Specifically, Foucault (1991 102, 103) defines governmentality thus:
The ensemble formed by institutions, procedures, analyses, and reflections, the calculations and tactics that allow the exercise of the very specific albeit complex form of power, which has as its target population, as its principal form of knowledge political economy, and as its essential technical means apparatuses of security. The tendency which, over a long period and throughout the West, has steadily led towards the pre-eminence over all other forms (sovereign, discipline etc.) of this type of power which may be termed government, resulting on the one hand, in the formation of a whole series of specific governmental apparatuses, and, on the other, in the development of a whole series of savoirs.
The process, or rather the result of the processes, through which the state of justice of the Middle Ages, transformed into the administrative state during the fifteenth and sixteenth centuries, gradually becomes governmentalised.

[9]   Foucault (1991) uses the example of Machiavelli's The Prince to illustrate this.

[10]   The NRMA publishes an abundance of such literature for example.

[11]   A large NSW based insurance firm.

References

Braithwaite, J. (1989), 'The State of Criminology: Theoretical Decay or Renaissance?', in *Australian and New Zealand Journal of Criminology*, Vol. 25, No. 3, pp. 333-55.

Braithwaite, J., Biles, D. and Whitrod, R. (1982), 'Fear of Crime in Australia', in H. J. Schneider (ed) *The Victim in International Perspective*, Walter de Gruyer, New York.

Burchell, G. (1993), 'Liberal government and techniques of the self', in *Economy and Society*, Vol. 23, No. 3, pp. 267-82.

Carrington, K., Gow, J., Hogg, R. and Johnson, A. (1996), *Crime, Locality and Citizenship: Interim Research Report*, Institute of Criminology: University of Sydney, Sydney.

Donzelot, J. (1991), 'Pleasure in Work', in G. Burchell, C. Gordon and P. Miller (eds) *The Foucault Effect*, Harvester Wheatsheaf, London.

Foucault, M. (1970), *The Order of Things: Archaeology of the Human Sciences*, Vintage, New York.

Foucault, M. (1977), *Discipline and Punish: The Birth of the Prison*, Penguin, Harmondsworth.

Foucault, M. (1978), *The History of Sexuality: Volume 1, an Introduction*, Penguin, London.

Foucault, M. (1984), *The Foucault Reader*, Rabinow, P., (ed) Penguin, London.

Foucault, M. (1991), 'Governmentality', in G. Burchell, C. Gordon, and P. Miller (eds) *The Foucault Effect*, Harvester Wheatsheaf, London.

Gainsford, J. 'Crime Fear Immense', in *Hills New*, May 26, 1998, p. 1.

Garofalo, J. and Laub, J. (1978), 'The Fear of Crime: Broadening Our Perspective', in *Victimology* 3: pp. 242-53.

Gordon, C. (1991), 'Governmental Rationality: An Introduction', in G. Burchell, C. Gordon, and P. Miller (eds) *The Foucault Effect*, Harvester Wheatsheaf, London.

Grabosky, P. (1995), 'Fear of Crime, and Fear Reduction Strategies', in *Current Issues in Criminal Justice*, Vol. 7, No. 1.

Hacking, I. (1995), *Rewriting the Soul*, Princeton University Press, New Jersey.

Hale, C. (1996), 'Fear of Crime: A Review of the Literature', in *International Review of Victimology*, Vol. 4, pp. 79-150.

Hawkesbury City Council (2001), *Hawkesbury Crime Prevention Plan*, Hawkesbury City Council.

Home Office (2001), http://www.crimereduction.gov.uk/personalsafety.htm.

Hough, M. (1995), *Anxiety about Crime: Findings from the 1994 British Crime Survey*, Home Office.

Jones, T., Maclean, B. and Young, J. (1986), *The Islington Crime Survey*, Gower, Aldershot.

Lee, M. (1999), 'The Fear of Crime and Self Governance: Towards a Genealogy', in *Australian and New Zealand Journal of Criminology*, Vol. 32, No. 3.

Lee, M. (2001), 'The Genesis of "Fear of Crime"', in *Theoretical Criminology*, Forthcoming.

Manly City Council (2001), *Manly Crime Prevention Plan*, Manly City Council.

Maxfield, M. (1984), *Fear of Crime in England and Wales*, HMSO, London.

Mugford, S. (1984), 'Fear of Crime – Rational or Not?', in *Australian and New Zealand Journal of Criminology*, Vol. 17, pp. 276-85.

Newcastle City Council (2000), *Newcastle Crime Prevention Plan*, Newcastle City Council.
    NSW Attorney General's Department (2001)
    [http://www.lawlink.nsw.gov.au/cpd.nsf/pages/cpddevelop2] accessed 01/07/2001.
NSW Department of Urban Affairs and Planning (DUAP) (2001), 'Crime prevention and
    the assessment of development applications: Guidelines under section 79C of the
    Environmental Planning and Assessment Act 1979', NSW Department of Urban Affairs
    and Planning.
NSW Police Service (1995), *Preventing Burglary.*
NSW Police Service (2001), *Prevention* [http://www.police.nsw.gov.au/prevention/],
    accessed 01/07/2001.
O'Malley, P. (1991), 'Risk, Power, and Crime Prevention', in *Economy and Society*, No. 21,
    pp. 252-75.
O'Malley, P., Weir, L. and Shearing, C. (1997), 'Governmentality, Criticism, and Politics',
    Economy and Society, Vol. 26, No. 4.
Rose, N. (1991), 'Governing by numbers: figuring out democracy', in *Accounting,
    Organisation and Society*, Vol. 16, No. 7: pp. 673-92.
Rose, N. (1999), *Powers of Freedom*, Cambridge University Press, Cambridge.
Rose, N. and Miller, P. (1992), 'Political Power Beyond the State: Problematics of
    Government', in *British Journal of Sociology*, Vol. 43, No. 2.
Sarre, R. (1997), 'Crime Prevention and the Police', in P. O'Malley and A. Sutton (eds),
    Crime Prevention in Australia, The federation Press, Annandale.
Shearing, C. and Stenning, P. (1985), 'From the Panopticon to Disney World: The
    Development of Discipline', in A. Doog and E. Greenspan (eds), *Perspectives in
    Criminal law*, Ontario, Canada Law Book Inc, pp. 335-49.
Sherman, R. (1994/95), 'Crime's Toll on the US: Fear, Despair, and Guns', in J. Sullivan
    and J. Victor (eds) *Annual Editions: Criminal Justice 95/96*, 57. Guilford,
    Dushkin/Brown.
Skogan, W. (1986), 'The Fear of Crime and its Behavioural Implications', in A. Fattah (ed)
    From Crime Policy to Victim Policy, Macmillan; London.
Stanko, E. (1997), 'Safety Talk: Conceptualizing Women's Risk Assessment as a
    "Technology of the Soul"', in *Theoretical Criminology*, Vol. 1, pp. 479-99.
Stanko, E. (1998), 'Warnings to women', in O'Malley, P. (ed) *Crime and the Risk Society*,
    Dartmouth, Sydney.
Stenson, K. (1993a), 'Social Work Discourses and the Social Work Interview', in *Economy
    and Society*, Vol. 22, No. 1.
Stenson, K. (1993b), 'Community Policing and Governmental Technology', in *Economy
    and Society*, Vol. 22, No. 3.
Toseland, R. (1982), 'Fear of Crime: Who is Most Vulnerable?', in *Journal of Criminal
    Justice,* Vol. 10, pp. 199-209.
Weatherburn, D., Matka, E. and Lind, B. (1996), 'Crime Perception and Reality: Public
    Perceptions of the Risk of Criminal Victimisation in Australia', in *Crime and Justice
    Bulletin* No.28, NSW Bureau of Crime Statistics and Research.
Wollongong City Council (2000), *Wollongong Crime Prevention Plan*, Wollongong City
    Council.
Zielinski (1995), 'Armed and Dangerous: Private police on the March', *Covert Action
    Quarterly*, Fall.

Chapter 3

The Control of Drugs in New Zealand

GREG NEWBOLD

Introduction

Modern attempts to monitor and control the use of mind-altering drugs have a history that is over 100 years old. However, the commencement of prohibitions on the casual and recreational use of such drugs is, for the most part, a 20th century phenomenon. As these prohibitions have developed, a variety of control strategies have been tried in different places at different times. Some have focussed on punishment and deterrence of drug offenders – which Anderson (1999: 89) calls the 'back end' approach – others have operated from the 'front end', and concentrated on treatment and therapy. There has been much debate about the effectiveness of drug control strategies, and it is not my intention to revisit it here (see, however, Inciardi, 1992: chs 8, 9; Abadinsky, 1993: 284-376; Mcdonald, Stevens, Dance and Bammer, 1993; South, 1994; Inciardi and McElrath [eds], 1995: Part X; Rosenberger, 1996; Jensen and Gerber [eds], 1998). My purpose in this chapter is to look specifically at illicit drugs and their control in New Zealand. After briefly reviewing the history of drug control measures in this country, I discuss and comment upon the many factors that impact on drug availability. It will be seen that many of the dynamics that exist in New Zealand, are applicable to other countries with similar political economies and culture.

History of Drug Control Measures

Like Britain, the recognition of a widespread 'drug problem' in New Zealand and the dedication of specific resources to deal with it, are relatively recent. Whereas a drug problem in parts of the United States was identified as early as the 1920s (Schmalleger, 2001: 588), it was not until the 1960s that serious concerns began in Britain (South, 1994: 396) and New Zealand.

In New Zealand, as in many other Western countries, opium, cocaine and cannabis were used in a variety of medical preparations and both were either unregulated or controlled very loosely in the 19th Century. A significant group of users were Chinese opium smokers, who had begun arriving in large numbers following the first major gold strikes in the 1860s, but Europeans also used drugs recreationally, usually by ingestion. In fact one of the first control laws was the *Distillation Act 1868*, which forbade the common practice of potentiating beer with substances like opium, cannabis, and tobacco.

In 1866, the first drug control legislation, the *Sale of Poisons Act*, required records to be kept of the sale of a number of toxic substances including opium and laudanum (tincture of opium), and five years later the *Sale of Poisons Act 1871* added morphine and chloroform. An amendment in 1900 extended the act to all opium alkaloids, including heroin. In 1901 the New Zealand government passed the *Opium Prohibition Act*. This act and its amendments, consolidated in the *Opium Act 1908*, banned the importation and smoking of opium, and required customs permits for importing non-smokable opium. Vendors were required to keep records of sales.

But importation of other drugs, like cocaine and opium alkaloids, remained virtually unsanctioned until 1921, when these were added to the gazette of 'patent' compounds that under the *Opium Act 1908* required a licence to import. Still, there were few restrictions on sale. Some people bought them in bulk and a number got addicted (Ashforth, 1970: 115). Not until 1927, following the recommendations of several international commissions and the League of Nations did the distribution of narcotics become effectively illegal outside of the medical profession (Morgan, 1997: 20). Under the *Dangerous Drugs Act 1927*, possession of prohibited drugs became punishable by a £50 fine, and growing or trafficking by a fine of £500 and 12 months' imprisonment. Included in the prohibited drugs schedule were opium, morphine, heroin, cocaine and cannabis.

Until the mid-1960s, illegal drug use was hardly noticeable in New Zealand. The first recorded illegal usage of marijuana did not occur until 1940, after introduction by American servicemen and merchant sailors. Later discoveries in the 1940s and early 1970s were of little consequence, however a slight rise in marijuana use among musical bands in the 1950s did give some cause for concern (Board of Health, 1970: 21-2). The only group known regularly to smoke opium were small numbers of Chinese.

For the first half of the 1960s there were few changes in drug abuse patterns. In most years, fewer than ten non-Chinese people were charged with drug offences. But in Britain (South, 1994: 396) and America (Abadinsky, 1993: 64-73), marijuana use was rising, and in 1960 New Zealand responded to these trends by stiffening the penalties established under the 1927 Act. The maximum prison penalty of twelve months for growing or trafficking an illegal drug was increased to seven years' imprisonment generally, and 14 years for supplying a minor.

The 1960s was a decade of rapid change. Television arrived in New Zealand in 1960, allowing visual images of the American civil rights movement and, from 1965, the anti-war movement and the associated rise of 'hippiedom', to be broadcast directly into people's living rooms. The 'Beatles' toured in 1964 and in 1966 the pirate radio station, Radio Hauraki, began the first broadcasts of all-hit music radio, 24 hours a day. As a result, New Zealand rapidly began catching up with changes in youth culture overseas. In 1964, the trial of John Gillies and Ron Jorgensen for the gangland-style killings of two men in Auckland produced evidence of sly-grogging, sexual vice and marijuana smoking. Gillies claimed that he would not have committed the murders, had he not been stoned on drugs (Yska, 1990: 99-100). That same year, stories of large-scale marijuana smuggling were reported in newspapers and commented on in parliament.

Concerned by the changes, in 1965 Detective Chief Inspector Bob Walton was despatched to the United States to study methods of controlling drugs, prostitution and gambling. Upon his return special police vice squads were formed and trained to investigate drug use and other vices (Yska, 1990: 84). One of the squads' first tasks was to raid and close down the known opium dens. By 1966 this was completed and about 100 Chinese came before the courts as a result. Thereafter, few Chinese were charged with drug offences, but increasing numbers of Europeans were. In addition, the burgling of pharmacies for drugs commenced, there were two drug-related deaths, and numbers of people admitted to hospital for drug dependence grew (Board of Health, 1970: 24-5).

In 1965, in accordance with its obligations to the Single Convention on Narcotic Drugs 1961, New Zealand replaced the 1927 Dangerous Drugs Act with the Narcotics Act. In this law, the sentence of three months' imprisonment for illegal drug use remained unchanged, but a maximum penalty of 14 years imprisonment was set for illegal production and trafficking. But no sooner was the act passed than reports of illegal drug use began suddenly to escalate. In 1965, ten people were charged with drug offences. In 1966 there were 28, in 1967, 50, and in 1968, 153 people were charged (Board of Health, 1970: 25). From about 1967, demand for marijuana among musicians and university students boomed and LSD, which had been popular in the United States since the early 1960s, began to appear in New Zealand as well. In 1965, the United States had effectively outlawed LSD. New Zealand followed in 1967, adding both LSD and mescaline to the schedule within the Narcotics Act.

In 1968, when reported drug offences trebled over the previous year, the government commissioned a Board of Health committee to investigate drug dependency and drug abuse and to make recommendations from its observations. Changes were occurring so fast, however, that by the time the report was released in February 1970 it was already out of date. By 1969, the hippie culture had reached New Zealand and drug offending was booming. Domestic production of marijuana was flourishing and between 1968 and 1970, total police-reported drug offences doubled. Concern was such that 12,000 copies of the Board of Health committee report were printed and snapped up by interested persons and agencies. The future looked grave and just two months after the committee presented the report, the government ordered a second inquiry. By the time this was presented in 1973, annual reported drug crimes had almost quadrupled.

More than half of reported offences involved marijuana possession, but from 1974 an increasing number of people were arrested for dealing in marijuana and other drugs. In 1972 a National Drug Intelligence Bureau had been established at Police National Headquarters in Wellington. By this time, with domestic cultivation of cannabis widespread, commercial importation had commenced as well. In Auckland, where most of the country's drug using culture was focussed, from 1970 onward, marijuana and LSD were not difficult to purchase. Also available in significant quantities were addictive opioids and cocaine deriving principally from chemist burglaries. Rock bands, university students and then young criminals created a burgeoning market for these illicit substances. Most marijuana was home-grown 'New Zealand Green', but by 1973, importation of marijuana and LSD on private yachts was common and the next year, several ships from the Royal Dutch Orient Line arrived with loads of high-quality Thai-produced marijuana wrapped on slivers of bamboo. Known as 'Buddha sticks', this form of marijuana soon came to dominate the New Zealand drug scene.

In 1972, members of an American commission on marijuana, the Shafer Commission, visited New Zealand and recommended a relaxation of anti-marijuana laws (Yska, 1990: 131). That same year, Britain passed a Misuse of Drugs Act which divided drugs into three classes according to potential for harm. In 1975, influenced by both Britain and the United States as well as by recommendations from the second Board of Health committee (1973: 100), New Zealand passed its own *Misuse of Drugs Act*, using a British-style classification and reducing penalties for most drugs. Henceforth, dealing Class A drugs – such as LSD and heroin – still carried a maximum of 14 years imprisonment, but penalties for Class B drugs – such as hashish, morphine and cocaine – were cut to ten years and the maximum for Class C drugs – such as cannabis plant – was cut to eight years. Under the act, police were empowered to search premises, etc, believed to contain controlled drugs and persons suspected of offending against the act, without obtaining a search warrant.

The relatively 'soft' approach taken toward the sentencing of drug offenders did not last long. In 1976, the police began talking of 'Mr Bigs' who were dominating the drug trade in New Zealand. The largest was Terrence Clark, a small-time criminal who, after being released from a five year burglary sentence in 1974, began coordinating the importation of Thai marijuana and later on, pure heroin from the 'Golden Triangle', on a scale unmatched in this country before or since. The so-called, 'Mr Asia' gang functioned in New Zealand for only a short time. The country is small and in 1975, Clark and one of his accomplices was arrested and charged with importing heroin. Although both were acquitted, by the end of 1975 Clark had moved his base to Australia. Under pressure following involvement in a series of murders in Australia, early in 1979 he flew to London where, some months later, along with several others of his gang, he was arrested for a murder there (Booth, 1980; Hall, 1981). In 1981, he and eight others were sent to prison for murder and/or drug offences.

It was the publicity attached to Clark's New Zealand activities, accompanied by evidence of major heroin importing by other organised criminal syndicates that prompted the government to increase the powers of detection of, and penalties for, trafficking in hard drugs. In 1978, a permanent drug liaison officer was established in Bangkok. That year also, an amendment to the Misuse of Drugs Act increased the penalty for trafficking in Class B drugs to 14 years and for moving Class A drugs, to life imprisonment. In addition, in the case of suspected Class A and B dealing offences, the use of tracking and listening devices by police and customs was legislated.

In the years following the 1978 amendment, the operations of customs and police proved effective in stemming the importation of marijuana and heroin to New Zealand. International cooperation and the new surveillance powers allowed the arrest and imprisonment of several New Zealanders with major drug involvement, not only in New Zealand, but in Australia and Great Britain as well. The breaking up of the Mr Asia empire in England in 1979 was one example. The arrest of Jimmy Shepherd in Australia was another. In 1986, Shepherd was sentenced to two consecutive 25-year terms for importing and distributing heroin to Australia. A third instance was the arrest of Brian Curtis in 1979. Curtis was apprehended after having imported three kilograms of heroin off a yacht that ran aground at Karamea in Westland, and was the first person sentenced to life imprisonment under the 1978 amendment. The sentence was later commuted to 16 years. In 1986, Wayne Beri, not long released from a 13-year sentence for heroin importing imposed in 1975 under the old Narcotics Act, was convicted of importing 307 grams of heroin to New Zealand. Much of the evidence against him had been obtained through listening devices. He got a sentence of life imprisonment that was upheld by the Court of Appeal. Finally, also in 1986, Peter Fulcher, formerly a leading member of the Mr Asia gang, received 14 years for importing heroin to New Zealand.

The big busts were truly effective and by the early 1980s, the police commissioner was commenting regularly in his reports that seizures of imported heroin were now rare. In fact, since 1985, the total heroin appropriations listed in police annual reports has only exceeded one kilogram on three occasions – the largest being 2.2kg seized in 1993. But staunching the flow of illegal drugs did not make drugs unavailable, it simply opened up alternative sources. From the early 1980s, 'homebaked' heroin – heroin produced from codeine phosphate – began to appear and from 1985 it featured regularly in police reports. Likewise, the end of the Buddha stick boom in the late 1970s saw its replacement with large-scale domestic cultivation. This soon became big business. From 1980, significant seizures of cannabis plants were reported annually, growing from 37,000 plants in 1980 to a peak of 352,000 plants in 1995.

By the early 1980s the demand for illegal drugs, particularly marijuana, was huge. A Heylen public opinion poll in 1984 found that 49 percent of 15-24 year-olds had used marijuana at some time (Department of Health, 1992: 28). Then in the 1990s, usage levels grew dramatically. In 1990, when the first comprehensive survey was conducted, 43 percent of 15-45 year-olds had tried marijuana, and 13 percent – a total of about 200,000 people – were current users. Current users increased to 17 percent – about 300,000 – by 1998 (Field and Casswell, 1999: 20). In other words, in 1998 there was a net increase of 50 percent, or 100,000 current users, over the figure estimated eight years before. In addition to this, lesser-used drugs, such as LSD and opioids, represented a much smaller but still growing and lucrative market.

In the light of the potential profits involved, it is not surprising that following the extinction of the wealthy Mr Asia syndicate in the late 1970s, other organised crime groups formed in its place. Motorcycle gangs in America had been dealing in LSD, cocaine, amphetamines ('speed') and other drugs, since the late 1960s (Barger, 2000; Grennan, Britz, Rush and Barker, 2000: 70). Several New Zealand gangs, most notably the 'Hells Angels', had formal links with their American counterparts but for several years after 1975, most of the New Zealand Angels were in prison on manslaughter-related charges, and the gang did not come back to strength until they started getting released about the turn of the decade. While in prison many, especially those in maximum security, came into contact with and sometimes befriended some of the country's biggest international drug dealers. After they were released, several Angels made use of their contacts to set up the organised importation of LSD and speed. But it was not just the 'Hells Angels' club, of course, that became involved in drug dealing and they may not have been the first. Gangs network a great deal, and during the 1980s many gangs, or members of gangs, in New Zealand became involved either in drug importation, cultivation or manufacture. Arrests and imprisonment of members for drug-related crimes soon followed (Newbold, 2000: ch. 6; Dennehy and Newbold, 2001: App.).

In the 1980s, marijuana cultivation and trafficking became a major source of income for Maori gangs. Several of the larger 'ethnic' gangs had grown wealthy through the exploitation of work incentive schemes, introduced in the late 1970s to combat rising unemployment. The closure of such schemes to gangs following a wave of negative publicity in 1986 may have been a factor that nudged these groups further into drug-related activity. Whatever the case, by 1987, the police were likening gangs to the Mafia, with multi-million dollar, international connections, sophisticated computer systems, and developments in organised criminal activity involving theft, extortion and drug dealing (Dennehy and Newbold, 2001: App.).

Drugs and Drug Control Today

It wasn't just the gangs that were involved in organised drug dealing, nor is it the case today. Then, as now, numerous operators outside of gangs manufactured, imported, and distributed drugs in an organised or semi-organised way. As the 1990s progressed, there is little doubt that drug dealing in New Zealand became more organised and controlled than ever before, and certain gangs have played key roles in this development. The 1990s also saw some new directions in the drug scene that have continued into the year 2000. The first is the rising presence of non-injectable morphine sulphate tablets (known as 'MSTs' or 'misties'). In most areas, where scarcity of codeine base or pressure upon bakers has made 'homebake' difficult to procure, MSTs have taken over as the most common source of opiate.[1] Prescribed frequently by doctors for chronic pain, MSTs are cheap to buy and can be converted to fairly pure injectable heroin in a simple, half-hour process.

It must be noted at this point that gangs almost never deal in addictive opioids. This is largely because of the stigma attached to them and the notorious unreliability of junkies. Although some sophisticated morphine-dealing operations have been uncovered, these are exceptions to the rule. The trade in morphine tends to be localised, involving small pockets of junkies, prostitutes and sickness beneficiaries, who deal principally with one another.

The availability of cheap, local morphine is the main reason that imported heroin in New Zealand is rare. One of the last major busts was in 1995, when Alan King was arrested for importing 2kg of heroin and for money laundering. In 1996 King, who had only recently been deported from Thailand after serving 11 years of a life sentence there for drug dealing, became the second person to have a confirmed sentence of life imprisonment for drug dealing imposed by the New Zealand High Court.

The second development of the 1990s has been the growing presence of the Class B drug, methamphetamine. Methamphetamine, also known as 'meth', 'crank' and 'speed', began trickling into New Zealand in the late 1970s. But few people came into contact with it and it did not become significant enough to appear in police reports until 1991. Since then, local manufacturing has fed a growing public appetite. Field and Casswell (1999: 39) report that whereas only one percent of those surveyed in 1990 aged 15 to 45 had used stimulants such as amphetamine, by 1998 the figure had grown to four percent. Produced by the kilogram, and normally heavily adulterated and sold by the gram, potential profits are astronomical. Thus, the 'crank' trade is still growing in spite of the large, double-figure sentences given to principals involved in it.

The final, and most recent significant development, is the appearance of another Class B drug, 'ecstasy' (MDMA). Synthesised as an appetite suppressant in Germany in 1912, 'ecstasy', or 'E', started to become popular as a party drug in Europe around 1985. It began arriving in New Zealand in small quantities soon after, but did not receive mention in police annual reports until 1995. Since that time, like methamphetamine, a huge demand for ecstasy has developed, in fact, the number of people aged 15–45 who had tried ecstasy grew five-fold – from .4 percent to two percent – between 1990 and 1998 (Field and Casswell, 1999: 39). With tablets selling for between $40:00 and $80:00 each, there are significant profits for importers who buy the drug for a fraction of that price overseas. Since the first big find of 5000 tablets in 1997, ecstasy busts have been quite regular, with more than 18,000 tablets seized since 1997. Sentences of up to 13 years have been imposed for trafficking in this drug.

Apart from prison sentences, a number of measures are in place in New Zealand to facilitate the prosecution of drug offenders and deter their activity. In 1980, a second overseas drug liaison office was established, this time in Sydney. Nowadays, drug liaison officers meet annually with their Asian counterparts, for the purposes of exchanging intelligence and coordinating activities. New Zealand is a member of INTERPOL, which formalises arrangements for international cooperation in criminal investigations and is a member of the Heads of Narcotics Law Enforcement Agencies (HONLEA), which is specifically aimed at international drug control. As a member of the United Nations, New Zealand is party to the

World Health Organisation's fight against international drug trafficking. For example, New Zealand liaises with the International Narcotics Control Board and is a signatory to the 1988 Vienna Convention Against Illicit Traffic in Narcotic Drugs and Psychotropic Substances. New Zealand also has a range of legislation which enhances its ability to extradite criminals between members of the British Commonwealth and other nations such as the United States, with which it has an extradition agreement. In addition, the Misuse of Drugs Act 1975 allows the prosecution of any person who conspires to commit an offence against the drug laws of New Zealand, whilst in another country (Newbold, 2000: 217-8). Thus, New Zealand has a range of agreements and laws in place to allow global and local coordination in policy and intelligence-gathering matters.

More recently, and not just related to drug dealing, the Proceeds of Crime Act 1991 allows the seizure of assets when the state can prove that property has been purchased through the proceeds of crime or has aided the commission of a crime. Since the act came into effect in July 1992, approximately $8.59 million worth of property has been confiscated under the act. In 1995, an amendment to the Crimes Act made money laundering an offence in New Zealand and the following year, the Financial Transactions Reporting Act made financial institutions responsible for reporting suspicious financial activity to the police. All of the above legislation has international applications, but for the most part they are used locally, particularly in relation to drug offending.

The Effectiveness of Drug Control Measures

It will be apparent from the above that New Zealand's drug control measures have been partially effective in combating this type of crime. The influx of marijuana and heroin, for example, was largely staunched by the mid-1980s by rigorous policing of the borders and comparatively large sentences. It is for the same reasons that cocaine has never been a problem in New Zealand: rigorous policing and penalties that are large by New Zealand standards. The drug became re-classified from Class B to Class A in 1987, and now carries a maximum of life imprisonment.

But allied to the above, it must be recognised that New Zealand's size and geographical location are also indirect factors in drug control. Unlike the United States and Australia, both of which are geographically close to drug-producing, third world countries, New Zealand is separated from its nearest large neighbour, Australia, by about 1900km of ocean. One of the most remote landmasses in the world, with an economy based largely on agriculture and fishing, it polices its borders and waters rigorously. Apart from specific drug-enforcement activity, therefore, day-to-day territorial controls add to the difficulty of importing controlled substances undetected.

A second factor is size: having a population of only 3.8 million affects New Zealand's attractiveness as a drug destination. The country can only absorb small amounts of narcotics like cocaine and heroin, without depressing their market value. Moreover, in the case of heroin, importers have to compete with locally-available MST and 'homebake', which are cheap and readily available. Cocaine must contend with amphetamine, which, at about $140:00 a gram, is a lot cheaper than cocaine at about $400:00 a gram. Thus, cocaine and imported heroin are rare and Australia is a far more commercially viable market. In a recent case, Tongan sporting hero Epalahame Liava'a and five others were convicted and sentenced to up to 12 years' jail for importing 4.5kg of cocaine – New Zealand's largest-ever cocaine bust. The bulk of this haul was destined for consumption in Australia.

The country's small population also makes it difficult for ongoing, large scale crime to continue undetected. Rising visibility was one of the reasons that the Mr Asia gang moved off-shore after it became successful. The last thing a criminal wants is a 'big name' and this is what tends to happen to large scale operators in small countries like New Zealand. One example of a failed large scale operator is Alan King, mentioned previously, who got life imprisonment in 1996 soon after his return from Thailand. Another is Peter Atkinson, who was released from a 13-year prison sentence in 1997. Not long after his discharge, Atkinson began a sophisticated, large-scale methamphetamine manufacturing operation, quickly becoming a household name in Auckland criminal circles. Not surprisingly, his activities were soon known to the police as well, who arrested him at the end of 1998. In December 1999 he was sentenced to 12 years imprisonment (later reduced to ten years on appeal).

Finally, unlike some Australian states, New Zealand does not have systemic corruption within its police force and customs service. Annual surveys by the Berlin-based organisation, Transparency International, have regularly found New Zealand to be one of the least corrupt of the 85 nations surveyed. The lack of corruption within New Zealand's policing and customs agencies is a major reason why syndicated crime in New Zealand – gang-related or otherwise – will always remain fairly low-key by international standards. Terry Clark, leader of the Mr Asia gang, was able to operate successfully in Australia, and be involved with at least five murders there without apprehension, partly because he had members of the Australian police on his payroll (Hall, 1981: 104; Kwitny, 1987: 251).

However, although they may reduce the amount of drugs entering the country, none of these factors is enough to stop the inflow when a ready and uncontested market is present. Examples are 'ecstasy' and LSD ('acid'). There are no known, large-scale manufacturing operations involving either of these drugs in New Zealand. There are no locally-available drugs that compete with them. Nearly all of the LSD and ecstasy consumed in New Zealand is imported. Prices for these drugs are high – $40:00 – $80:00 for an ecstasy tab and around $50:00 for an acid trip – but they are quite readily available in parts of New Zealand, most notably in the largest city of Auckland (population: one million). As observed, reported ecstasy usage has increased four-fold since 1990. Those aged 15–45 who report having used LSD at least once have grown more than threefold, to five percent (Field and Casswell, 1999: 39).

What this suggests is that if a market exists and there is profit available, some importers will run the customs/police gauntlet, and often they will succeed. Increased risks and the reduced supply that results, simply inflate unit prices.

We have also seen that, where customs/police activity has succeeded in cutting drug influx, this reduction has been associated with, and I suggest largely caused by, the emergence of reasonably-priced local alternatives. In the case of marijuana, it was 'New Zealand Green'; in the case of heroin, it was homebake and misties; in that of cocaine, which has never really taken hold in New Zealand due to its distance from South America, local methamphetamine. Border controls are not an issue with local drugs, and police activity has not significantly impacted on supply. Marijuana is widely available and broadly used, particularly among 18–24 year-old males. Around 65 percent of this group report having used marijuana; 45 percent in the last 12 months (Field and Casswell, 1999: 22). We have seen that methamphetamine has increased as well and it, too, is widely available in the big cities.

Police and justice figures reflect the increasing prevalence of the more dangerous types of drugs in recent times. Police-reported marijuana offences (principally use and possession) stabilised during the 1990s, but non-cannabis crimes grew by 45 percent. Justice Department data tell the same story: in the ten years between 1989 and 1998, convictions for marijuana usage were stable but cannabis dealing convictions grew by 60 percent and dealing in other drugs (principally Class A and B), by 82 percent. Convictions of low seriousness actually dropped, while those of high seriousness rose dramatically (Spier, 1999: 17, 53).

Although reported illegal drug use is rising, I suggest however that there is still little evidence that drug abuse constitutes a major public health problem. Approximately 92 percent of all reported drug offences are marijuana-related, which the Ministry of Health (1996: 12, 28) acknowledges has low levels of dependence and few deleterious effects among casual users. Addiction to opiates is low and fatalities are few. Accidental deaths from opioid overdose normally number less than ten a year and for all drugs, including prescribed barbiturates, there are about 30 deaths per year (Toxic Substances Board, 1989: 5; Department of Health, 1992: 52). Since it first started becoming available in the mid-1980s, there have been just two deaths attributed to ecstasy in New Zealand.

An interesting case is heroin and morphine, which are cheap and easy to acquire within certain circles, and significantly problematic in Australia, Britain and the United States. MSTs sell for about a dollar a milligram, and a non-habituated user can get high for as little as $15:00 on injected heroin converted from MST base. One would think that, with the drug being so cheap and so addictive, New Zealand would have a serious opioid addiction problem. This is not the case, although usage may be rising. In the Field and Casswell survey (1999: 43), the number of 15–45 year-olds who had ever used any opiate grew from three, to four percent. Current users grew from .5 to .6 percent. Greatest area of growth was in the 15–17 year age group: from one percent to three percent between 1990 and 1998. From these figures it may be deduced that there are around 11,000 'current users' of opiates in New Zealand. Not all of these are addicted and not all are illegal users. Many are taking prescribed opiates or opioids. In fact, in 1998, Pharmac, the Crown agency that manages New Zealand's Pharmaceutical Schedule, issued nearly 468,000 prescriptions for opioids, a figure that had grown by 72 percent since 1993 (Newbold, 2000: 188). It is from legal prescriptions that the majority of MSTs sold illegally derive. Adamson and Sellman (1998: 160) say that in 1996 there were four times as many registered methadone recipients as there were in 1991. Increased prescribing of MST must be at least part of the reason.

Nonetheless, chronic abuse levels are still apparently low. The number of registered drug addicts in New Zealand in 1996 was about 2800 (Adamson and Sellman, 1998: 160). Recognising that many current addicts are not registered, it is still unlikely, given Field and Casswell's figures, that more than 6000 addicts exist in New Zealand at any one time. At .16 percent, this is a fairly small fraction of the country's national population. Addicts may need up to $100:00 worth of drugs a day and for some, offending levels must be high. There is a perception that large numbers get this money through crimes such as burglary and theft. According to Adamson and Sellman (1998: 160), however, in 1996, 2352 registered addicts were receiving prescribed methadone, and an unknown number, we know, are addicted to their prescribed morphine. Others, as Adamson and Sellman (1998) confirm, support themselves (and often their partners) by prostitution. Only a few, I suggest, would be able to survive long by stealing and selling goods worth $100 on the black market, every day of the week.

If these facts are accepted, it is difficult to argue that New Zealand has a serious drug problem.

The 'Drug Problem' and Law Enforcement

If sentence length is any indication of perceived crime seriousness, it appears that the New Zealand judiciary, by and large, accepts that drugs are not a major problem. Penalties for Class A and B drug offending at the upper levels can be severe, but overall, treatment of drug offenders is not harsh. Just 15 percent of cannabis dealers are sent to prison, for an average of thirteen months. Fifty-four percent of dealers in 'other' drugs are imprisoned, for an average of only 33.5 months. Moreover, the judicial attitude appears to be softening. The percentage of dealers in 'other drugs' sent to prison, as well as the average sentences given to them, all declined in the 1989-1998 period (Spier, 1999: 54). Drug offenders in New Zealand are normally eligible for parole after serving one-third of their sentences, and may expect a release date after about half. Thus they are not in prison for long. In 1997, only 7.3 percent of all inmates were doing time for drugs as their major offence (Lash, 1998: 28).

These figures are in sharp contrast to those of the United States, where a significant heroin and cocaine problem exists, and where a reinvigorated 'war on drugs' since 1986 has created harsh sentences even for minor offenders (Jensen and Gerber, 1998). US state and federal legislatures have declared a 'zero tolerance' policy on drugs, meaning that simple possession can result in lengthy imprisonment (Inciardi, 1993: 31; Inciardi and McElrath, 1995: 319). One result is a burgeoning prison population, with inmate numbers increasing from .75 million to 1.8 million between 1985 and 1998. In 1998, 62.5 percent of all federal prison inmates were incarcerated for a drug offence, up from 53 percent in 1990 (Office of National Drug Control Policy, 1999: 25). Reported usage of drugs overall, as well of specific drugs such as cocaine and marijuana, dropped by about 40 percent between 1985 and 1990, but then stabilised and remained virtually unchanged through the 1990s.

Discussion

It is not clear to what extent the tough American laws have been responsible for the change in drug abuse patterns. Crack use is down, but both heroin and amphetamine use are up. These changes may have more to do with social trends than with law enforcement. In 1997, 14 million out of a total of 270 million Americans were estimated to be current users of illegal drugs (Office of National Drug Control Policy, 1999: 12-13, 26, 30, 32-33), and are apparently undeterred by the drug laws. The high social cost associated with the tough policies, and the injustices arising from them, have been the subject of considerable comment (eg. Inciardi, 1992; Irwin and Austin, 1994; Rosenberger, 1996; Jensen and Gerber, 1998).

In New Zealand, factors affecting the availability or otherwise of various types of drug are only partially affected by law enforcement strategies. Of course, law enforcement policy must have some effect: if it didn't drugs would be a lot cheaper and more accessible than they are. Law enforcement not only impacts on the prices and quantities of drugs available, however, it also affects the types of drugs that are around. We have seen that in New Zealand, rigorous police and customs activity was largely responsible for the replacement of imported heroin and marijuana with local varieties. It is these same factors that have made cocaine rare and expensive here. However, as the Americans have discovered, draconian sentencing laws and expensive drug control policies cannot stamp drugs out and are unlikely even to dramatically affect user levels. There are a number of other, interrelated, factors that influence what drugs are used, to what extent they are used, and by whom. The principal factors are:

1. Price. The price of a drug, relative to other drugs, affects usage because most customers are casual, with limited finances at hand. Expensive drugs like cocaine and ecstasy can only be used regularly by people who are affluent or high up the dealing chain. Others must abstain or seek a cheaper alternative. Moreover, some drugs last longer than others, and thus give a better 'bang for the buck'. Cocaine, for example, only lasts an hour or so, whereas a few snorts of meth can keep a person going all night.

2. Alternatives. The presence or absence of alternatives also affects usage. Drugs compete on a market basis with other drugs. Few people will pay $400:00 for a gram of cocaine, when they can purchase amphetamine for $140:00 a gram or Ritalin – a commonly-prescribed stimulant used in the treatment of Attention Deficit Hyperactivity Disorder (ADHD) – for a dollar a milligram. Likewise, users will seldom buy grams of imported heroin, when misties can be purchased for about a dollar a milligram.

3. Intoxicating Effects and After-Effects. A major factor in the marketability of a drug, of course, is the effect it has on the user, both in the long and short term. Some drugs 'feel' better than others, and some people prefer certain effects over others. Some, for example, prefer the laid-back opiate 'stone'; others like being speeded up. Some enjoy the psychotic adventure of LSD; others are frightened by it. Some like 'blobbing out' on marijuana; others loathe it. After-effects are also a factor. The amphetamine comedown, for example, is notoriously bad, leaving the user feeling drained the next day and perhaps off-colour for several days – creating what is sometimes known as 'terrible Tuesdays'. This causes many people to decline amphetamines, especially those with jobs. Ecstasy, on the other hand, is renowned for the feelings of euphoria it produces, and the absence of a heavy day-after hangover. This is one reason why it has become so popular in places like Europe, where it is cheap and plentiful. A final factor is

addictiveness. Because heroin is known to be highly addictive, many people refuse even to try it. They read the anti-heroin literature and spurn it because they fear it.

4. Availability. Markets for drugs are created by availability. Methamphetamine was around for at least 15 years before it became popular. This is because there wasn't much of it around. It was not until organised criminals began importing and then making amphetamine in bulk in the 1990s that this drug suddenly came into demand. The situation with ecstasy is similar. Ecstasy is widely-used in Europe because it is cheap and easy to get. However in New Zealand, due to problems with importation, availability is sporadic but the market is growing. Because it feels good and has few after-effects, people who try it want it again. So the more people who try it, the more they want it.

5. Popular Trends. Whether or not a drug is trendy or 'cool' is a major factor in its perceived attractiveness, especially among young people. LSD was extremely popular in the 1960s and 1970s, because of its association with the highly-publicised 'hippie' culture of north America, and because of its association with popular music of the time (eg. 'acid rock'), cult heroes (eg. Timothy Leary, Ken Kesey, and the Beatles), and the rebellious emotions of the anti-war movement. After the Vietnam War, which ended in 1974, usage of the drug largely fizzled out. It was replaced by heroin, which became the new drug-of-the-moment, popularised this time by the music of cult figures such as Lou Reed and bands like the Rolling Stones. In the mid-to-late 1970s, 'shooting skag' (injecting heroin) became an extremely cool thing to do among young people, even those from the middle classes. If we look at 'crack' cocaine, it has been suggested that its divorce from 'cool' was a major reason that usage has dropped in the United States: the 'crack generation' has grown older and today's youngsters see it as their parents' thing and thus, highly uncool (Witkin, 1998). Nowadays, ecstasy's link with teenage 'rave' culture and music is a factor that makes its usage highly cool and desirable.

Conclusion

So where illegal drugs are concerned, there are a variety of factors that determine availability, price and demand. Police activity is one; penalties are another. But it has to be recognised that drug control is not simply a matter of law enforcement and that many other dynamics are involved. For this reason, rigorous and rigid control strategies may simply deflect a problem elsewhere – as we have seen happened with marijuana and heroin – or create another problem, without actually solving the initial one. I have mentioned the zero-tolerance policies of the United States. These have resulted in a prison population that is exploding out of control, with huge expense and associated social dislocation. Drug use patterns have not been demonstrably affected, in fact, it appears that the changing profile of drug use in America – such as from crack to amphetamine – may have less to do with law enforcement strategy than with independent social trends.

So questions about drug control can never be answered simply. At the most fundamental level, people use mind-altering drugs – including alcohol – because they like them, and dealers sell these drugs because there is a dollar in it. It is unlikely that this situation will ever change. The nature and popularity of drugs may shift but whether legal or not, in some form or another, drugs will be in demand. Architects of social policy must know this: in a society such as ours, recreational drug use will always exist. Most drugs are dangerous in one way or another – some more dangerous, some less, or less dangerous in some ways and more in others. A well-managed drug control policy should aim at minimising the drugs with the most harmful effects, or minimising those drugs' harmful potential. Whatever the case, eradication is not a realistic objective and I have argued that attempting it may spawn more problems than solutions. The goal of a serious drug control policy, in my argument, should be management of drugs, both legal and illegal, in full recognition of the complex dynamics that such a task involves. If that is performed effectively, then we will not have a drug-free society, but we may have one where the deleterious potential of drugs is minimised.

Note

[1] The term, 'opiate' refers to opium and alkaline derivatives of opium, such as morphine and heroin. 'Opioid' refers to a wider category of drugs, and includes pharmaceutical non-opiates that produce an analgesic effect. Examples include methadone, omnipon, palfium and pethidine.

References

Abadinsky, H. (1993), *Drug Abuse: An Introduction*, Nelson-Hall: Chicago.

Adamson, S.J. and Sellman, J.D. (1998), 'The Patterns of Intravenous Drug Use and Associated Criminal Activity in Patients on a Methadone Treatment Waiting List', *Drug and Alcohol Review*, Vol. 17, pp. 159-66.

Anderson, D.C. (1999), 'The Mystery of the Falling Crime Rate', in M.L. Fisch (ed), *Criminology 99-00* (3rd ed), Dushkin McGraw-Hill: Guilford, CT, pp. 89-93.

Ashforth, J.I. (1970), 'A Short History of Drugs and Drug Abuse Control in New Zealand', in Board of Health, *Board of Health Committee on Drug Dependency and Drug Abuse in New Zealand* (First Report), Government Printer: Wellington, pp. 111-26.

Barger, R. (2000), *Hell's Angel: The Life and Times of Sonny Barger and the Hell's Angels Motorcycle Club*, Fourth Estate: London.

Board of Health (1970), *Board of Health Committee on Drug Dependency and Drug Abuse in New Zealand* (First Report), Government Printer: Wellington.

Board of Health (1973), *Drug Dependency and Drug Abuse in New Zealand*, (Second Report), Government Printer: Wellington.

Booth, P. (1980), *The Mr Asia File: The Life and Death of Marty Johnstone*, Fontana/Collins: Auckland.

Dennehy, G. and Newbold, G. (2001), *The Girls in the Gang: Women's Experiences in New Zealand Gangs*, Reed: Auckland.

Department of Health (1992), *Drug Statistics 1992*, Department of Health: Wellington.

Field, A. and Casswell, S (1999), *Drug Use in New Zealand: Comparison Surveys, 1990 and 1998*, Alcohol and Public Health Research Unit: University of Auckland, Auckland.

Grennan, S., Britz, M.T., Rush, J., and Barker, T. (2000), *Gangs: An International Approach*, Upper Saddle River, NJ, Prentice-Hall.

Hall, R. (1981), *Greed: The Mr Asia Connection*, Pan: Sydney.

Inciardi, J.A. (1992), *The War on Drugs II: The Continuing Epidemic of Heroin, Cocaine, Crack, Crime, AIDS, and Public Policy*, Mayfield, Mountain View: California.

Inciardi, J.A. (1993), *Criminal Justice* (4th ed), Harcourt, Brace, Jovanovich: Forth Worth.

Inciardi, J.A. and McElrath, K. (eds) (1995), *The American Drug Scene: An Anthology*, Roxbury: Los Angeles.

Irwin, J. and Austin, J. (1994), *It's About Time: America's Imprisonment Binge*, Wadsworth: Belmont, Ca.

Jensen, E.L. and Gerber, J. (1998), 'The War on Drugs Revisited: 'Objective' and Socially Constructed Harm', in E.L. Jensen and J. Gerber (eds), *The New War on Drugs: Symbolic Politics and Criminal Justice Policy*, Anderson: Cincinnati, pp. 197-203.

Jensen, E.L. and Gerber, J. (eds) (1998), *The New War on Drugs: Symbolic Politics and Criminal Justice Policy*, Anderson: Cincinnati.

Kwitny, J. (1987), *The Crimes of Patriots: A True Tale of Dope, Dirty Money, and the CIA*, Simon and Schuster: New York.

Lash, B. (1998) *Census of Prison Inmates 1997*, Wellington: Ministry of Justice.

McDonald, D., Stevens, A., Dance, P., and Bammer, G. (1993), 'Illicit Drug Use in the Australian Capital Territory: Implications for the Feasibility of a Heroin Trial', *The Australian and New Zealand Journal of Criminology*, Vol. 20, No. 2, pp. 127-45.

Ministry of Health (1996), *Cannabis: The Public Health Issues 1995-1996*, Ministry of Health: Wellington.

Morgan, J.L. (1997), *A Social History of Drug Use in New Zealand and the 'Manufacture of Consent': A Dunedin Case Study, 1960-89*, Unpublished MA thesis, University of Otago, Dunedin.

Newbold, G. (2000), *Crime in New Zealand*, Palmerston North: Dunmore.

Office of National Drug Control Policy (1999), *National Drug Control Strategy 1999*, Office of National Drug Control Strategy: Washington DC.

Rosenberger, L.R. (1996), *America's Drug War Debacle*, Avebury: Aldershot.

Schmalleger, F. (1999), *Criminal Justice Today: An Introductory Text for the 21st Century*, Prentice Hall: Upper Saddle River, NJ.

South, N. (1994), 'Drugs: Control, Crime, and Criminological Studies', in M. Maguire, R. Morgan and R. Reiner (eds), *The Oxford Handbook of Criminology*, Clarendon Press: Oxford, pp. 393-440.

Spier, P. (1999), *Conviction and Sentencing of Offenders in New Zealand 1989 to 1998*, Ministry of Justice: Wellington.

Toxic Substances Board (1989), *Health or Tobacco: An End to Tobacco Advertising and Promotion*, Toxic Substances Board: Wellington.

Witkin, G. (1998), 'The Crime Bust: What's Behind the Dramatic Drop in Crime?', *US News and World Report*, May 25, pp. 28-40.

Yska, R. (1990), *New Zealand Green: The Story of Marijuana in New Zealand*, David Bateman: Auckland.

Chapter 4

Korrectional Karaoke: New Labour and the Zombification of Youth Justice[1]

JOHN PITTS

> There's the music, and you have your own little line, you can sing it, and everything is written for you, and that is the way life appears to a lot of people and feels to a lot of people.
>
> Dennis Potter (1994)

> Un partito, uno voce (one party one voice).
>
> Benito Mussolini (1938)

Introduction

In 1998 the Labour government in the UK introduced the *Crime and Disorder Act*. This Act brought into being multi-agency Youth Offending Teams in each local authority area and created the Youth Justice Board of England and Wales to oversee their development and to assume control of secure and penal provision for juveniles; henceforth to be known as the 'secure estate'. The Act also ushered in new penalties and interventions which aimed to induce a new, younger, population into the youth justice system, via pre-emptive civil measures, which targeted their 'incivilities', augmented by 'parenting orders'. Informalism was abandoned in favour of earlier, formal, intervention by the police, via reprimands and final warnings. Diversion from custody into non-stigmatising 'alternatives' was abandoned. Instead, an expanded range of community penalties, which could be imposed on a maximum of two occasions, were introduced. After this, a new semi-indeterminate Detention and Training order was to be imposed and the age at which it might be imposed was lowered from 15 to

12, with reserve powers given to the Home Secretary to lower it to 10 if circumstances required.

The Necessity of Success

Anyone browsing the Youth Justice Board (YJB) website (www.youth-justice-board.gov.uk/newsletter/cover_article.html) in 2000 would have learnt that 'One of Britain's leading criminologists' had described the Pilot Youth Offending Teams (YOT's) as an 'unqualified success' and a fine example of 'joined-up government'. Scrolling down, the browser would have found this view endorsed by Home Secretary Jack Straw and Mark Perfect, the YJB Chief Executive.

In fact, the YOT evaluation was far more critical than this up-beat YJB press release suggests. This is hardly surprising. Their many achievements notwithstanding, nobody with a passing knowledge of the problems and dilemmas with which YOTs are presently grappling could conclude that they represent an 'unqualified' success. There are problems with the sufficiency and duration of funding. Professionals and managers from different agencies, and at different levels within those agencies, sometimes hold markedly different views about the purpose of YOTs and how such purposes might be realised (Bailey and Williams, 2000). Tight, albeit frequently unmet, Home Office time and Volume targets work against the establishment of realistic programmes for young people or effective victim-offender mediation. There is a paucity of protocols to guide work with the Voluntary sector and the secure estate. Moreover, there is ambiguity within the legislation itself and some vagueness and confusion at the YJB concerning priorities. These difficulties are compounded from time to time by erratic sentencing and political interventions aimed at exploiting the fear of youth crime for electoral advantage (Bailey and Williams, 2000; Youth Justice Board, 2001). Most seriously, perhaps, is the fact that less time seems to be spent in face-to-face-contact with youngsters in trouble than before New Labour came to power; the main problem Youth Offending Teams were introduced to remedy (Audit Commission, 1996).

Promises to Keep

Publication of the YOT Evaluation was preceded by considerable prevarication and uncertainty at the YJB. The publication date was shifted back several times and, had the general election not been delayed by the 'foot and mouth' epidemic, publication would have been scuppered by the law which prevents governments from publishing research during an election campaign. The YJB's anxieties about the content of the report which can be read as revealing only that making big, complicated changes quickly is difficult, flowed from the fact that reform of the youth justice system was a central plank of New Labour's 'covenant' with the electorate; the 'five pledges' upon which its 1997 election strategy was built. It was this commitment which led the Prime Minister, Tony Blair, in a front-page article in the *Sunday Express* in March 1999, entitled 'How we're fighting teenage tearaways', to declare that:

> We will deliver on our pledge on court delays, ... before, hardened young offenders could wait months between arrest and sentence with an average delay of 142 days ... Our aim, as a first step this year is to hit our target of 72 days for persistent offenders in 50% of cases (*The Sunday Express*, 1999: 6).

Somewhat rashly, the Prime Minister invited the electorate to sanction the government if it failed to 'deliver' on this pledge. Thus when, at the end of 2000, it emerged that the time between arrest and sentence had been reduced to around 96 rather than the promised 72 days, an obviously delighted Anne Widdecombe, the shadow Home Secretary, came out fighting. On the BBC's Today Programme, Lord Warner of Brockley, Labour peer and chair of the YJB, blustered that the time-scale for the promised reduction had been five calendar years rather than one parliamentary term but Ms. Widdecombe was not to be fobbed off, administering a monumental verbal drubbing to the hapless peer. Meanwhile, behind the scenes, the YJB was frantically dispatching 'gagging orders' to YOT managers, forbidding them to speak to the press about the unmet time targets.

This profoundly uninteresting fracas was the logical outcome of New Labour's commitment to a strategy of 'good governance' (Mair, 2000). 'Good governance' aims to circumvent the in-fighting, party political horse-trading, managerial drift and professional self-interest of a more traditional politics, in order to establish a 'direct' relationship with the electorate. This relationship involves making promises, being held accountable and being judged on 'hard outcomes'.

But who determines what these outcomes are to be? John Humphrys has observed that:

> The political technicians and strategists are now adept at identifying the relatively small number of people who can swing an election and put their clients in power, and they are the people they will listen to most carefully. All of Gould's focus groups consisted only of people who had voted Tory in 1992 and had become 'floaters'. So no one else gets a look in (2000: 251).

If the policy choices on offer are fashioned with an eye to ensnaring the ephemeral loyalties of this small but electorally significant rightward-leaning constituency, we should expect those policies to resonate with the central tenets of traditional Conservatism. Thus, politics as a struggle between opposing interests or a public competition of ideas collapses. In consequence, we witness what Slavoj Zizeck (2000) has called 'the zombification of social democracy'.

Populist Criminal Justice Policy

The implications of 'good governance' for youth justice policy are all too clear. New Labour's criminal justice policy-making perpetuates the movement away from 'elitism' towards 'populism' set in train by their Tory predecessors:

> The 'elitist model' had its heyday in the two and a half decades after 1945 ... This elite is often attributed with defending and promoting liberal, humane and welfarist policies against the demands of a more punitive public culture (Ryan, 1999: 3-4).

New Labour, as Gerry Johnstone (2000) observes, is only too keen to engage the public in the policy-making process.

> The Home Secretary, Jack Straw (the minister responsible for penal policy), has suggested that the elites, who from their comfortable social position pushed penal policy in a liberal and humane direction, were oblivious to the concerns of those less well positioned who suffer most from shocking rises in crime rates. ... Accordingly, Straw declared that, in devising its plans to tackle crime, the government would listen not just to 'interest groups' but also and primarily to 'ordinary people' living in areas undermined by crime and disorder (2000: 162).

As a result, both policy ends and policy means must accord with the dictates of an invariably retributive 'common sense'. The senior civil servants, criminal justice and penal professionals, pressure groups, judges and magistrates, who once determined the shape of criminal justice policy, are now moved to the margins of the policy-making process. New policy initiatives are no longer justified by reference to the criteria of these 'experts'. Now the experts are called upon to advise on the means whereby populist policy goals may be realised, rather than the ends to which policy should strive. Whereas, in an earlier period, growing penal populations were represented as a shameful error on the part of the authorities because they were both wasteful and inhumane, now a steadily rising penal population is celebrated as a political success. This is a celebration which serves to drown out the proponents of both traditional liberalism and progressive minimalism (Currie, 1985; Simon, 2000).

In this new era of populist 'good governance', policies must go all the way down. David Marquand (2000) has written of a 'Prussian discipline' within the Labour government, enforced, as often as not, by a new political class, part political apparatchik, part public servant, brought into being to keep public services, and their privatised surrogates, firmly 'on-message'. It is their job to establish 'robust' and 'rigorous' mechanisms for ensuring that neither policy ends nor policy means are subverted by managerial drift or professional self-interest. There is to be no slippage between intention and implementation; no space for discretion, innovation, cupidity, stupidity or idleness. Everybody at all levels – the policy makers, administrators, managers, professionals, private and Voluntary sector agencies, and even Volunteers if they are needed – must be heard to be singing 'from the same hymn-sheet'. Moreover, this hymn must be sung with optimum efficiency, economy and effectiveness because, like 'law and order' and sexual continence, fiscal prudence is dear to the hearts of the Tory defectors whose ephemeral loyalties these policies aim to secure. However, the attempt to meet all of their demands simultaneously presents formidable problems.

The Contradictions of Populism

The populist demand for greater surveillance, control and punishment has resulted in an overall increase in the numbers of juveniles incarcerated and an extension of incarceration to a new, younger, population. However, incarceration becomes progressively less productive, in both fiscal and rehabilitative terms, as penal populations grow younger. A report on the first cohort of 12-14 year olds to leave the new, £2,400:00 per head, per week, Secure Training Centres reveals a 30% reconviction rate within the first six weeks (Goldson and Peters, 2000).

Moreover, the rapid influx of children and young people into the 'secure estate', since the mid-1990s, has exacerbated the crisis of control already brewing in Young Offenders Institutions. This means that, even as their populations grow younger, the spread of violence, intimidation, extortion, rape, drug taking and drug dealing continues in institutions whose stated purpose is the inculcation of discipline into the previously undisciplined. Meanwhile the supposedly politically popular, although previously untried, pre-emptive measures introduced in the 1998 Act (the parenting order, the child safety order, the anti-social behaviour order) are driving up the costs of the youth justice system, despite the absence of any hard evidence that they will increase its effectiveness (Henricson, Coleman and Roker, 2000). Taken together, these developments drive a coach and horses through governmental claims that the system they are bringing into being will offer optimal economy, efficiency and effectiveness.

The Quest for Congruence

These developments offer an example of the tensions between the ideological and operational dimension of contemporary youth justice. Nonetheless, the attempt to achieve congruence between a populist, criminal justice 'agenda' and the practices of those who run and staff the agencies of the youth justice system continues apace. This project is being advanced by a novel range of inter-related strategies.

News Management

We have already noted the role played by the Youth Justice Board in delaying the publication of the YOT Pilot evaluation, 'spinning' a news story which deviates in significant ways from the actual findings, and 'gagging' the YOT managers. For its part, the Home Office has developed a covert 'shoot the messenger' strategy which aims to discredit Labour MPs, senior civil servants and public figures who wander 'off message'. Sir David Ramsbotham, the outspoken Chief Inspector of Prisons who has, on a number of occasions, called for the removal of under-18s from Young Offender Institutions, is regularly 'briefed against' by junior Home Office ministers who 'portray him as a dotty toff who has lost the plot'. Most recently, the Home Office announced that Sir David's contract was not to be renewed because he would shortly be entering a well-earned retirement. Unfortunately, nobody told Sir David and, shortly afterwards, his contract was extended for a further year. Former Conservative Home Secretary, Douglas Hurd, president of the Prison Reform Trust, gets the same anti-elitist flak when he criticises prison conditions and, just prior to the 2001 general election, the liberal Lord Chief Justice, Lord Woolf, was coming into the malevolent sights of Alistair Campbell, New Labour's chief 'spin-doctor'.

The Inculcation of Culture

One of the few 'big ideas' informing UK criminal justice policy at the dawn of the 21st century is 'cultural change'. In her consultative document *A New Choreography*, Eithne Wallis, the newly appointed director of the newly re-configured National Probation Service, states that:

> Nothing short of deep-rooted culture change in the organisation can deliver these reforms and outcomes. Many probation areas have already made a good start and we will acknowledge and build on these achievements. Sometimes, however, I shall be leading the Service against the grain of its past history and a tradition … As National Director, my primary strategic objective is to build the capacity of the NPS to deliver the Home Secretary's priorities and requirements (2nd draft, Nov. 2000: 5).

In a similar vein, the unpublished YOT Pilot report is at pains to stress the importance of the development of 'a new, correctional, practice culture relevant to the *Crime and Disorder Act'* within the YOTs. Temporarily abandoning their scientific neutrality, the authors assert that this 'new culture':

> ... is not about dealing with crises or exceptional cases; about non-intervention; about keeping cases open for long periods of time or about placing victims in a secondary role. ... [it] ...is about new and clear views of what managers and practitioners take for granted as routine work ... The Pilot Youth Offending Teams have moved to embrace this new culture of work but much more needs to be done.

Whether it is appropriate for notionally disinterested academic evaluators to specify so forcefully the nature of the new culture the Youth Offending Teams should be attempting to realise is, of course, debatable. The struggle to impose cultural homogeneity within the YOTs is rooted in the assumption that the development of a shared 'vision', ethos and mode of professional practice, which accords precisely with Home Office and YJB policy goals is an unequivocally desirable outcome. However, the realisation of this new culture, the report suggests, has been impeded by professionals who cling to discredited, anachronistic, practices. Yet, as Roy Bailey and Brian Williams (2000) found in their study of two Midland YOTs, divergent perceptions of how Youth Offending Teams should discharge their functions were not simply a product of idiosyncratic professional histories or aberrant professional priorities. They also derived from real ambiguities within the 1998 Act, real differences of view between senior officers in the partner agencies and real problems encountered by young people and victims. For their part, the education and health professionals seconded into the YOTs couldn't see how or why they could or should develop the requisite 'offence-focus' in their work.

It may be that what the YOT evaluations actually reveal is the impossibility of imposing a homogeneous culture upon teams comprising different professionals who are required, sometimes by law, to represent the interests of different protagonists in the legal process. It seems that in its effort to construct a corporate youth justice system, the YJB has systematically confused the building of an effective multi-agency team with the eradication of professional difference and the denial of structural conflict. An effective multi-agency team makes their differences explicit and creates a forum in which these differences can be discussed intelligently and some decision reached. A further barrier to the development of the homogeneous, 'correctional', cultures prescribed by the Youth Justice Board and the Home Office is the growing clamour from young people and their advocates, emboldened by the United Nations Convention on the Rights of the Child (UNCRC) and the new UK Human Rights Act, to have a voice in decisions taken about them by public bodies (Crimmens, forthcoming). However, the development of such a 'culture of critical discourse' (Habermas, 1983) which inevitably requires each protagonist to question both themselves and the assumptions which inform their practice, is not what the Home Office and the YJB have in mind at all. Yet, it is hard to see how the desired cultural hegemony could ever be sustained, since a defining characteristic of a culture is its capacity for adaptation to changing circumstances. The alternative to such cultural evolution is stasis and the collapse into an even more 'target-happy', 'outcome-led' bureaucratised practice, which will almost certainly result in even less time being spent in face-to-face contact with young people in need and in trouble.

The quest for cultural change is more than a straightforward attempt to re-fashion practice in accordance with the dictates of 'what works' or 'economy, efficiency, and effectiveness'. It also marks a repudiation of a set of ideas about crime and justice which have their origins in the seismic cultural shifts which took place in the 1960s. In the sphere of criminal justice Howard Becker's Whose Side are We On? (1967) and David Matza's Becoming Deviant (1969) launched a debilitating critique of the kinds of correctionalism currently in vogue in the UK, while posing an intriguing choice to justice system professionals: whether to be part of the solution by establishing solidarity with those who had fallen foul of the law, or part of the problem by colluding with the system's spurious correctional pretensions. These were ideas which came to inform the minimalist 'delinquency management' and 'back to justice' strategies developed by youth justice professionals in the 1970s and 1980s. The problem as perceived by the Home Office and the YJB in 2001 is to prevent this potentially dissident workforce 'going native' once again, by ensuring that they remain 'on message'. This is to be achieved by instituting a cultural change at the core of which is a far more pervasive managerial and political control.

De-professionalisation

New Labour's apparent ambivalence, if not antipathy, to youth justice professionals, has its origins in the neo-conservative critique of the welfare state that gained currency in the 1980s, according to which:

> ... the true purpose of the state is to further the interests of its constituent groups. A cadre of human service professionals such as health and care personnel, social workers, psychologists, counsellors and administrators [who] would be out of work if the welfare state was abolished (Stoesz and Midgley, 1991: 33).

One way to dislodge this parasitic by-product of the welfare state is to dismantle the structures which sustain it. De-professionalisation holds many advantages for criminal justice system policy makers and managers with an iconoclastic and homogenising bent. Non-professionals have little or no knowledge of alternative ways of doing things, as a result the potential for disagreement with, or deviation from, prescribed method or procedures is minimised. This means, for example, that the integrity of the Home Office accredited 'offending programmes', discussed below, is far less likely to be subverted by the exercise of 'professional discretion'. Such training as these new recruits receive is essentially practical and any ethical issues which arise can be resolved by reference to the relevant 'values statements' or codes of practice. Over time, this recruitment strategy spawns a new division of labour in which non-professionals 'deliver' the 'programmes' and the dwindling number of professional workers become, essentially administrative, 'case managers'. This produces a cheaper, more flexible and far more manageable workforce.

Increased throughput, tight time targets, escalating demand for information and data, burgeoning bureaucracy and 'initiative fatigue' mean that, more than ever before, face to face work in youth justice is being undertaken by unqualified sessional workers and Volunteers (Porteous, 2001), or is sub-contracted to private or Voluntary sector agencies, staffed largely by unqualified workers. The annexation of the Voluntary sector by government to provide mainstream criminal justice services was already evident in the 1980s (Pitts, 1988; Nellis, 1989). In the 1990s, dwindling charitable donations have increased the sector's reliance upon state funding. However, nowadays, this funding is secured via a process of competitive tendering for non-negotiable central and local government contracts. The rise of 'contract culture' has meant that Voluntary sector organisations are under immense pressure to act as low-cost providers of mainstream correctional services rather than exemplars of innovative practice or advocates for young people in trouble with the law.

Centralisation

The advent of the Youth Justice Board and the National Probation Service has transformed an assortment of local justice systems with, sometimes complex, local accountabilities into two, inter-related national systems with far greater accountability to the centre. This represents a significant move in the direction of a national system of youth justice, with the potential to inject a greater degree of equity into a system previously characterised by significant variations in provision, quality of service and sentencing outcomes (Audit Commission, 1996).

Although the Crime and Disorder Act (1998) hands new responsibilities to local authorities and local multi-agency partnerships, it is the Home Office, via the Youth Justice Board, which prescribes the goals they should pursue, the targets they should achieve and the time-scales within which they should achieve them. The procurement of the means whereby these goals and targets are to be achieved remains a local concern. However, the anxieties engendered by this simultaneously 'hands-on' and 'hands-off' mode of governance, leads to an unprecedented concern with implementation which, as a result, comes to be specified in ever closer detail in an attempt to minimise the scope for innovation and professional discretion. Thus, what initially appears to be an exercise in devolution, upon closer inspection, takes on the aspect of a franchising operation. 'Product support' is provided via a steady flow of 'evidence-based' data about 'what works' and 'pilot studies' of new administrative arrangements and modes of intervention, while 'quality control' is vouchsafed by statutory audit, and god help the laggard local authority or hapless police chief whose performance is found wanting by the Youth Justice Board auditors. Meanwhile, growing numbers of local councillors and chief executives are asking 'whatever happened to local government'?

Ironically, as a result of the electoral anxiety which pervades its ranks, New Labour's finely-tuned, optimally managed, 'evidence-based' structures can be subverted at a stroke if the opinion polls mirror back to the party, or its leader, that they are no longer regarded as the 'the fairest of them all' by that fickle element of the electorate which can swing the election. Thus, in 1999, with New Labour's popularity-rating slipping appreciably for the first time since the general election, Jack Straw suddenly introduced Michael Howard's 'three strikes and out' sentencing policy for juvenile offenders.

Narrowing the Aetiological Focus

In the contemporary discourse, aetiological theory has given way to the specification of 'risk factors'; the statistical correlates associated with youth offending. These 'risk factors' derive from the Cambridge Study of 411 South London boys undertaken by David Farrington and Donald West between 1961 and 1985 (West and Farrington, 1973). It is undoubtedly the case, as David Farrington asserts, that the 'risk factor prevention paradigm [has the great advantage of being] easy to understand and to communicate, and it is readily accepted by policy makers, practitioners and the general public' (2000: 7). However, as he also acknowledges, it is not possible at present to distinguish between those risk factors which are causes and those which are effects. Yet, if we are unable to accord some degree of causal primacy to 'parenting', 'truancy', 'drug abuse', 'homelessness', 'low income' and the like, or theorise the ways in which these correlates interact, we are little nearer understanding the causes of youth crime and our choice of methods of intervention must remain haphazard. In the event this, by no means insignificant, problem has been resolved by a process of political and scientific attrition.

In the Home Office consultative document Tackling the Causes of Crime (1996) eight key risk factors are identified: 'parenting', 'truancy', 'drug abuse' 'lack of facilities', 'homelessness', 'unemployment', 'low income' and 'economic recession'. These 'risks' are similar to those cited in the Audit Commission Report Misspent Youth (1996) which is hardly surprising since they both derive from the findings of the Cambridge Study. However, in the Audit Commission report the risk factors are divided into 'foreground' and 'background' factors. Familial and developmental factors occupy the foreground, while factors such as family income, employment and the socio-economic status of the neighbourhood are relegated to the background. In 1997 New Labour published its No More Excuses White Paper. No More Excuses drew heavily upon the 1996 Audit Commission Report and Crime and the Family, written by three New Labour insiders

(Utting, Bright and Hendrickson, 1993), which was also based upon the Cambridge Study. And concluded that 'the tangled roots of delinquency lie, to a considerable extent, inside the family'. In consequence, No More Excuses reduces the multiplicity of risk factors originally identified by West and Farrington to three main groupings. Parenting, Schooling and Peers, with the key risk factors identified as 'being male', having 'poor parental discipline', 'criminal parents' and 'poor school performance'.

This is remarkable because a significant body of contemporary research, utilising huge databases, suggests that the neighbourhood of residence may well have as significant an impact upon serious juvenile offending as the quality of parenting. In a study of 15,000 young people in Philadelphia (over 30 times the size of the West and Farrington cohort) Jones, Harris and Grubstein, (2000) found that 'risk factors' will operate quite differently in different cities and, indeed, different neighbourhoods:

> The results showed clearly that significant variations exist among neighbourhoods throughout the city in terms of the propensity of high-risk early delinquents to actually become chronic offenders (2000: 7).

One of Jones' major findings was that in certain well-resourced, higher socio-economic status neighbourhoods, all predictions of future chronic delinquency based on a risk factor assessment failed to materialise. Wikstrom and Loeber (1997) in their Pittsburgh Youth Study, utilising a database of 18,000 young people, found a clear neighbourhood effect upon offending, with serious offending by children and young people with the lowest individual risk factors occurring significantly more frequently in the lowest socio-economic status neighbourhoods.

Nonetheless, in an interview with the *Observer*, Jack Straw felt able to assert that:

> all the serious research shows that one of the biggest causes of serious juvenile delinquency is inconsistent parenting. We need to bring parenting out as a public issue so people feel able to talk about it. It is not easy, but one of my tenets in politics is that we should try the difficult issues (*Observer*, 1st February, 1998: 10).

Clearly, families play an important role in determining whether, or to what extent, children and young people become involved in a broad range of socially deviant and illegal behaviours. However, the causal primacy ascribed to the 'criminogenic' lower class family in New Labour's youth justice strategy suffers from what Elliott Currie (1985) has termed the 'fallacy of autonomy'. This is because it denies or ignores the relationship between socio-economic stress, neighbourhood poverty and the biographies of young offenders (Braithwaite, 1979 and 1981; Field, 1990; Hope, 1994; Wikstrom and Loeber, 1997; Sampson, Raudenbush and Earls, 1997; Pitts and Hope, 1998; Hagedorn, 1998; Young, 1999), the peculiar, mutually-reinforcing, negative contingencies set in train by socially deviant acts perpetrated by lower class children and young people (Hagan, 1993; Sampson and Laub, 1993) and the role of state agencies in the construction and amplification of their 'deviant careers' (Muncie, 1999; Goldson, 1999 and 2000).

The appeal of the strangely skewed criminological perspective which now constitutes New Labour's *de facto* aetiological theory of youth crime is fairly clear. In a time when politicians are unwilling to countenance robust social and economic intervention to counter social problems, and yet eager to demonstrate that they are equally 'tough' on both crime and the 'family', an analysis which identifies poor child-rearing practices and weak parental control as the fundamental problem is a political godsend.

Restricting the Rehabilitative Options

Although the risk factor prevention paradigm would not seem to point unequivocally towards any particular intervention programme, its proponents appear to be unanimous in their espousal of the transformative powers of cognitive-behavioural interventions (see for example, Farrington, 1996). These programmes aim to develop the types of 'cognitive social competence' in offenders which will enable them to exert 'self-control'. However, the logical link between the risk factor prevention paradigm and these programmes has yet to be satisfactorily explained. We are therefore left to infer that the numerous and disparate social, economic and psychological risk factors identified by West and Farrington, have the single, simple, effect of undermining the young offender's capacity for self-control; the very deficiency, which incidentally, cognitive behavioural programmes are designed to remedy. This simple and convenient explanation is made yet more implausible when we recognise that some of the leading aficionados of the risk-factor paradigm are also major purveyors of the, often costly, cognitive behavioural remedy (Ross, 1988; Hawkins and Catalano, 1998).

Whatever their logical fit, there can be little doubt that the risk factor prevention paradigm and cognitive behavioural programmes are ideas whose time has come. Once again, Eithne Wallis, director of the National Probation Service, captures the spirit, pace, style and syntax of New Labour's correctional thrust perfectly when she asserts that:

> This is the leadership challenge now facing the newly created National Probation Service for England and Wales. The scale of change and reform unleashed through the Criminal Justice and Court Services Bill is unprecedented in the Service's history and the service delivery targets are formidable. The 'What Works' portfolio of evidence-based offender programmes is ground breaking in its scale, on the fast moving world stage of correctional services (2000: 6).

It is intended that these evidence-based, cognitive behavioural, programmes, accredited by the newly formed Community Justice National Training Organisation (CJNTO), will become the 'national curriculum' of the National Probation Service by 2004 (Wallis, 2000). Their development will be paralleled by the spread of similar programmes, accredited by the H.M. Prison Service Offending Behaviour Unit, which are currently operating in 100 UK prison department establishments. In prisons, and increasingly in the probation service, sessions are video-taped and sent to the Home Office where they are evaluated. The monitors are particularly concerned with the integrity of programme implementation in that the programme should run exactly as intended by its designers. Thus those personnel who, quite literally, deviate from the 'script' are brought to book since they may well jeopardise programme integrity, and hence the accreditation of the institution or probation area. We are witnessing the emergence of a 'one-size-fits-all' national (correctional) curriculum for offenders in prison and the community and, its corollary, a substantially enhanced capacity for senior managers to quantify and control the day-to-day, face-to-face, work of probation officers, prison officers and ancillary workers. With the advent of the new 'Intensive Supervision and Surveillance Programmes' to be introduced for young offenders in the new parliament, it is more than likely that these programmes and these managerial regimes will spread to the YOTs.

In accrediting a limited range of ideas and practices, and tying the allocation of resources to their successful introduction and execution, 'accreditation' effectively discredits alternative ideas and practices and prevents innovation from below. The homogenisation of correctional intervention is justified on the grounds that the programmes commended by CJNTO and the Prison Service Offending Behaviour Unit are those to which 'research points as the most thorough and best designed programmes showing the most promising results' (Farrington, 1996: 4).

Indeed, this phrase has become a kind of official mantra amongst Home Office ministers, the YJB, senior figures in the welfare, justice and community safety industries and the denizens of some university senior common rooms. However, the apparent confidence in these interventions, cognitive skills training (and its derivatives), restorative justice and mentoring, appears to be rooted in a partial reading of the research evidence and an over-estimation of their 'promise'.

The most frequently cited evidence of the effectiveness of cognitive skills training is derived from the correctional programme designed by Robert Ross and undertaken in a Canadian jail in the mid-1990s (Fabiano, Porporino and Robinson, 1991). What this evidence actually shows is that prisoners who volunteered for, and 'completed', cognitive skills programmes clocked-up a 19.7 percent re-conviction rate, compared with in excess of 50 percent for prisoners who did not volunteer. However, a third group, who volunteered for the programmes but were placed on a waiting list, registered a reconviction rate of 23 percent. When other contingencies and inconsistencies are taken into account the measurable impact of the cognitive skills training programme evaporates (Pawson and Tilley, 1997). Sophisticated meta-analyses of cognitive-behavioural programmes conducted with young offenders in North America suggest that they will succeed with only a limited range of motivated participants and only if intensive aftercare or 'relapse prevention' programmes are instituted. Even then, re-conviction rates are likely to exceed 50% (Fabiano *et al*, 1991; Gendreau, 1996; Lipsey and Wilson, 1998; Matthews and Pitts, 1998; Vanstone, 2000).

The other measures which underpin, or otherwise support, the youth justice provisions of the *Crime and Disorder Act* (1998) are restorative justice and mentoring. In his overview of restorative justice programmes undertaken for the Home Office, Tony Marshall (1999) notes that research on the relationship between participation in restorative justice programmes and re-conviction is inconclusive. This finding is echoed by Lipsey and Wilson (1998), in their meta-analysis of the ten best evaluated US 'restitutive' intervention programmes. Indeed, whatever its merits in terms of victim-offender satisfaction, there is little to suggest that restorative justice has a particularly positive effect on re-conviction rates (Van Hooris, 1985).

Unsurprisingly, perhaps, the evaluations of mentoring cited by the Youth Justice Board, which is funding over 100 such programmes, are remarkably upbeat, deriving as they do mainly from studies undertaken by members of the US-based National Mentoring Association. However, in the main, these studies have been undertaken by the agencies providing the mentoring programmes. As such, they may tend, for understandable reasons, to 'accentuate the positive' and overlook, or underplay, areas where no change occurs or where problems actually worsen. Other American research, on the effectiveness of mentoring with young offenders, is far more equivocal. An analysis of the ten 'best-evaluated' mentoring programmes, carried out for the US Department of Justice in the early 1990s (Brewer, Hawkins, Catelano and Neckerman, 1995), suggests that they failed to achieve their goals in terms of academic attainment, 'dropping out', behavioural change or employment. This analysis also points to 'interaction effects', citing evaluations which reveal significantly increased delinquency for young people with no previous offences, although significantly decreased recidivism for youngsters with prior offences (Goodman, 1972; Fo and O'Donnell, 1974).

The problem is not that these correctional options don't 'work' at all. Like the interventions they have supplanted, for example: social casework, social group work, adventure education, motor projects etc., they sometimes, in some cases, help to reduce the incidence and severity of some young peoples' offending. However, far too much has been claimed for them and the suggestion, implicit within the contemporary correctional discourse, that if 'properly administered', these techniques will simply arrest the development of 'offending careers', is implausible. However, this belief has led to the creation of a youth justice system in which the number of community penalties a young person may receive is reduced to two, alternatives to custody are eliminated, custodial options are expanded and custodial sentences lengthened in the belief that only the most intractable young offender could be unresponsive to these evidence-based interventions. It should come as no surprise then, that we are currently witnessing a youth imprisonment bonanza unsurpassed since the early 1980s (Pitts, 1988; Goldson and Peters, 2000).

In reality we can seldom be sure of what 'works', with whom, under what circumstances and why. In a rational world this realisation would trigger the development of a broad range of measures, designed to operate at many different levels. Instead, the overweening desire of government to control policy all the way down to the point of implementation means that a rich repertoire of responses to the complex problem of youth crime is reduced to a narrow range of correctional techniques, the popularity of which resides ultimately in the fact that they accord with the tenets of a conservative 'political correctness'.

Speaking Truth to Power

Edward Said (1994) argues that the role of the intellectual is 'to speak the truth to power'. If there is to be a productive relationship between social science and governance, social science must provide illumination rather than the scarcely veiled political legitimation currently on offer. Illumination is an active process, involving a critique of policy assumptions and policy ends as well as policy means. The social science discussed here proceeds from the same 'common sense' beliefs which inform the government's populist policies and, as a result, it tells us exactly what the Conservative defectors who populate Mr. Gould's focus groups always suspected – that inadequate and incompetent parents produce inadequate, incompetent, and sometimes dangerous children – and in the process it demonises them. As Jock Young observes:

> Demonisation is important in that it allows the problems of society to be blamed upon 'others', usually perceived as being at the edge of society. Here the customary inversion of causal reality occurs: instead of acknowledging that we have a problem in society because of basic core contradictions in the social order, it is claimed that all the problems of society are because of the problems themselves. Get rid of the problems and society would be, *ipso facto*, problem free! (1999: 111).

Can This Really be the End?

The advent of this new youth justice is presented as a kind of 'year zero', the beginning of history, on the one hand and the 'end of history'; the fullest expression of post-ideological, evidence-based, good governance, to which there is simply no alternative, on the other. But the end of history has been erroneously predicted many times before. Perhaps the main lesson to be drawn from the history of the UK youth justice system in the post-war period is that the coalescence of social, cultural, political and intellectual currents into legal and administrative structures and professional practices, far from signalling the coming of age of a historical project, often foreshadows its demise. Then, as now, even as the new laws are placed on the statute book, the political administrative and fiscal downside of the project is becoming evident. Usually, the early promise of the rehabilitative or correctional interventions the project has spawned, has not been realised. Meanwhile, the political, academic and professional constituency which gave impetus to the project is unravelling and the political imperatives which created the conditions for its emergence will almost certainly be changing.

Thus, the 1960s saw the development of a strategy of welfarist social interventionism which culminated in the *Children and Young Person's Act* (1969). However, the early 1970s witnessed a corrective backlash, resulting in a custodial bonanza which culminated in the previously unparalleled punitiveness of the *Criminal Justice Act* (1982). No sooner had the 1982 Act hit the statute books than soaring custody rates and a looming fiscal crisis spawned a cross-party 'minimalist' alliance which achieved unprecedented reductions in the numbers of youngsters formally processed and imprisoned. These latter developments were enshrined in the 1991 *Criminal Justice Act*, the aims of which were almost immediately subverted by the punitive renaissance of the early 1990s a succession of modifications to the law pertaining to the sentencing of juveniles which culminated in the *Crime and Disorder Act* (1998).

It is tempting, but probably unwise, to see this as a kind of Hegelian dialectic; an oscillation from thesis to antithesis to synthesis. Nonetheless it is intriguing to watch the perpetual re-configuration of policy elements to meet the changing political, economic and administrative contingencies with which governments must deal. Welfarist interventionism ousts classicism only to be supplanted by justice-oriented minimalism, which is, in turn, met by justice-oriented interventionism. The logic of this dialectic would appear to dictate that the next development will be 'welfarist minimalism' in which the elusive 'hard core' will be forced into re-opened Child Guidance Clinics to recount their dreams. Or maybe not.

The New Correctionalism: Eulogy or Epitaph

More ominously, it may be that New Labour's flirtation with correctionalism is drawing to a close and that the shift towards American-style 'post-modern penology', predicted by some commentators, is now underway (Simon, 2000; Pratt, 2000). As New Labour enters its second term, it is evident that correctionalism is being sidelined in favour of greater 'surveillance' and 'incapacitation'. The investment of £45 million over three years, from April 2001, to enable fifty urban YOTS to operate 24-hour Intensive Supervision and Surveillance Programmes for fifty hardcore young offenders represents a move away from correctionalism. This cash injection of £250,000 per annum for the selected urban YOTs notwithstanding, a shift from a weekly two hour meeting between the YOT worker and the young person to 7-day, 24 hour, surveillance represents an 840% increase in staffing. It is inconceivable that this move will not undermine still further the capacity of YOTs to develop the holistic, correctional regimes which are their *raison d'etre*. The promised 400 additional places in Secure Training Centres, their already legendary counter-productiveness notwithstanding, the 'three strikes' sentencing strategy for repeat juvenile offenders to be introduced in June 2001 and the *de facto* one-strike 'breach' conditions introduced in the *Criminal Justice and Court Services Bill* (2000) all attest to the growing centrality of penal incapacitation. Of course, these developments will be girded round with the rhetoric of rights, even as they systematically violate both the letter and the spirit of the *Children Act* (1989), the UN Convention on the Rights of the Child, the provisions of the European Court of Human Rights and the UK *Human Rights Act* (2000). But, in the hands of New Labour, young people's rights are routinely subordinated to the strident demands of authoritarian populism. The January 1999 Social Services Inspectorate report on the first Secure Training Centre recommended that it be shut down and the construction of three further centres should cease because such facilities were inimical to the rights and best interests of the children confined there. Similarly, as we have noted, successive reports from Sir David Ramsbotham, Chief Inspector of Prisons, have recommended that children or young people under 18 should be removed from Prison

Department establishments as soon as possible for the same reasons. If evidence of a New Labour's commitment to a post-modern penality were needed, the shelving of these damning reports and plans to expand this provision in its second term provides just that.

'Korrectional Karaoke' is, first and foremost, an attempt to peddle simplistic, but politically acceptable, solutions to remarkably complex social, economic and cultural problems. As Richard Titmuss once observed, 'the denial of complexity is the essence of tyranny' and this tyranny is presently being visited upon many of the poorest and most vulnerable children and young people in our society (Jones, 2001). Yet, nothing stays the same for long and as I write 'Korrectional Karaoke' is transmogrifying into a far more ominous 'Retributive Rap'.

Note

[1]   An earlier version of this chapter appeared under this title in the journal *Youth Justice*, Vol.1, No.2, of October, 2001.

References

Audit Commission (1996), *Misspent Youth*, The Audit Commission: London.

Bailey, R. and Williams, B. (2000), *Inter-agency Partnerships in Youth Justice: Implementing the Crime and Disorder Act 1998* Social Service Monographs research in practice/Community Care.

Becker, H. (1967), 'Whose Side are We On?', in *Social Problems* Vol. 14, No. 3, pp. 239-47.

Braithwaite, J. (1981), 'The myth of social class and criminality reconsidered', in *American Sociological Review* Vol. 46, pp. 36-57.

Braithwaite, J. (1989), *Reintegrative Shaming*, Cambridge University Press: Cambridge.

Brewer, D., Hawkins, J., Catalano, B. and Neckerman H. (1995), 'Preventing Serious, Violent and Chronic Juvenile Offending: A Review of Evaluations of Selected Strategies: Childhood, Adolescence and the Community', in J. Howell, B. Krisburg, J. Hawkins and J Wilson, *Serious, Violent and Chronic Juvenile Offenders*, Sage Publications: London.

Crimmens, D. (forthcoming), *Having Their Say: Young People, Rights and Participation*, Russell House Publishing: Lyme Regis.

Currie, E. (1986), *Confronting Crime: An American Challenge*, Pantheon: New York.

Fabiano, E., Porporino, F. and Robinson, D. (1991), 'Canada's Cognitive Skills Program Corrects Faulty Thinking', in *Corrections Today*, Vol. 53, August, pp. 102-8.

Farrington, D. (1996), *Understanding and Preventing Youth Crime*, Joseph Rowntree Foundation: York.

Farrington, D. (2000), 'Explaining and Preventing Crime: The Globalisation of Knowledge', in *Criminology* Vol. 38, No. 1, February, pp. 1-24.

Field S. (1990), *Trends in Crime and Their Interpretation*, Home Office Research, Study No. 119, HMSO: London.

Fo, W. and O'Donnell, C. (1974), 'The Buddy System: Relationship and Contingency Conditioning in a Community Intervention Program for Youth with Non-Professionals as Behaviour Change Agents', in *Journal of Consulting and Clinical Psychology*, Vol. 42, pp. 163-196.

Gendreau, P. (1996), 'The Principles of Effective Intervention With Offenders', in A. Harland (ed.) *Choosing Correctional Options That Work*, Sage Publications: Thousand Oaks.

Goldson, B (1999), 'Youth (In)justice: Contemporary Developments in Policy and Practice', in Goldson B. (ed.) *Youth Justice: Contemporary Policy and Practice*, Ashgate: London.

Goldson, B. and Peters, E. (2000), *Tough Justice: Responding to Children in Trouble* The Children's Society: London.

Goodman, A. (1972), *Companionship Therapy: Studies in Structured Intimacy*, Jossey Bass: New York.

Habermas, J. (1983), *Moralbewusstein und Kommunikatives Handeln* Suhrkamp: Frankfurt.

Hagan, J. (1993), 'The Social Embededness of Crime and Unemployment', in *Criminology*, Vol. 31, pp. 455-91.

Hagedorn, J. (1998), *People and Folks: Gangs, Crime and the Underclass in a Rustbelt City*, Lakeview Press: Chicago.

Hawkins, D. and Catclano, R. (1998), *Effective Prevention for Today's Youth Problems*, Developmental Research and Programmes: Seattle.

Henricson, C., Coleman, J. and Roker, D. (2000), 'Parenting in the Youth Justice Context', in *The Howard Journal of Criminal Justice* Vol. 39 No. 4, November, pp. 325-8.

Hope, T. (1994), *Communities Crime and Inequality in England and Wales*. Paper presented to the 1994 Cropwood Round Table Conference Preventing Crime and Disorder, September 14-15, Cambridge.

Humphrys, J. (2000), *Devil's Advocate* Arrow: London.

Johnstone, G. (2000), 'Penal Policy Making: Elitist, Populist or Participatory?', in *Punishment and Society* Vol. 2, No. 2, April, pp. 161-80.

Jones, A. (2001), *An Analysis of the Offending Careers of Young People Placed On the Child Protection Register of One London Borough*, University of Luton (unpublished M.Phil Thesis).

Jones, P., Harris, J. and Grubstein, L. (2000), *Identifying Chronic Juvenile Offenders*, Paper presented to the 2000 British Criminology Conference, Leicester, July, produced at the Crime and Justice Research Institute, Philadelphia, PA, USA.

Lipsey, M. and Wilson, D. (1998), 'Effective Intervention for Serious Juvenile Offenders: a Synthesis of Research', in R. Loeber and D. Farrington (eds), *Serious and Violent Juvenile Offenders: Risk Factors and Successful Interventions*, Sage Publications, Thousand Oaks.

Mair, P. (2000), Partyless Democracy, in *New Left Review*, Vol. 2. March/June.

Marquand, D. (2000), 'From Baldwin to Blair', in *New Left Review*, Vol. 3. May/April.

Marshall, T. (1999), *Restorative Justice: an Overview*, Home Office Research Development and Statistics Division: London.

Matthews, R. and Pitts, J. (1998), 'Rehabilitation, Recidivism and Realism: Evaluating Violence Reduction Programs in Prison', in *The Prison Journal*, Vol. 78, No .4, December, pp. 390-405, Sage Publications.

Matza, D. (1969), *Becoming Deviant*, Prentice Hall: New Jersey.

Muncie, J. (1999), *Youth and Crime: A Critical Introduction*, Sage Publications: London.

Nellis, M. (1989), 'Juvenile Justice and the Voluntary Sector', in Matthews, R. (ed.) *Privatising Criminal Justice*, Sage Publications: London.

Pawson, R. and Tilley, N. (1997), *Realistic Evaluation*, Sage Publications: London.

Pitts, J. (1988), *The Politics of Juvenile Crime*, Sage Publications: London.

Pitts, J. and Hope, T. (1998), 'The Local Politics of Inclusion: The State and Community Safety', in *Social Policy and Administration*, Vol. 31 No. 5.

Porteous, D. (2001), 'Mentoring, Factor F', in V. Chauhan and J. Pitts (eds) *The Russell House Companion to Work with Young People*, Russell House Publishing: Lyme Regis.

Pratt, J. (2000), 'The Return of the Wheelbarrow Men: or, the Arrival of Postmodern Penality?' in *The British Journal of Criminology* Vol. 40, No. 1, Winter, pp. 127-45.

Ross, R. (1988), 'Reasoning and Rehabilitation', in *International Journal of Offender Therapy and Comparative Criminology* Vol. 32, pp 29-35.

Ryan, M. (1999), 'Penal Policy Making Towards the Millennium: Elites and Populists: New Labour and the New Criminology', in *International Journal of the Sociology of Law* Vol. 27, No. 1, pp. 1-22.

Said, E. (1994), *Representations of the Intellectual*, Vintage: London.

Sampson, R. and Laub, J. (1993), *Crime in the Making: Pathways and Turning Points*, Harvard University Press: Boston.

Sampson, R., Raudenbush, S. and Earls, F. (1997), 'Neighbourhoods and Violent Crime: A Multi-Level Study of Collective Efficacy', in *Science*, Vol. 277, August 15.

Simon, J. (2000), 'From the Big House to the Warehouse: Re-thinking Prisons and State Government in the 20th Century', in *Punishment and Society* Vol. 2, No. 2, April, pp. 213-34.

Stoesz, D. and Midgley, J. (1991), 'The Radical Right and the Welfare State', in H. Glennester and J. Midgley (eds) *The Radical Right and the Welfare State*, Harvester Wheatsheaf: London.

Utting, W., Bright, J. and Henricson, C. (1993), *Crime and the Family: Improving Child Rearing and Preventing Delinquency*, paper No.16, Family Policy Studies Centre, London.

Van Hooris, P. (1985), 'Restitution Outcome and Probationer's Assessments of Restitution: The Effects of Moral Development' in *Criminal Justice and Behaviour* Vol. 12, pp. 259-87.

Vanstone, M. (2000), 'Cognitive-Behavioural Work with Offenders in the UK: A History of Influential Endeavour', in *The Howard Journal* Vol. 39, No. 2, May, pp. 171-83.

Wallis, E. (2000), *A New Choreography: Integrated Strategy for the National Probation Service for England and Wales – Strategic Framework 2001-2004*, Draft 2, November, Consultation Document, The National Probation Service: London.

West, D. and Farrington, D. (1973), *Who Becomes Delinquent?*, Heinemann: London.

Wikstrom, B. and Loeber, C. (1997), 'Individual Risk Factors, Neighbourhood SES and Juvenile Offending', in M. Tonry (ed.) *The Handbook of Crime and Punishment*, Oxford University Press: New York.

Young, J. (1999), *The Exclusive Society*, Sage Publications: London.

Youth Justice Board (2001), *Pilot Youth Offending Team Evaluation Undertaken by the Universities of Sheffield, Hull and Swansea*, Home Office: London.
Zizeck, S. (2000), 'Casting Out Haider', in *New Left Review* Vol. 2, March/April.

Chapter 5

Expect the Unexpected:
DNA, Guilt and Innocence

BARBARA ANN HOCKING AND HAMISH MCCALLUM

Introduction

There can be no more persuasive example of a hi-tech solution to crime control than DNA technology. In the criminal sphere, DNA has been hailed as a miracle of proof – capable of solving the mystery of the unsolvable crime (Chester, 2000). With such law-enforcement glowing credentials, the prospect that DNA might also provide a form of empowerment for convicted prisoners seems unlikely – but with DNA, it is a case of expect the unexpected! As uses of DNA have accelerated and police powers expanded to accommodate increased DNA sampling and testing, the refrain has been 'if you're innocent you have nothing to fear'. The refrain refers to the role of DNA in crime control. In this chapter, in keeping with the theme of this book, we consider that role together with its unexpected consequence: namely, that DNA may not actually impact greatly on crime statistics as it may serve to prove innocence as well as guilt. The point is that DNA is actually most persuasive as a technology of exclusion rather than inclusion and that 'non-matches' are more clearly justice related than 'matches'. Convicted prisoners have seized upon this potential in their attempt to prove innocence, as have law enforcement officers in their efforts at detection. A number of unexpected, unresolved tensions emerge from the use of DNA, most particularly concerning powers, rights and responsibilities with respect to DNA samples and tests.

The Genetic Age

The contemporary era has been called the 'biotech century' and the age of genetic commerce. It has been referred to as an age in which our biological understandings of the word 'genetics' have changed (Katz Rothman, 1998: 21). It is claimed that where once 'gene' was 'the name given to the force that transmits qualities from parent to child, whether among people or among pea plants' the term now signifies 'stretches of DNA that code for the production of specific proteins' (Katz Rothman, 1998: 21). DNA has also been referred to as '… that famous double helix, that intertwining spiral staircase whose image shows up on everything from ads to sociology textbooks' (Katz Rothman, 1998: 21). New genetic technologies are playing a key role in the clinical medical area, giving rise to urgent calls for resolution of its complex legal issues and comprehensive regulation of genetic research and bio-informatics (Kirby, 1993: 894; Chalmers 1999: 202-39; Lemmens and Austin, 2001). The new advanced genetics, as an integral development in contemporary medicine and health care, has been called 'one of the substitute forums for religion' (Somerville, 2000: 4) because it provides diverse possibilities stretching even to 'immortalizing our genetic selves' (Somerville, 2000: 75) through human cloning.

The uses of DNA are many and varied. In France it has been claimed that DNA helped to 'trap the Beast of the Bastille' (MacIntyre, 1998) and has solved the mystery of deceased singer Yves Montand's 'love-child', where his body was dug up and taken to a laboratory for DNA tests to settle a 22 year old woman's claim to be the film legend's unacknowledged love child (Whitney, 1998). In Australia, DNA has assisted in the search for an Aboriginal warrior's grave. Emeritus Professor of Anthropology at Sydney University, Richard Wright, will use radar and DNA sampling in the search for the remains of the Aboriginal warrior Yagan in farmland near Perth. Yagan was shot by white settlers 166 years ago, decapitated, his body buried and his head sent to London. The head was returned to Australia after Aboriginal people went to collect it more than a century later (*Sydney Morning Herald*, 1999). Legal applications of DNA technology extend to fields as diverse as ecology and conservation (for example, wildlife smuggling situations (Chester, 1998; Saunders, 1998: 4) and in the identification of ivory poachers (*Sydney Morning Herald*, 2000; Carpi and Mital, 2000) and a role in proof of substitution of low value seafood species for high value seafood species (for example, passing shark off as coral trout). The issue is that of a DNA fingerprinting database of all legally kept wildlife, coupled with electronic tagging and legislation, enabling smugglers to be prosecuted on the DNA evidence. In its many and varied incarnations, the advanced genetic technologies are being universally hailed as miracles of science and law across the jurisdictions. Despite such optimism, governments have sought to establish the benefits and potential dangers of genetics technology. Thus, various government inquiries have been established including the current Australian Law Reform Commission and the Australian Health Ethics Committee of the National Health and Medical Research Council joint inquiry into issues surrounding advances in genetic information (Australian Law Reform Commission: [http://alrc.gov.au/news/index.htm]).

Every Which Way – it's DNA!

As the uses of DNA in crime control have accelerated, claims of its powers have comparably expanded, often in dramatic terms. For example, it has been claimed that shortly we will be able to picture a suspect's face from the genetic information they leave behind – even from a speck of dandruff (*Sydney Morning Herald*, 1999). Praise for DNA emanates from both lawyers and scientists. It has been enthusiastically described by eminent scientist Richard Dawkins in these terms: '… a new kind of evidence increasingly coming into the criminal courts: evidence from DNA fingerprinting, and it is extremely powerful' (Dawkins, 1998: 85).

DNA profiling allows examination of human biological material at its most fundamental level and is distinguished by its particularly low false-positive rate (Freckelton, 1989: 360-3). It has been considered a solution to crime because it is 'capable of infallibly identifying the source of biological samples taken from crime scenes' (Freckelton, 1989: 363). Importantly, where it seeks to include, DNA establishes a statistical probability about a suspect: only when it seeks to exclude, does DNA establish a certainty. The words 'Volume, speed and light' have been applied to DNA technology and the trend in applying DNA testing to an increasingly diverse range of criminal offences can be explained by the rapid developments with respect to human DNA:

Thanks to PCR, today's routine work needs genetic material from a mere 600 cells containing about a nanogram of DNA; a speck of blood just 2 square millimetres in size will do nicely (Watson, 2000: 851).

Genetic Identification

Because of its accuracy, DNA testing has been said to have 'changed the landscape of criminal investigations' (Bassan, 1996: 246). It 'genetically' identifies crime perpetrators by comparing bodily substances taken from the scene of the crime with bodily substances collected from suspects (Bassan, 1996: 246). Its primary role has been in relation to identification, often a key issue in criminal trials (Bassan, 1996: 246). Traditional provisions for obtaining identifying particulars did not extend to genetic samples but as the science has developed, the investigatory powers have been extended accordingly. Perhaps because of the traditional caution with which the law has treated visual identification evidence, for example the High Court reiteration in *Domican* (Domican v The Queen (1992) 173 CLR 555) about the need for a warning, the law has subjected DNA to what appears to be far more stringent criticism and scrutiny than has been accorded comparable forms of physical identification evidence such as fingerprinting and voice identification. The explanation for this lies partially in the fascinating battles in the scientific community itself over the recognised ethnic complication associated with databases. A key requirement for calculating the probability that a match occurs between an evidentiary sample and a suspect is a database giving the frequency of each of the genetic markers in the general population. The law has reflected public acknowledgment that while we have databases for the mainstream majority population, they may be far less accurate for members of certain ethnic groups, as the frequency of many genes, and their pattern of co-occurrence is known to differ substantially between ethnic groups (Lewontin, 1994). However, advances in genetic technology, particularly increases in the number of markers used for identification, have rendered many of the issues concerning ethnic differences in gene frequencies moot (for an example, see Weir, 1996).

Not Junk: Admissible as Scientific Evidence

The law has long grappled with a test for admissibility of novel categories of scientific evidence and battled to keep out 'junk' science (Mercer, 1997: 48). Precisely what constitutes 'junk' science has been the subject of some debate. As Alldridge says: 'It can be agreed that soothsayers and witch doctors should not be allowed to testify in their professional capacity, and that experts on skidmarks caused in road traffic accidents should. But somewhere in between a line must be drawn' (Alldridge, 2000: 153). In Freckelton's view, Australian courts have engaged in a 'quest for scientific rigour' (Freckelton, 1997: 141), despite 'lapses in the face of the beguiling temptation posed by simplistically positivist assumptions of what 'scientific evidence' can offer to the courts' (Freckelton, 1997: 141). Furthermore, once the scientist does testify, they must do so within the parameters of their expert knowledge and not presume expertise within the periphery of their actual knowledge. This limitation has been particularly pronounced in Australian law since the Chamberlain convictions of 1987 which seriously discredited its expert witnesses. Indeed, Freckelton considers that it will no longer be acceptable in Australian courts for any expert witness to form 'reliable opinions on matters which lay on the outer margins of their fields of expertise' (Freckelton 1997: 1164).

The cross-jurisdictional trend towards admitting DNA as evidence in criminal cases has its genesis in the major United States case of *Castro*. The United States Supreme Court held that DNA identification tests were admissible and capable of producing reliable results. However, the particular evidence established or demonstrated an exclusion of the accused as the source of the blood on the crime scene sample. Because the evidence established an exclusion, the second stage population genetics question did not really arise for consideration. This early case both pointed to the power of DNA as a weapon of exclusion or elimination of suspects and to the need in law to formulate a means of explaining probability theory.

Uses of DNA to Establish Guilt

DNA has become increasingly common in major criminal cases where identity of an alleged perpetrator of a crime is concerned. English law has progressed to the point that DNA alone can form the basis of conviction, although the serious complexities of Bayesian Theory (Balding and

Donelly, 1996; Stockmarr, 1999) have not been considered appropriate for a jury. Bayes theorem concerns conditional probability, and whilst its details may seem highly technical, the essence is straightforward: if a suspect is identified as a result of a DNA match, the matching probability needs to be interpreted much more stringently than in a case in which an individual is already a suspect, and then a DNA match is obtained. While also involving circumstantial evidence and eye-witness identification, an early DNA case in Australia was the prosecution of the 'backpacker murderer', Ivan Milat. In 1996, there was no existing genetic reference database for Australia so they used people who donated blood to the Red Cross and also people (409 of them) who had given samples as a result of being involved in criminal casework. It appears that they tried to 'round up' people to provide the samples. Hunt CJ held that the statistical validity of such a database depends on whether it is representative of the population at large that it was adequate. The link with Milat was that a victim's blood matched blood found on a rope at Milat's house. In the *Milat* case ([1996] 87 A Crim R 446) validation was given in evidence, but Hunt CJ recommended limitations on the use of the DNA evidence.

Solving Past Unsolved Crimes

DNA has been particularly effective in solving unsolved crimes. Two such cases occurred in Queensland. In 1998 Brisbane's *Courier Mail* reported that DNA had solved the unsolved murder of Janet Phillips after advances in technology in the intervening decade provided a key link between the perpetrator of the rape and murder and the victim (White and Bradford, 1998). Sperm taken from the victim was stored and later matched with the blood of the accused, giving an 'exact' match according to Judge Bill Lee of 'one chance in 6 billion' (White and Bradford, 1998).

In November 1998, Ambrose J handed down the decision in *White* in the Supreme Court of Queensland. Here DNA analysis had advanced to the point where conclusions could be expressed such that the odds against a matched sample being from someone else were at least 4.2 times 10^{17} (4.2 followed by 17 zeros!). As this number greatly exceeds the human population of the earth, the number can be interpreted as meaning that there is virtually no chance that two individuals have this particular DNA profile, and that the sample therefore must belong to the suspect. The results from White's earlier tests in 1991 were retested using this advanced DNA technology. The original tests did not allow for a conclusion more accurate than one which would exclude 94% of the population. As a result, White was not committed for trial.

A jury convicted a man accused of the brutal murder of a Brisbane veterinarian solely on the basis of DNA evidence (Oberhardt, 1999). The allegation that the accused was the killer was not made until four months after the death. It was also made on the basis that bloodstains found at the scene of the murder were made by the deceased's blood and the appellant's blood. This followed, the Crown alleged, from the results of DNA profiling. The court heard allegations that DNA evidence proved beyond doubt that the accused was at the murder scene, in a pet surgery, on the ground floor of the murdered woman's home. The accused Fitzherbert refused to give a blood sample to police during initial investigations. Police then raided his home and seized items including a handkerchief from the pocket of a pair of trousers (Chester, 1998). A DNA sample of the mucus on the handkerchief was enough to obtain a court order for a blood sample. Nine tests were undertaken of the accused's blood, comparing his DNA to that of the blood that was found at the scene. The Court was told that the chances of anyone else having the same DNA as that of the blood sample found at the scene was about one in 1400 million (Chester, 1998). The matter of his refusing the first test was not raised at the trial. A scientist of twenty years standing gave evidence about the DNA tests they had conducted, and the prosecutor said that the statistical chance of another match to the accused's DNA profile was 14 billion to 1 (Chester, 1998).

It appears from reports of the case that the sole line of defence argument from the accused's barrister was that the jury should question why only a Caucasian database was used. On appeal to the Supreme Court of Queensland the sole issue was whether the DNA evidence was reliable, with the appellant alleging fraud. He maintained that the recorded results of DNA testing relied on by the Crown were faked. However, in dismissing the appeal, all three judges noted that the case had not been one where the laboratory documents now sought to be relied upon to vitiate the conviction were unavailable to, or not utilised by, the defence before the trial. The statistical basis to the DNA profiling had been dealt with in defence counsel's cross-examination at the trial. The accused appealed against his conviction alleging fraud with respect to analysis of documents generated in the course of the DNA profiling. His arguments met with little sympathy. Perhaps not surprisingly, in the case concerning the murder of a

    Hard Lessons

young schoolgirl, Keyra Steinhardt, by Leonard John Fraser before the Queensland Supreme Court only a short time after Fitzherbert, again involving DNA evidence, it has been observed that the prosecution 'used DNA as the foundation of its case and then built a fortress on top of it with other evidence' (*Courier Mail*, 2000).

The Databases

Such cases of unsolved crimes where DNA provides enough evidence for a conviction are occurring more frequently and provide a strong momentum for a DNA database (Niesche, 1998; Doneman, 1998). In keeping with the global developments in this area, it was reported that Australian criminals are next 'in line for DNA' (*The Australian*, 1997). Various statutes already establish criminal DNA data banks in the United States (Bassan, 1996: 279). While it is accepted that DNA cannot provide an overall solution to the problem of identification in criminal trials, it can place an accused at the scene of the crime. If other elements of the crime can then be proved against him or her, for example, motive and intention, in the case of murder, admissibility of DNA matches will strengthen the case. Police have therefore long been keen to maintain gene banks of DNA. While their arguments are usually couched in terms of crime control, clearly DNA has a double role in law enforcement. Indeed, the Australian Prime Minister, John Howard, has pronounced that the database will have the effect of 'protecting innocent people' (Madigan, 2001).

It is important to recognise that there are two entirely different applications of DNA databases in forensic science. First, there may be a database that stores DNA profiles of individuals, together with the individuals' identities. Such a database can then be searched to identify suspects whose DNA matches an evidentiary sample. Second, the calculation of match probabilities requires the existence of a database that gives the frequency of occurrence in the general population of each of the alleles used in the DNA profile. As we have explained earlier, allele frequencies are known to differ between ethnic groups, and it may be important to obtain such a database for several ethnic groups within a diverse community. Databases of this second type do not require the identity of the individuals contributing the sample to be linked to the samples. It is the use of databases of the first type that causes the most concern to civil libertarians (see, for example, http://www.justiceaction.org.au/ja_dna/papers/ndx_papers.html), but even those of the second type cause some concern. The Privacy Commissioner of New South Wales is currently enquiring into how allele frequency information obtained from blood donations ended up being used in criminal proceedings. It is not clear that all the individuals donating these samples consented to their use for this purpose (Ryle, 2001).

A key issue in the DNA database context is uniformity of regulation: without such uniformity, the effect of DNA databases in crime control is minimised. Australian police ministers are to meet with the Federal Government in March 2002 to develop consistent State laws on the basis that currently inconsistent state laws jeopardise the operation of the national DNA database (Chulov, 2002).

More Power to the Police

An inevitable consequence of the expansion in the uses of DNA in the criminal law is a related increase in and rethinking of police powers. There has been considerable debate as to whether police should be able to compulsorily obtain a sample in the event of a refusal by a suspect. Search and seizure powers in the *Fitzherbert* case enabled Queensland police to seize a handkerchief, tissue from which then facilitated obtaining the necessary court order for a blood sample. While the law varies throughout Australia, the rule in Queensland, laid down in the *Police Powers and Responsibilities Act (Qld.) 1997* s 64., states that where a detainee is in custody for an indictable offence and a magistrate approves the procedures, and a police officer asks a doctor or dentist to perform procedures, then a doctor acting in good faith may do any of the following that provide evidence of the commission of an offence: take samples of the detainee's blood, saliva or hair. However, the law in this area is constantly subject to pressure for reform. Again in Queensland, following *Fitzherbert*, new DNA powers were extended to police, to empower them to take swabs from the mouths of criminals or suspects (Franklin and Scholz, 2000). Under current laws only doctors can take DNA samples with an individual's approval or a magistrate's order. Under the new system, police, nurses and doctors are to have the power to take swabs (Franklin and Scholz, 2000). An attempt by Queensland prisoners to argue that the power to compulsorily test did not apply to them as they were convicted in magistrates courts for summary offences not for serious offences, failed

(*Courier Mail*, 2001). While the right to silence prevails in Australian legal systems, any formal recognition of it can be undermined by resorting to compulsory DNA testing for certain offences. A clear example of this can be found in Victoria, where a magistrate ordered a DNA test on a man accused of killing a security guard at an abortion clinic when the man resolutely refused to provide police with any personal details (*The Australian*, 2001). In Australia, the current Federal Government's Crimes Amendment (Forensic Procedures) Act 2001 (Cth) is one legislative attempt to regulate in this area yet while it deals with many major database and DNA issues in the federal context, even at the bill stage it was presaged that it did not provide an adequate dispute resolution procedure with regard to problems that arise in respect of sampling (Gans, 2001). Nor does it regulate non-forensic procedures with respect to obtaining a sample from a suspect. The key legal term in this context is that of informed consent but this has yet to be analysed in the range of new contexts in which this information is being gathered.

Related to this is the emergence of mass testing in the interests of crime control. While there have been many mass testing DNA exercises in Britain, they are relatively new in Australia. The first mass DNA test in Australia took place in April 2000 during the search for a rapist in the north-western New South Wales cotton-growing town of Wee Waa. The test involved 500 men who voluntarily took part in the police DNA program. The men were asked to give saliva samples. The man who ultimately confessed to the rape had apparently taken a test but confessed before results were known, apparently under pressure from the inevitability of the test results (Kennedy, 2000a). The DNA samples were destroyed five months after the mass testing, thus honouring a commitment of New South Wales police to the 2000 residents of the town and all the men who took part in the test that their samples would be destroyed (Kennedy, 2000b).

The fate of the information gathered in these law enforcement exercises remains unclear, and concerns have been raised about privacy protection[1] and other possible uses of the samples for further testing by law enforcement agencies. Although the issues raised by the use of forensic samples have been characterised as 'often very specifically connected to criminal law and evidence' it has also been noted in this context that the United States military is now one of the largest collectors of DNA samples (Lemmens and Austin, 2001).

Squeaky-Clean Processes and Protocols

Scientific evidence is not infallible in legal hands. Magnusson has identified five key areas where doubt may arise as to the utility of DNA testing and matching. These include general technical incompetence, broken chain of events, measurement error, logical error and statistical error (Magnusson, 1994: 11). Admissible evidence is dependent upon correct processes and protocols; otherwise an appeal on grounds of lack of process is likely. In the O.J. Simpson case, the defence asserted that the blood on Simpson's console and the rear gate had been 'planted' by police, from blood drawn from Simpson the day he was questioned by police (Clarke, 2000: 378). The *Los Angeles Times* report described expert witness testimony for the prosecution by prominent statistician Bruce Weir, as: 'dry as sand and about as digestible' (Aranella, 1995). In Weir's view, O.J. Simpson was acquitted despite very strong DNA evidence linking his blood to the crime. Although numerical statements describing the strength of this evidence were made, the DNA profiles included so many loci that the need for presenting numbers in this case, and in others using similarly high numbers of loci, is, in Weir's view, 'probably unnecessary' (Weir, 1995: 365). Weir advocates that if numbers are to be presented, they should be given in the form of likelihood ratios (Weir, 1995: 365). Apart from this, Weir contends that the Simpson case made it essential that the integrity of DNA evidence (with regard to collection, potential contamination or tampering) be beyond doubt (Weir, 1995: 365). The expert is not there to protect the police process.

While the high-profile case may be unique to America, a similar argument of police misconduct was alleged on appeal in *Fitzherbert*. However, the Queensland Court of Appeal dismissed the argument of fraud concerning the analysis of the documents generated in the course of the DNA profiling. In *Hytch* ([2000] QCA 315), a Queensland jury convicted Paul Hytch in 2000 for the murder of Rachel Antonio, only to have another jury acquit Hytch just one year later (Ketchell, 2001). The different outcome was largely the result of criticism of the testing techniques at the John Tonge Centre, which were claimed to fail in as many as one per cent of cases due to inability to identify the sex of the samples. Related criticisms were made of the lack of uniformity of the Centre's practices with national practices, and the probability that samples had been contaminated in the laboratory (Sholz, 2001). Even in the first trial, much had been made of the continuity of testing due to the fact that beyond the testimony of witnesses that each DNA sample reached the laboratory, 'there was no direct admissible evidence that what was in the gel which the scanner read and translated into a graph was any of those samples' (*Hytch* [2000] QCA 315 4 August 2000: 15).

Genetic Information and the Composite Picture of the Criminal

The potential of DNA to provide extensive information beyond the immediacy of the criminal investigation is still being recognised. Britain's Forensic Science Service (FSS) has announced that research is underway into determining facial characteristics from DNA 'fingerprints' left at crime scenes. If this became reality, police would be able to construct a composite picture of a suspect's face from the genetic information contained in a single speck of dandruff (*Sydney Morning Herald*, 1999). The report goes on to say that the FSS notes that DNA samples are already used to tell police if a suspect was likely to be from a particular racial group. At this stage, however, the proposal is science fiction: the loci used for DNA identity testing are neutral loci, which have no affect whatsoever on any characteristics of the individual that carries them. It is, however, theoretically possible that, 'since facial characteristics are at least partially determined by genes, science may be able to tell if someone has a round face, or something about the shape of their earlobes. Skin, hair and eye colour could all be revealed by DNA profiling as well as other features such as a Roman nose or pointed chin' (*Sydney Morning Herald*, 1999). The linking of complex attributes such as these to known DNA sequences is an area of intense current research, following the successful sequencing of the human genome project. Despite the hype in the popular press, lawyers and police should not expect an identikit photo to emerge from the DNA in a speck of dandruff in the foreseeable future.

The extent to which human genetic make-up predetermines behaviour and psychological attributes remains highly contentious. Key future issues include predictions of predisposition to crime and finding a 'criminal gene'. At least one paper in *Science* (Vol. 260, 18 June, 1993) has claimed: 'evidence found for a possible 'aggression gene.' In this regard, Justice of the High Court of Australia and prolific writer in this area, Michael Kirby, has noted that:

> The discovery of genetic causes of many disorders raises the possibility of identifying genes associated with antisocial behaviour. What are the implications of discovering criminal actions may be caused or profoundly influenced by a genetic characteristic? Is it back to the drawing boards for assumptions about deliberate criminal wrong-doing? (Kirby, 2001: 13).

An Unexpected Twist? Using DNA to Prove Wrongful Conviction

DNA testing is most powerful as a means of excluding persons from criminal liability. Thus: 'non-matches are much more justice orientated than matches' (Smith, 2001). As Hytch illustrates, DNA can exonerate persons accused of crimes just as surely as it can convict. DNA can provide a statistical probability that a suspect was at a particular location and a statistical probability of identification in that context. So it can also prove that a person was not present at the crime scene. Thus it has been instrumental in eliminating potential suspects and in establishing some wrongful convictions. Yet its full potential in proving innocence is only just emerging. It is arguable that uses of DNA to prove innocence is the inevitable counterpart to its emergence as a major crime-fighting technique, although issues of equal access will remain of key concern.

Innocence in the USA

The role of DNA in proving innocence has been particularly critical in the United States given the widespread use of capital punishment. Hence the occasional headlines: 'DNA clears man after decade on death row' (*Sydney Morning Herald*, 2000). In California, ninety-nine prisoners were freed after DNA evidence helped expose a police corruption racket that manufactured prosecutions to inflate conviction statistics (Riley, 2000). The main source of information on exemptions through DNA evidence in the United States is the 1996 US National Institute of Justice (NIJ) Report 'Convicted by Juries, Exonerated by Science: Case Studies in the use of DNA evidence to Establish Innocence After Trial'.

Innocence in Australia

While there have been Australian situations where DNA testing has eliminated all the prime suspects in a murder case (*Sydney Morning*

Herald, 1999) and eliminated potential suspects in the Wee Waa rape case, there have been only a few cases where it has featured as a tool to exonerate. The 'Innocence Project' at Queensland's Griffith University Law School secured the release of a Western Australian man jailed for the rape of his 14-year old niece, after uncovering new evidence including DNA matters (Stolz, 2002). While in an earlier Queensland case, DNA had in fact not featured in securing the conviction. In *R* v *Frank Alan Button* ([2001] QCA 133) semen stains were not tested in a rape investigation and Button was convicted largely on the basis of an alleged confession and presence at the house at the time of the offence. His lawyers insisted upon subsequent testing of bedding and those tests revealed that Button was not the perpetrator. The Queensland Court of Appeal identified the two-fold purpose of DNA testing as first: 'identifying the perpetrator of crime, and secondly, that of excluding a possible offender as being the perpetrator of crime'.

The Prisoners' Legal Service in the State of Queensland sought court orders to stop the Queensland Police Service from compulsorily taking DNA samples from all prisoners, claiming that extensions to police powers in that State were meant to apply only to serious offenders (Monk, 2001). However, the Queensland Supreme Court decided that it was irrelevant that the person had been convicted summarily of an indictable offence. The Prisoners' Legal Service has also called for prisoners' DNA to be sampled to establish innocence, as in *Brogden* v *Commissioner of the Police Service Supreme Court of Queensland* (Brisbane, 27 April 2001, S3142/01, Wilson J, unreported), allowing individual prisoners to apply to have the evidence against them tested against their DNA. An 'Innocence Panel' was established in New South Wales early in 2002, and during its first twelve months, applications were limited to those convicted of sexual assault and murder on the basis that those two crimes offered the greatest chance of DNA matching (*Courier Mail*, 2001). However, there was some controversy arising from this Panel when certain extremely unpleasant crimes were revisited in the wake of applications from those convicted.

Issues of Access

The appeal of DNA as a weapon of vindication for convicted prisoners may however be misleading. The matter of demands by prisoners for DNA testing so they can use it to disprove guilt is not regulated and currently depends on the independent actions of their lawyers. They are not likely to have the funds to pursue such initiatives in the fight for justice, nor are such claims likely to provoke concerted public sympathy. It was sympathy for crime victims that prompted key changes to DNA in evidence in Canada. Victim well-being was a key argument in the aftermath of the Supreme Court of Canada's insistence on due process and subsequent exclusion of bodily samples used for DNA testing, where police failed to obtain them in accordance with due process (Roach, 1999: 79). Indeed, as Roach has observed, 'Like blood testing for drink driving, DNA testing has strong victims' rights implication [and in Canada] it was sympathy for the victims that eventually forced parliament to act'. Sympathy for victims of crime is a very different governmental imperative from sympathy for the wrongfully convicted. It is difficult enough for defendants to refute the DNA tests advanced by the prosecution since they cannot universally afford the type of justice afforded O.J. Simpson. Still more difficult is it for those already convicted to insist upon a DNA test to support their claim of wrongful conviction. The political status of DNA is that it has been 'embraced … as part of a get-tough-on-crime push' (Bearup, 1998: 23). It follows from this that: 'Improving policing with DNA is a vote-winner, but using it to flush out miscarriages of justice and free the innocent seems less of a concern'.

DNA cases may prompt us to reflect upon what is proven 'beyond reasonable doubt' in both legal and scientific context. A key example is the United States case of Castro, where Jose Castro was accused of murdering a neighbour and her two year old daughter. The case against him concerned blood found on his watch, which was identified using DNA typing as being blood of the adult victim. A commercial firm, Lifecodes Corporation of Valhalla, New York performed the DNA testing, producing results indicating the odds of finding the pattern found on the watch of the murdered woman were 1 to 189,200,000 odds that inevitably 'made the identification sound pretty decisive' (Hubbard and Wald: 146). Eminent geneticist and mathematician, Eric Lander, was then called as an expert witness for the defence, and he calculated the odds entirely differently: coming up with the odds of a random match as one in twenty four (Ibid.). An unprecedented 'expert witness conference' then took place, with experts from both the prosecution and defence evaluating the data, arriving at a consensus that challenged the adequacy of Lifecodes' contention of a match. The evidence was therefore ruled inadmissable. Castro however pleaded guilty and received a lengthy term of imprisonment (to the dismay of his lawyers according to Hubbard and Wald: 146).

Conclusion

In its use as a technology of inclusion, DNA science has steadily been translated into law. While it was once observed 'science has outpaced the law' (*Sydney Morning Herald*, 2000) there are now effective records of forensic uses of DNA profiling where probabilities of a match with a suspect's DNA are explained to a jury, drawing upon the data in the DNA database. In that context, DNA has provided a momentum for uniformity of regulation and clarity of exposition to juries. In its use as a weapon of exclusion, DNA equally has shown the clear capacity to exonerate the innocent. That it has been seized upon by those already convicted as part of the fight to clear their names is not unexpected, but the effect of those claims may yet prove so. What remains is therefore a fully unexpected issue: whether DNA may provide a new right of access to justice for those wrongfully convicted of crimes where DNA has some role in the fact-finding process.

Note

[1]   See R.S. Murch and B. Budowie, 'Are Developments in Forensic Applications of DNA Technology Consistent with Privacy Protections?' in M.A. Rothstein, (ed) *Genetic Secrets: Protecting Privacy and Confidentiality in the Genetic Era* (New Haven: Yale University Press, 1997, 212 at p. 222.

References

Alldridge, P. (2000), *Relocating Criminal Law*, Ashgate, Aldershot.
Aranella, P. (1995), *Los Angeles Times*, June 23.
Australian Law Reform Commission: [http://alrc.gov.au/news/index.htm].
Balding, D. and Donelly, P. (1996), 'Evaluating DNA profile evidence when the suspect is identified through a database search', in *Journal of Forensic Sciences* Vol. 4, pp: 603-7.
Bassan, D. (1996), 'Bill C-104: Revolutionizing criminal investigations or infringing on charter rights?', in *University of Toronto Faculty of Law Review* Vol. 54, pp: 246-79.
Bearup, G. 'Beyond Suspicion', *Sydney Morning Herald*, December 28, 1998.

Carpi, A. and Mital, J. (2000), 'The expanding use of forensics in environmental science', in *Environmental Science and Technology* [print] Vol. 34, June, pp: 262A-266A.

Chalmers, D. (1999), 'The Challenges of Human Genetics', in Freckelton, I., and K. Petersen, *Controversies in Health Law*, The Federation Press, Sydney.

Chester, R. (1998), 'DNA defence for wild ones', *Courier Mail*, 7 October, p. 4.

Chester, R. (2000), *Courier Mail*, 12 February, p. 5.

Chulov, M. (2002), 'Police seek DNA law uniformity', *The Australian*, 27 February, p. 3.

Clarke, M. (2000), *Without a Doubt*, Viking, London.

Courier Mail, 11 September 2000.

Courier Mail, 28 April 2001.

Dawkins, R. (1998), *Unweaving the Rainbow*, Penguin, London.

Doneman, P. (1998), 'DNA code cracks our most baffling cases', *Courier Mail*, 7 November, p. 11.

Franklin, M. and Scholz, N. (2000), 'New DNA powers handed to police', *Courier Mail*, 8 February, p. 1.

Freckelton, I. (1989), 'DNA profiling: optimism and realism', in *Law Institute Journal*, pp. 360-3.

Freckelton, I. (1997), 'Judicial Attitudes Toward Scientific Evidence: The Antipodean Experience', in *U.C. Davis Law Review*, pp: 1137-41.

Gans, J. (2001), 'What's Wrong With Australia's Model Forensic Procedures Bill?', Paper presented at the ANZSOC Conference, Melbourne, February.

Hubbard , Ruth and Elijah Wald (1999), '*Exploding the Gene Myth*', Beacon Press.

Katz Rothman, B. (1998), *Genetic Maps and Human Imaginations*, W.W. Norton and Company, New York.

Kennedy, L. (2000a), 'Wee Waa rapist's plea', *Sydney Morning Herald*, 12 July, p. 4.

Kennedy, L. (2000b), 'Wee Waa's DNA Samples go up in smoke', *Sydney Morning Herald*, 20 September, p. 5.

Ketchell, M. (2001), 'Family weeps as Hytch cleared', *The Sunday Mail*, 17 June, p. 4.

Kirby, M. (1993), 'Legal Problems: Human Genome Project', in *Australian Law Journal*, Vol. 67, p. 894.

Kirby, M. (2001), 'The human genome project-the big legal issues', *The Proctor*, Vol. 21, April, p. 12-13.

Lemmens, T. and Austin L. (2001), 'Of Volume, Speed and Light', Paper for the Canadian Biotechnology Advisory Committee, February.

Lewontin, R. (1994), 'Forensic DNA typing dispute', *Nature* Vol. 372, p. 398.

MacIntyre, B. (1998), 'DNA samples trap Beast of the Bastille', *Weekend Australian*, 28-29 March, p. 18.

Madigan, M. (2001), 'CrimTrac signals crook times for felons', *Courier Mail*, 21 June, p. 6.

Magnusson, E. (1994), 'Reasonable Doubt, Legal Doubt and Scientific Doubt', in *Australian Journal of Forensic Sciences* Vol. 26, No. 11.

Mercer, D. (1997), 'Keeping "Junk" History Out of the Courtroom', in *University of New South Wales Law Journal* Vol. 48.

Monk, S. (2001), 'Prisoners in court to stop DNA test', *Courier Mail*, 18 April, p. 8.

National Institute of Justice (NIJ)[USA] Report 1996 [www.ojp.usdoj.gov/nij/].

Niesche, C. (1998), 'DNA dragnet closes on killers', *The Weekend Australian*, 17-18 October, p. 7.

Oberhardt, M. (1999), 'Accused should fear DNA data, court told', *Courier Mail*, 31 July, p. 3.

Riley, M. (2000), 'DNA testing gives freedom to 64th inmate', *Sydney Morning Herald*, 21 September, p. 25.

Roach, K. (1999), *Due Process and Victims' Rights: the new law and politics of criminal justice*, University of Toronto Press, Toronto.

Ryle, G. (2001), 'Red Cross edgy over DNA blood samples', *Sydney Morning Herald*, November 16.

Saunders, M. (1998), 'DNA tests to put the bite on wildlife smugglers', *The Australian*, 7 October, p. 4.

Science, (1993) Vol. 260, 18 June.

Sholz, N. (2001), 'DNA doubt raised in killing trial', *Courier Mail*, 9 June, p. 3.

Smith, W. (2001), 'Unlocking the cells', *Courier Mail*, 16 June, p.30.

Somerville, M. (2000), *The Ethical Canary*, Viking, Ringwood.

Stockmarr, A. (1999), 'Likelihood ratios for evaluating DNA evidence when the suspect is found through a database search', in *Biometrics* Vol. 55, pp: 671-7.

Stoltz, G. (2002), 'Students go in to bat for wrongly jailed', *The Courier Mail*, 2 March, p. 16

Sydney Morning Herald (1999), 'Search for warrior's grave', 13 September, p. 5.

Sydney Morning Herald (1999), 'DNA research: The star prosecution witness: dandruff', 16 September, 1999, p. 7.

Sydney Morning Herald (1999),'Postcards clue to murder riddle', 30 September, p. 6.

Sydney Morning Herald (2000), 'DNA clears man after decade on death row', 14 February, p. 12.

Sydney Morning Herald (2000), 'DNA stretches limit of rape laws', 26 February 2000, p. 30.

Sydney Morning Herald, (2000), 'DNA could be used to combat ivory poachers', 24 August, p. 9.

The Australian 3 April 1997.

The Australian (2001), 'Magistrate orders DNA test on abortion clinic killing accused', 18 July, p. 2.

Watson, A. (2000), 'A New Breed of High-Tech Detectives', in *Science* Vol 289, August, p. 850.

Weir, B. (1995), 'DNA statistics in the Simpson matter', in *Nature Genetics* December, pp: 365-8.

Weir, B. S. (1996), 'The second national research council report on forensic DNA evidence', in *American Journal of Human Genetics* Vol. 59, pp: 497-500.

White, A. and Bradford, S. (1998), 'Murderer convicted on DNA evidence', *Courier Mail*, 9 May.

Whitney, C. (1998), 'Body exhumed for DNA match with "love child"', *Sydney Morning Herald*, 13 March, p. 9.

Chapter 6

Parental Restitution:
Soft Target for Rough Justice

ANTHONY McMAHON

In an effort to 'get tough' on juvenile crime and to placate growing 'public concern', western neo-liberal governments have introduced a range of legislative measures designed to extend and strengthen sentencing options available to the court. While such legislation has been directed mainly towards the sentencing of offenders, the notion of responsibility extends to the role played by parents in the control and supervision of their children (see the chapter by Pitts in this book). Cohen (1985), for example, has noted a more penetrative and incisive extension of social control which has incorporated the voluntary and/or coerced participation of an active citizenry in the war against crime. Central to this strategy was 'a greater direct involvement of the family, school and various community agencies in the day-to-day business of prevention, treatment and socialisation' (Cohen 1985: 77). The family, therefore, has a central role in the ideology of community control of crime since parents are seen to represent the principle guarantors of the child's moral character. The management of offending, mainly as prevention, has devolved increasingly onto parents, among others, with the expectation that they could be held directly accountable when things went wrong (Hil and McMahon, 2001).

Governments in Britain, Australia and the United States, have provided for the greater use of parental restitution by the courts as a means of punishing parents for the criminal actions of their children, thereby extending the boundaries of culpability to include the family as a whole. In so doing the legislation necessarily absolves the State from any direct or indirect responsibility for generating the conditions that might lead to crime and instead places the blame squarely on the shoulders of young people and their parents (Cook, 1997). In this sense, parental restitution constitutes a formal recognition by the legal and judicial authorities that the neglectful actions of parents have contributed directly to the irresponsible behaviours of their children.

In contrast to this crude understanding of the connections between families and crime, this chapter seeks to report on simplistic assumptions that tend to be associated with socio-legal discourses on restitution. The study found that the parents/guardians of juvenile offenders are rarely oblivious to the offending of their children and are in fact actively engaged in various strategies designed to curtail continued criminal behaviour. While there has been popular and political enthusiasm for legislation to compel parents to pay restitution, the actual exercise of the restitution proceedings in court has the unintended consequence of charging concerned, conscientious parents for supposedly neglecting their children. A significant outcome of this process, also not intended by the legislators, was the realisation by the judiciary that finding parents liable for restitution was too difficult to prove in court.

Making Parents Pay

This chapter is based on research undertaken in North Queensland, Australia, in 1998. Just prior to this research, the Queensland State Government, like many other governments, sought to implement new measures to reduce juvenile crime and the causes of crime. Two years previously, parents and their offending children were targeted by the then Queensland Attorney General, when he commented that proposed legislation would hold both the offenders and their parents responsible for crimes. He emphasised that the community has 'had enough' (*Townsville Bulletin*, May 30, 1996). Another local newspaper editorialised:

> Parents in Townsville and Thuringowa may find themselves in the dock alongside juvenile offenders under new laws announced last week. And they may also have to pay up to $5000 compensation where courts decide it is appropriate for crimes committed by a child. Attorney General Denver Beanland on Wednesday launched the start of a four-week consultation period for amendments to the *Juvenile Justice Act 1992*. These changes are tough, yet fair, Mr Beanland said (*Townsville Sun*, June 5, 1996).

All Australian states and territories have legislative provision which enable courts to order parents to make restitution for the crimes of their children. In Queensland, provision for parental restitution in cases of juvenile crime has long been part of the State's legislative framework. Thus, Section 62 of the *Children Services Act 1965* states that restitution or compensation could be imposed on parents or guardians where a failure to exercise adequate care, supervision and guardianship could be demonstrated by the court. The *Juvenile Justice Act 1992* includes similar provisions, although it was more concerned with the principle of 'wilful neglect' of parents in relation to cases of juvenile crime. Like the previous legislation, the *Juvenile Justice Act 1992* asserted a clear causative link between the negligent actions of parents and guardians and the offending behaviours of their children. Section 197(1) of the Act stated:

> If it appears to a court that finds a child guilty of an offence relating to property or against the person of another, on evidence admitted or submissions made in the case against the child –
> a. that wilful failure on the part of a parent of the child to exercise proper care of, or supervision over, the child was likely to have substantially contributed to the commission of the offence; and
> b. that compensation should be paid to any person for –
> (i) loss caused to the person's property whether the loss was an element of the offence charged or happened in the course of the commission of the offence; or
> (ii) injury suffered by the person, whether as the victim of the offence or otherwise, because of the commission of the offence;
> the court, of its own initiative or on application by the prosecution, may decide to call on the parent to show cause, as directed by the court, why the parent should not pay the compensation.

The Act thus implicated parents (under the principle of 'wilful failure') in the instigation, if not the commission, of their children's offending behaviour. However, the Act offered no clear definition as to what might constitute 'wilful failure' on the part of parents and guardians in cases of juvenile crime, or how a 'substantial contribution' to the commission of the criminal act might be assessed. In allowing for such a broad framework of interpretation, the Act opened up the possibility for considerable variation in decision-making by the court. The Act further stated that parents may be required to pay compensation to victims for damage, loss or injury resulting from the criminal actions of their children.

Mindful of the fact that some parents may find it extremely difficult to meet restitution or compensation payments, the Act provided for consideration of 'the parent's capacity to pay the amount, which must include an assessment of the effect any order would have on the parent's capacity to provide for dependents' (s.198(7)). Other Australian states and territories have similar provisions (Hil, 1996).

Holding Parents Responsible

Internationally, the increased emphasis on penalizing the parents of juvenile offenders has received support from those seeking a tougher approach to law and order. It has also been condemned by those who see such developments as worsening the plight of many already hard-pressed families. Notwithstanding the latter, it appears from the move toward increased parental responsibility in legislation and judicial action, that the link between parental supervision and juvenile crime has now become an axiomatic feature of many criminal justice systems.

In the United States, the proposition that some parents should be held responsible for the criminal actions of their children has been widely accepted by a number of state legislatures. One of the first states to make the explicit link between childrens' crimes and parental supervision was California. The Parental Responsibility Act 1988 made parents criminally liable for failing to supervise their offending children adequately. Culpable action on the part of parents in respect of their children's offending could result in imprisonment of up to one year or a maximum fine of $2500. Although the law was challenged by various legal and welfare organizations on the grounds that it was subjective and an intrusion into the privacy of family life, the Californian Supreme Court upheld the law (Yea, 1997). Since 1988, at least 17 other states have passed laws that hold parents criminally responsible for the crimes of their children. States have also strengthened provisions that allow courts to pay the cost incurred by courts or the corrections system in dealing with their children. Arizona, Alaska, Idaho, Dakota, New Hampshire and Virginia have passed laws that make the parents of offenders responsible for victim restitution. In Kentucky, parents may further be required to meet the adjudication costs incurred by their children's appearance in court (Yea, 1997).

The growing emphasis given to parental responsibility in respect of juvenile crime in the United States has found expression in a number of celebrated court cases. For example, in Indiana, the parents of a repeat juvenile offender were fined $30,341 for the cost of incarcerating their son. While the Judge in the case stated that the parents were not held responsible for their son's crimes, their actions had nevertheless led to his offending. As the Judge stated, 'The effect is to make parents aware of their responsibly for their children. They can't pass it off to some social agency. That's a smokescreen' (Collins 1990: 21). One of the underlying messages associated with a number of the laws that seek to penalize parents is that the contemporary family is, for a host of reasons, ill equipped to care for its children. As a senior representative of the National Center for Juvenile Justice stated, 'We want them (parents) to be something they used to be, but the mechanism is gone. The father is not always the breadwinner and the mother is not home nurturing. That's all gone' (Collins, 1990: 34). A somewhat different view was aired in the wake of another celebrated judgment in which the parents of a Detroit teenager offender were each fined $100 and ordered to pay $1,000 court costs for their failure to properly supervise their son. A spokesperson for the American Civil Liberties Union not only questioned the constitutional basis of the parental responsibility laws but also pointed out that the fining or jailing of parents would do little to address the particular skills required of a parent, especially when confronted with a son or daughter who offends (Meredith 1996). Moreover, writing in the influential Stanford Law and Policy Review, Davidson (1996: 28) argued that, 'It is simply inappropriate to rush into legislative solutions that punish parents for their children's criminal acts without ensuring that effective services are readily available to families at all income levels...to help them to be better parents'.

In Britain the recent focus on the family as the chief cause of delinquent behaviour occurred during the premiership of Margaret Thatcher during the 1980s (Pitts, 1988). Growing concern over rising juvenile crime and outbursts of violent inner city disturbances led to calls for tougher law and order measures aimed at punishing offenders and their apparently negligent parents. The links drawn between poor parental supervision and juvenile crime led to specific provisions in two major pieces of legislation designed to combat growing levels of lawlessness among the young. The Criminal Justice Act 1991 stated that in cases where a young person under the age of 16 has been convicted of an offence the parents should be bound over to exercise 'proper' care and control of him (sic). Parents are bound over for a sum of money up to £1000 which is to be forfeited if the child re-offends. Although the Act required the consent of parents in order to impose bind over orders, refusal to accept such an order could be met by a fine! In fact, therefore, parents were given little choice. The second major piece of legislation (this time passed under the conservative administration of John Major) was the Criminal Justice and Public Order Act 1994. The Act built on the 1991 legislation by requiring parents who are bound over to ensure that the child complies with the sentence of the court. Under the Act parents would be required to forfeit their monies if the child failed to meet the conditions of an order, let alone if s/he re-offended.

The election of New Labour in June 1997 meant a continuation rather than reform of many of the previous government's law and order policies. Indeed, a Labour discussion paper published shortly before the election noted the central importance of the family and styles of parental supervision in the creation of crime and delinquency among the young. Drawing on a number of criminological studies of offenders the authors concluded that, 'The evidence is now strong that the character of parental supervision in the pre-teen years holds the key to later delinquency. This raises the question about whether as a matter of public policy there should be more intervention in the upbringing of some children' (Straw and Anderson, 1996: 5) and proceeded to discuss a range of policy proposals aimed at ensuring parental compliance in the upbringing of law abiding children. Central to these were Parental Responsibility Orders which were aimed at those parents who 'have not been prepared to accept guidance and counselling to help them cope with their behaviour'. The order would require parents to attend counselling or guidance sessions. 'They [parents] would learn...how to set and enforce consistent standards of behaviour and how to respond more effectively to challenging adolescent demands' (Straw and Anderson, 1996: 18). Despite the changed emphasis in the policies from control to responsibility, it is clearly evident that, like Australia and the United States, the British approach to juvenile justice has embraced the central idea that the family, as the supposed main instigator of anti-social behaviours, requires punitive legislation to ensure parental compliance in the crusade against crime.

Families' Experiences of Restitutio Proceedings

Despite the rhetoric concerning parental responsibility, in Queensland at least, courts have been reluctant to order parents to pay restitution. As part of a wider study of the parents of juvenile offenders, Hil and McMahon (2001) found only seven instances of parents in Queensland being asked to show cause why they should not be required to pay restitution for their children's offending. We were able to interview four of the seven parents. Three of the four parents had been ordered by a magistrate to show cause when, in 1996, the then Queensland Attorney General was in Townsville and talking tough about juvenile crime and parental responsibility. This instance, reported in the *Townsville Bulletin* under the headline 'Juvenile Act trialled', noted that a Townsville Magistrate was requiring three parents to appear in court 'to argue why they should not pay for the crimes committed by their children' (*Townsville Bulletin*, May 30, 1996).

The circumstance that initiated the response by the magistrate was the stealing and destruction of a car. Three boys were involved: John Watts, Carl Webb and Richard Marcos (not their real names). As John Watts' mother remembers:

> They had stolen the cars and taken them for joy rides, and then returned to the place of their next car and the boys were sort of caught in the act after one car exploded in flames and they were seen walking away. During the Children's Court hearing, the magistrate decided that he would ask us to show cause and we were told by him to obtain legal counsel. There was myself and another family, we went and obtained solicitors and the third family also got a barrister. And then their barrister and solicitor approached my solicitor as to whether I would share the cost of the barrister for the appearance in court because it was really quite costly. I think my share of his fee was like $300. John was pleading guilty.

Interestingly, when interviewed for this research, Mrs Watts had a copy of the *Juvenile Justice Act 1992* ready to hand and from which she read:

> It says, 'Section 197 permits a court which finds a child guilty of certain offences of his own initiative or an application by the prosecution to decide to call upon a parent to show cause why the parent should not pay compensation. The court may do so if it appears to the court that the wilful failure on the part of the parent of a child to exercise proper care of

or supervision over the child is likely to have substantially contributed to the commission of the offence.' I mean, at this time we had been involved with Family Services (the Queensland department responsible for juveniles who offend) for quite a period of time asking for help, telling them our situation, what problems we were having, and then to be asked this sort of stuff. So I went to my solicitor and gave him John's background and also what attempts we'd made to do something about correcting his behaviour.

When we went back to court, the barrister baffled the magistrate. Well, not really, he just went on, you know how barristers always talk in mumbo-jumbo language? Mumbo-jumbo language about the legality of how the summonses and things were served and why was one partner served and not the other partner and all this sort of stuff. And at some point not so far past that, (while the barrister) was still going on about this and other things, the magistrate then withdrew the charges without even hearing them. So the show-cause thing was then thrown out. $600 later we don't get proved guilty or innocent.

The reason the magistrate said that he gave for withdrawing the charges or dropping the matter or putting it aside, or whatever they call it, was that he had subsequently, and why he didn't get his facts right in the first place, read the report from Family Services which indicated to him that he was barking up the wrong tree, obviously.

Carl Webb's mother was one of the other parents at the court on that day.

We were all there; there was myself, one of the other boy's mother and the grandma, and then the other boy's mother and father. So there were five of us. Five adults, I believe, in the court. And the magistrate said that this law had been passed and he felt that we would be charged because the children had caused a fair bit of damage and costs. I don't deny that, but I was a bit taken aback because as I said at the time (Carl) wasn't living under my roof. I was, well, a little bit taken aback because I really didn't know what would happen. It wasn't until afterwards when I got home and I started to think about, well, what could I have done to have prevented or tried to stop what was going on. I couldn't (have prevented it) because he wasn't here for me to have any control over.

Mrs Webb was shocked at being asked to show cause. She found the accusation unfair and the process unfair and expensive.

> If I'd have been a different type of personality, I would say I probably would have had a nervous breakdown. But I'm a fairly stoic sort of personality and I just had to take it day by day. I think the biggest kick in the butt from all that was that I needed to get a lawyer to prove my innocence from what (the magistrate) had charged me with and from the fact that he charged me, not my husband as well was, I felt, a bit unfair because even though (the husband) didn't live at home most of the time he still was a part of the family. He still was aware of what everything that was going on. I mean, I speak to him at least twice a week by telephone. He was aware of what was going on.

> I had to get a solicitor to defend myself because we weren't financially poor enough to get Legal Aid. There was myself and one of the other mums. She actually went to a different lawyer. Then the two lawyers conversed with each other and then they both got a barrister to defend the things. My court costs were $2,500 which was a large whack out of our pocket at the time. The other girl, I believe, she was charged $800, so she must have had a better lawyer or a lawyer that was perhaps a little bit less greedy or what, I don't know. But that in turn put lots of extra pressures on the family.

Mrs Marcos, the mother of Richard, was the third parent in the court that day. She, too, felt it was unfair of the magistrate to ask the parents to show cause.

> Yes, that was my first time, you know (in court). Ever since in my life that's the first time I experience going to the court. Yeah. So I was nervous and all that, you know. I'm really nervous.

Mr and Mrs Marcos had a solicitor from Legal Aid because they could not afford to employ one. Mrs Marcos went on to say:

> It was unfair for us. Yeah, it is unfair for us that time. Because you know, as I said, as a parent we had nothing to do with it, you know, got nothing to do with it because we have raised him in a good manner to respect others, that's what always I've told him. That is our house rule here at home. But his behaviour we cannot do anything about. Yeah.

When the three families came back to court to 'prove their innocence' in Mrs Webb's terms, the magistrate did not proceed.

> Because then after that, they just threw it out of court anyway because the lawyer said that virtually the magistrate had to prove that we were unfit parents, you know. Now, that's a very hard thing to do. Um, so it was just quashed. Nothing was proceeded with. But then I felt that I had been wronged and I felt angry at the system to be even charged with it. So I said to my lawyer, 'What recourse have I got to do that?' In fact, it cost me a lot more than just $2000. That was just the one lump sum. It cost me, I reckon, in other follow-up fees probably another $500 or $600 on top of that. And I said to him, 'What recourse have I got to recoup' because I felt that it was unjust that I should have to pay that sort of money just to get somebody up there to say that I was innocent because as far as I was concerned I should not have been charged with it to start with. Because if (the magistrate) had done his homework properly, you know, he would have realized that Carl's address was not my address.

Something in the Air

Mrs Watts is very cynical about why the three families were asked to show cause. She says they had no warning that this might happen.

> I'd been quite a few times (in court) prior to that and now heaps more times after that and never been asked to show cause again. I think it must have just been politically in the air at the time. They were discussing this in the media and probably in Parliament and the magistrate thought, 'Oh, well, we might give this a little bit of a run,' not forgetting how much it was going to cost ordinary working people, and there's no provision in the *Juvenile Justice Act* to award costs in court.

Mrs Webb has much the same suspicions.

> It was just like, oh, wow, this is something new. This might be something I could use to prove a point or whatever. I don't know... so I still feel bitter about that. Certainly I wasn't prepared for it. I mean, I was prepared to see the worst for my child. I certainly wasn't prepared for anything for myself to be charged. I mean, that was a shock.

Surprisingly, both John Watts' and Carl Webb's mothers agree that some parents should be made to pay restitution for the crimes of their children. Mrs Watts says it depends on the situation but 'I'm sure that there's cases where the parents should be asked to'. Carl Webb's mother thinks much the same.

> In certain circumstances. If a parent can be proven to be neglectful and bring up the child to steal and rob – I mean, there are parents I dare say that bring their children up because they do it themselves – in those circumstances, I think the parent should be accountable because then the child sees no differently, you know. If dad can do it, then why can't I?
>
> But, at the same time, it's very difficult because if a child does commit a crime, as in burn down somebody's house, how do you then say, 'Well, yes, that's going to be the responsibility of the parent to pay that'. I mean, you can't do that. I think (restitution) should be in community service. It's very difficult to put a money thing on it. But, I still think that the community does lose out by parents that are not doing the right thing. They should be brought to somebody's attention to try and help (them). If they can't help the parent, well then the child should then be given some sort of support.

A Letter of Demand

The other family interviewed in regard to parental restitution had an interesting story to tell. The Ryans are an Aboriginal family whose son, Luke, had been breaking into houses and stealing. Eventually, the Children's Court magistrate decided that Luke's parents should be made to pay $2,500 as restitution for their son's offences. Unlike the previous families, they were not told in court about the penalty but received a letter in the mail demanding payment. They took the letter to the Legal Aid solicitor who said, 'Don't take any notice of it because Luke's a juvenile. But when he turns 18, if they'd like to get it back, they can'.

> Oh, we were panicking, hey? And then, that's when we went and seen a solicitor again, and he said, 'Don't take any notice of it'. And that was the first time we heard about that when we got the letter from the court. He (the magistrate) never told us face to face in court. We were at home one day and that's when that letter came. Oh, it sickened us. Where were we going to get two and a half grand, you know, just like that by a certain

> period of time. We thought it was a joke. You know, true. Well, that was our first impression, you know. We said, 'No, this can't be right. No way in the world, because they never said anything at the court about it, you know, and we were always there. Always'.

> That's what I mean, it come as a complete surprise, you know. It come out of the blue. Like, you know, the police prosecutor or even the Magistrate, he never come up to us there and said, 'Oh, Mr and Mrs Ryan, you'll be getting something in the mail soon'.

Of further interest, after the letter had been sent, one of the Family Services' officers came to the Ryan's' house to ask about their assets. One can't help feeling it was a scheme devised by court and welfare officials, outside court, to make the parents pay for the offences of their child. Mrs Ryan was angry at the whole episode.

> To tell you the truth I felt pissed off. You know, I was looking at the system and said, 'Oh, you know, you can't come back to the parents then surely?' Even Luke said, 'Never mind, mum, I'll go to work and I'll get a job, I promise, I'll pay it all back'. He was panicking then because he realized what was happening, you know. He got a bit upset when he seen all that.

The Ryans ignored the letter of demand and heard no more about it.

Why Restitution Proceedings do not Work

In general, the principle of parental responsibility is now firmly established in juvenile justice systems. However, the introduction of penalties for parents has attracted considerable criticism. As one commentator has noted,

> rather than dealing with the issue of crime informally at a local level, the imposition of 'external solutions' is likely to bring more juveniles (and their parents) into contact with the justice and welfare systems (O'Connor 1992: 329).

Generally, such criticism is directed at the assumptions that parental neglect is a direct and major factor in the occurrence of juvenile crime and that restitution is an effective means of dealing with juvenile crime. In relation to the former, the Australian Association of Social Workers notes that:

> The assumption that a parent can guarantee a child's behaviour at all times is simplistic, and is likely to affect disproportionate numbers of those on low incomes who are least able to pay fines. Convicting parents for not exercising proper care transforms failure as a parent into a crime, and punishes parents without offering help (Australian Association of Social Workers, 1995: 1).

Likewise, the Australian Catholic Prison Ministry and the Church Network for Youth Justice (1996: 4) point out that parental restitution is likely to '...further alienate families who are most in need of support and encouragement...'. And in a similar vein, the NSW Council of Social Service (NCOSS) notes of the *Children (Parental Responsibility) Act* that, '...the impact on families already under stress is unimaginable in practical (financial) terms but is also likely to be considerable in terms of already fragile intra-family relationships' (New South Wales Council of Social Services, 1995: 8).

In Queensland, proposals to make parents liable for up to $5000 restitution in cases of property damage caused by juveniles have been condemned by a number of key justice organizations in the state. Thus, the Brisbane Aboriginal Legal Service, Youth Advocacy Centre, Queensland Council for Civil Liberties and the Victims of Crime were united in their opposition to parental restitution, principally on the grounds that it is likely to make the plight of many already hard-pressed families considerably worse (Courier Mail May 3, 1996). An editorial in the Townsville Bulletin, a regional paper not noted for its liberal stance on juvenile crime, pointed out that the newly proposed penalties in Queensland might be applied differentially to offender's parents: 'The proposal that parents be required to pay up to $5000 for their offspring's errant ways is ... flawed. For a start it would seem that only the parents of means will be required to pay. Those well off financially will go scot free' (Townsville Bulletin July 3, 1996).

The four examples detailed in this chapter show not only that the courts appear somewhat reluctant to evoke parental penalty in cases of juvenile offending, but also that parents themselves see very little ameliorative value in such measures. In Queensland there appear to be a number of reasons for this, not the least being that it may be difficult to prove that parents are contributing to the delinquency of their children. Certainly, this seems to have been the case for the Watts, Webb and Marcos families. The situation in the Ryan's case suggests an attempt by officials to coerce an Indigenous family into paying restitution without going through the due process of the law. Moreover, the findings suggest that penalising parents constitutes something of a crude judicial response to many of the complex problems facing families, particularly those trying to grapple with the problems of a son or daughter offending. It is difficult to see, even with the most generous benefit of the doubt, how penalising parents can contribute in any meaningful way to preventing further offending. While such measures may placate those who locate the causes of crime in the context of family dysfunction or of simple parental neglect they do little in a practical sense to support parents attempting to deal with an offending child.

Thus, this study from North Queensland seems to have highlighted at least three unintended consequences of parental restitution proceedings. The first unintended consequence is that conscientious parents have been singled out and charged with offences that in no way mirror what has gone on in the family home in regard to caring for or disciplining of their children. The second unintended consequence is that the judiciary has come to the realisation that proving parental neglect so as to enforce restitution proceedings is very difficult and may be too difficult to pursue at all. The third unintended consequence appears to be that a crude emphasis on parental responsibility and restitution allows vigilantes in the community to take the law into their own hands to compel parental control. It is particularly disturbing when the vigilantes appear to be the very members of the community paid to uphold the due process of law.

Conclusion

Legislative provision for parental penalty has been a prominent feature of juvenile justice systems over recent years. The idea that parents should be held responsible for the offences of their children has found its way into the statute books of countries such as Australia, Britain and the United States. Yet, it appears difficult to prove legally that parents are contributing to the delinquency of their children and parents who have had experience of parental restitution legislation not only reject the idea that they should be held financially responsible for the offences of their children but, if these examples are any indication, are prepared to fight this suggestion in court.

Much criticism has also been levelled at the notion of parental restitution by a range of social and welfare organizations as well as by parents at the receiving end of the justice process. Such criticism casts serious doubt on whether parental penalty can be effective in preventing further offending among juveniles; indeed, it is more likely to create new problems such as increased family tensions (possibly resulting in youth homelessness) and financial hardship. It does little or nothing to help and support those parents who, despite their own efforts, have not succeeded in preventing the offending of their children. Proposing parental restitution also tends to individualise the supposed causes of crime by taking attention away from the social origins of offending and placing all the blame (and responsibility) on the shoulders of children and their parents. In so doing, of course, crime becomes transformed into a simple moral issue strikingly consistent with many of the individualistic explanations of offending currently in public circulation.

References

Australian Association of Social Workers (1995), 'Impounding Children Like Stray Dogs: The Children's (Parental Responsibility) Act', *Social Policy Bulletin*, No. 4, June.

Cohen, S. (1985), *Visions of Social Control: Crime, Punishment and Classification*, Cambridge, UK, Polity Press.

Collins, C. (1990), When Parents Pay for their Children's Mistakes, *State Government News (California)* June.

Cook, D. (1997), *Crime, Poverty and Disadvantage*, Child Poverty Action Group, London.

Davidson, H. (1996), No Consequences – Re-Examining Parental Responsibility Laws, *Stanford Law and Policy Review*, Vol. 7, No.1.

Hil, R. (1996), *Making Them Pay: A Critical Review of Parental Restitution in Australian Juvenile Justice*, Centre for Social and Welfare Research, James Cook University, Townsville.

Hil, R. and McMahon, A. (2001), *Families, Crime and Juvenile Justice*, Peter Lang, New York.

Meredith, R. (1996), 'Parents convicted for a youth's misconduct', *New York Times*, October 5, 1996.

New South Wales Council of Social Services (1995), 'Making Parents Responsible', *NCCOS News*, Vol 22, No. 1, February.

O'Connor, I. (1992), *Youth, Crime and Justice in Queensland*, Criminal Justice Commission, Brisbane.

Pitts, J. (1998), *The New Politics of Juvenile Justice*, Macmillan, London.

Straw, J. and Anderson, S. (1996), *Parenting: A Discussion Paper*, New Labour Headquarters, London.

Yea, A. (1997), Holding Parents Responsible, *NCLS Legislator*, Vol. 5, No.7.

Chapter 7

In Pursuit of the Responsibilised Self: Boot Camps, Crime and Punishment

RICHARD HIL

Introduction: Back to Shock Work

This chapter examines the emergence over recent years of a rash of boot camps across a number of western countries. Touted by various governments as the latest great penal hope, boot camps have proliferated in the wake of calls to 'get tough' on crime. Euphemistic references to the 'boot' have thus been endorsed as a deliberate masculinist cue for the introduction of a range of military-style disciplinary projects. Early morning reveille ('rise and shine'), 'square bashing', boot polishing, endless room tidying, meticulous bed-making and a culture of enforced deference to authority are common features of boot camps. Such practices are complemented by an assortment of educational and training programmes designed to address the offending and other 'anti-social' behaviours of residents.

The rapid growth of boot camps in North America, Canada, Australia and New Zealand reflects not only an established punitive-correctional impulse to reform recalcitrant individuals through shock and coercion, but also a governmental desire to be seen as 'tough' on young offenders. The latter, as will be noted, is integral to changing cultures of crime control in western neo-liberal states where the old certainties of penal-welfare have been gradually replaced by new and more punitive approaches to law and order. Boot camps are symptomatic of a changing penal philosophy in which antiquated and recycled ideas of punishment have percolated into the latest round of attempted crime reduction. The fact that boot camps are less than 'successful' in reducing crime, and indeed that they may occasionally do the reverse, is perhaps less important than the appearance of doing something tough to offenders – Thomas Mathieson (1990) has referred to this as the 'action function' of government.

Underpinned by notions of 'shock treatment', 'culture shock' or 'shock incarceration', boot camps are an emblematic feature of changing 'correctional' times in which 'the old ways' (reform through welfare, treatment and alleviation of deleterious social conditions) are seen as weak and ineffective in the face of the contemporary tyrannies of 'high crime', 'risk' and 'ontological insecurity' (Simon, 1995; Hogg and Brown, 1998; Young, 1999).

In order to demonstrate the many practical and philosophical problems associated with boot camps I will first outline the socio-political contexts in which they have emerged over the past decade and a half. I will then proceed to look at some of the claims made in respect of boot camps and outline arguments and findings contained in the voluminous research on such initiatives, especially in relation to the United States. Finally, I will return to the political mileage that has been made from boot camps and the prospects for other forms of 'youth justice' that are perhaps more sensitive to the contexts and environments in which many young offenders find themselves. Following Foucault (1977), my underlying argument is that the question of the 'effectiveness' of boots camps is secondary to a consideration of such initiatives as yet another aspect of contemporary neo-liberal governance. Boot camps are best considered in the wider context of punitive discourses and disciplinary practices that have shifted from the penal-welfare approaches of earlier decades to a hybrid system of punitive justice in the contemporary era.

Boot Camps and Changing Cultures of Crime Control

The past twenty years or so have witnessed a number of dramatic changes to cultures of crime control in most western countries (Hogg and Brown, 1998; Garland, 2000). Fictitious representations of a 'golden age' of pre-second World War peace and harmony in which crime was contained by the agencies of the 'sovereign state' have been gradually replaced by a ubiquitous (and actuarial) sense that the reality of everyday life is now governed by the risks associated with 'high crime' (Garland, 1996). To make matters worse, it is widely perceived by the public, and indeed acknowledged by agencies of the state themselves, that the state can no longer provide the necessary guarantees and resources to adequately police 'at risk' neighbourhoods and communities. The functions of policing and other forms of regulation and control therefore have to be relocated to various sites in the social body, most notably the family, school and neighbourhood (Cohen, 1985).

Overseen by regulatory governmental practices of 'inclusion', 'partnerships', and localised 'anti-crime' alliances, devolution of this sort has been a prominent feature of western crime control over recent years (Crawford, 1999; Garland, 2001). Individuals, families and neighbourhoods are thus absorbed into the crime control project; they are actively encouraged (via 'Neighbourhood Watch', 'Crime Stopper' initiatives and other pseudo-informal 'community' networks) to watch and gaze over others in anticipation of crimes about to be committed. This culture of regulated 'inclusion' and community vigilance has had the occasional unintended spin-off such as self-appointed and covert vigilante groups bent on reducing and/or preventing crime through violent means (Rose, 1994; Johnson, 1996; Hil, 1999).

Threat and risk in the face of high crime is, however, experienced differentially across the class divides of late modernity. In the gentrified inner-city condominiums and middle class estates brisling with home security and high insurance premiums the experience of crime is dramatically different to the zones of exclusion occupied by the poor and marginalised (Silbey, 1996). Given that the urban poor experience the most direct consequences of crime (physical attacks, break-ins, property damage, vandalism, graffiti etc.) it is hardly surprising that the perception of high crime is at its most intense among such populations (Rock, 1994; Walklate, 1998). Despite this, the nature and extent of crime remains something of a mystery. The reasons for this are well known: demographic changes, alterations to methods and criteria of recording, changes to policing policy and practise, changes to criminal codes, discretionary policing and so forth (Enders, 2000). Self-report studies and victim surveys further suggest the existence of a large and untapped 'dark figure of crime' which lends support to the popular (and occasional criminological) view that crime is a deeply embedded and ubiquitous feature of everyday life (Coleman and Moynihan, 1996).

David Garland (2000) argues that changes to cultures of western crime control have occurred largely in the wake of actuarial assumptions about high crime as well as in response to social, economic and political transformations associated with 'late modernity' (see also Garland and

Sparks, 2000). In relation to the former, Garland (2000: 367-8) identifies a number of significant changes to the epistemological and operational foundations of crime control in neo-liberal states over the past decade or so. Specifically, he notes that:

- High crime rates are regarded as a normal social fact.
- Emotional investment in crime issues is widespread and intense, encompassing elements of fascination, fear, anger and resentment.
- Crime issues are politicised and publicly represented in emotive terms.
- Concerns about victims and public safety dominate public policy.
- The criminal justice state is viewed as inadequate or ineffective.
- Private, defensive routines are widespread and there is a large market in private security.
- A 'crime consciousness' is institutionalised in the media popular culture and the built environment.

As Garland (2000: 308) observes, this fearful and insecure culture of high crime – or what Young (1999) refers to as a condition of 'ontological insecurity' – remains a deeply embedded and enduring feature of contemporary life in western states:

> Once established, this view of the world does not change rapidly. It is not much affected by year-to-year changes in the recorded crime rate, even where these involve reductions in real rates of criminal victimisation. This explains the apparent absence of a relationship between crime rates and fear of crime sentiments. Our attitudes to crime – our fear and resentments, but also our commonsense narratives and understandings – become settled cultural facts that are sustained and reproduced by cultural scripts and not by criminological research and official data.

Faced with this quasi-apocalyptic vision, politicians and crime control mandarins respond to the perceived reality by calling for and implementing policies that are deemed suitably 'tough' to counter the threat of crime in our midst. Less reliance is placed on 'expert' criminological opinion and more on the 'signs and symbols' of punishment as a politicised curative for the menace of high crime (Pratt, 2000). A sense of 'judicial vengeance' pervades the sensibilities of 'the public' as well as the actions of criminal justice administrators (Hudson, 2000). Increasingly, talk of the 'needs' of offenders' has been usurped by the rhetoric of the 'back to justice' movement which proposes that offenders should be held directly responsible (and therefore accountable) for their actions. The individualisation of justice over recent years has been distinguished by a shift from the 'penal-welfare' culture of the 1960s and 1970s (with its emphasis on social welfare intervention and notions of 'treatment' and 'rehabilitation'), to a hybrid and highly politicised system of crime control based on 'targeted' policing and punitive judicial action. The latter are evidenced in measures such as 'zero tolerance' policing, mandatory sentencing, 'truth in sentencing', longer gaol terms, and more stringent supervision orders etc., as well as in pro-active approaches to law and order, like risk-based crime prevention and various modalities of 'local governance'.

The philosophical shift in judicial discourse from welfare to justice has arisen alongside similar changes in other domains of social regulation (health, welfare, employment) where governments have actively promoted the devolutionary notion of personal (rather than social or governmental) 'responsibility'. However, it is in the domain of criminal justice that the nebulous notion of 'individual responsibility' has been advocated most enthusiastically. In recent years it has become increasingly evident that various conceptions of 'individual responsibility' now cut across virtually all aspects of criminal justice policy and practice, from the role that parents should play in curtailing crime among their offspring to the active participation of entire communities in the crime control project. The morally charged cult of 'responsibilisation' has also been apparent in liberal and humanitarian approaches to 'restorative justice' as well as in probation and detention centre orders, and in various crime prevention/reduction initiatives (Garland, 1996; Hil, 1998). This notion extends both to explanations of the 'causes of crime' (s/he is regarded as a rational-calculating 'actor') and to ways of preventing and/or reducing offending. Thus, the actual or potential ('at risk') offender is required to engage in forms of self-regulated behaviour that will prevent further criminal action. Failure to act responsibly is, of course, likely to be greeted by the full force of the criminal law (Hil and McMahon, 2000).

Significantly, the discursive practice of responsibilisation has been applied most vigorously to juvenile offenders (Ritter, 2001). Its current manifestations, however, must be seen in the context of entrenched actuarial assumptions about the presence of high crime in the social body. The fact that notions of individual responsibility reflect antiquated ideas of personal reform and redemption as a means of dealing with crime is no accident, particularly since neo-classical explanations of crime conveniently gloss over the structural and governmental conditions associated with such behaviours. From the perspective of the powerful, it is expedient to view crime as originating form *within* the individual rather than *through* institutional arrangements. Certainly, the return to practices of crime prevention and reduction based on the requirement of personal change (via personal growth, development and treatment), and the emergence of practices that seek to 'reintegrate' the individual 'back into the community', are reflective of current approaches to crime control that have their origins in the mid-nineteenth century articulations of the confession, personal enlightenment and self-redemption (Hunt, 1999). Indeed, the idea that offenders can be reformed through regimes of self-regulated 'normalisation' is a feature of the earliest systems of juvenile crime control in countries like Australia (Seymour, 1988). Then as now, the immediate environments and wider social, economic and political contexts of criminal action were regarded as secondary (or entirely irrelevant) to the moral and redemptive aspects of self-regulation and individual responsibility. The emergence over recent years of wilderness programs, bush camps, boot camps and the like, are contemporary expressions of regulatory and reformative projects that have long sought to discipline and 'normalise' the most marginalised sections of the youth population (Bessant, Sercombe and Watts, 1998).

The remainder of this chapter will focus on the claims made on behalf of boot camps and how these stack up against the available evidence.

Reform Through Regimentation, Self-discipline and Fear

Boot camps have proliferated in a number of western countries over recent years, especially in the United States. The US government's commitment to boot camps is evidenced by the fact that under the Clinton administration $24.5 million was allocated to the expansion of such programs (Heyslip, 2000).

By 1993 there were over 50 military style boot camps across north America with a total capacity of just under 11,000 residents. Thirteen boot camps were designed specifically for women. Most camps accommodate between 100-250 inmates and are designed mainly for non-violent young offenders (Gowdry, 1999: 2). Most of these programs are based on the goals of cost reduction, reduction of prison overcrowding, rehabilitation of offenders and general deterrence (Austin, 1993). Designed primarily as tough, military-style programs for both young and adult offenders, boot camps are distinguished by their attempt to 'breakdown individualism' among inmates and to ensure deference to authority, 'self control' and general conformity (Hoffman, 1990). One of the primary aims of the boot camp is to induce 'stress' among new inmates and by the same token to ensure that the use of systematic shock and trauma brings about a suitable degree of docility and conformity among inmates. Despite early attempts to disguise the military style of boot camps by referring to them euphemistically as 'work camps', 'challenge camps' or even 'motivational camps', it was apparent such programs constituted a return to modes of discipline and punishment based upon the deliberate and systematic infliction of pain to the body and mind. Although there was considerable variation between boot camp programs they nonetheless shared a number of common features, including a commitment to drill and ceremony, separation of detainees from the general prison population (in fact most boot camps in the US are physically annexed from prisons), and commitment to 'a rigorous daily schedule of hard labour and physical training' (Travis, 1996: 40).

In a study of disciplinary practices in boot camps in Cleveland, Ohio; Denver, Colorado and Mobile, Alabama, it was found that usual practices involved a combination of 'military regimentation and conditioning with rehabilitation and a range of after-care and follow-up services' (Felker, 1999: 6). Typically, inmates moved through a three-stage program starting with 'selection', 'screening' and 'intake', to a period of 'intensive training', through to after-care and 'supervision in the community'. During the period of intensive training (usually three months) inmates are subjected to paramilitary discipline aimed at building 'self discipline, responsibility, self-esteem and team work by employing military structure, discipline and physical fitness training' (Felker, 1999: 7). In each camp the level of 'verbal conformation' and 'intimidation' used by officers varied, although it was common to all such camps. The regulation of order and cleanliness was of particular importance in the daily grind of the camps:

> Recruits scrubbed, cleaned and polished living areas and policed outdoor
> areas. The programs considered work assignments that required little
> supervision such as cleaning administrative offices, to be an earned
> privilege .... Physical training was an important adjunct to the programs
> military regimens. Youths participated in daily physical conditioning
> activities, beginning with exercise and runs early in the morning (Felker,
> 1999: 10).

As observed in the dramatised representations of the military type
experience in prime-time television documentaries like *Boot Camps*, such
initiatives are designed specifically to induce terror, fear and trauma in
residents in order to bring change in attitude and behaviour. Atkinson
(1995) describes the 'typical' boot camp approach as follows:

> Boot camps seek to capitalise on the transformative power of stress
> [shock] to inculcate behavioural and attitudinal change. In general,
> prisoners experience stress at the start of the period of incarceration. That
> stress is exacerbated in the structured, authoritarian environment of boot
> camps. In the early days of boot camp detention uncertainty prevails and
> previous behavioural responses are found to be inadequate for gaining
> control of the new situation. It is a watershed time when detainees are
> down and when, it is argued, the conditions of change are optimised
> (1995: 2).

Interestingly, as even the most sanitised media representations of boot
camps reveal, the level of trauma experienced by detainees is often acute
and many (especially young people) quickly succumb to the physical and
emotional demands that are placed upon them. The rehearsal of some of
the worst aspects of militaristic initiation rituals appears to operate openly
and with considerable justification and support from the managers of boot
camps. As Atkinson (1995: 2) notes:

> Negative strategies are reportedly no longer used with military recruits,
> yet degradation, harassment and physical punishment are abiding features
> of modern correctional boot camps.

This suggests an institutionalised 'double standard' in which the rights of
young people are often rendered secondary to the imperative of 'breaking'
those who appear to be hardened villains (Mackarel, 1995). This 'moral
holiday' on the part of those who operate boot camps suggests

a regulatory approach that, at best, seems to tolerate actual or potential breaches of some of the most fundamental rights articulated in the United Nations Charter of the Rights of the Child (UNHCRC). Boot camps and other 'shock' regimes like the notorious 'day in prison' programs rest on a profoundly mistaken belief that shock strategies will result in long term personal change, irrespective of the socio-cultural circumstances of an individual (for a critical discussion of 'shock treatment', see Hil and Moyle, 1992). Additionally, the use of abusive methods to bring about personal change is likely in the long term to bring about the very behaviours boot camps and other 'shock therapies' are designed to eradicate. Using violence on young residents who have often been brutalised both in their own families and by welfare and educational institutions is likely to provide a ready excuse for use of such behaviour in conflict situations (Mathius and Mathews, 1991). Moreover, it has been argued (Travis, 1999: 4) that the use of verbal intimidation and various forms of degradation are an anathema to any notion of 'treatment'. Thus:

> ... boot camps cannot provide a mechanism for treatment because many of the characteristics of the programs (confrontation [and] punishment instead of reward) are antithetical to treatment... When boot camps are bad, they can be abusive, destructive and even dangerous for inmates and staff (Travis, 1996: 5-6).

Further, as evidence on the military type regimes of the 'short, sharp, shock' experiments in England during the 1980s demonstrated, efforts to shock young offenders into conformity though the use of ritualised modes of degradation and humiliation, often produce short term docility and conformity and long term anger, resentment and criminality. Perhaps not surprisingly, the rate of recidivism among the subjects of the 'short, sharp, shock' were often worse than many other approaches to youth crime prevention (Muncie, 1999; Mackarel, 1995).

Despite the fact that similar outcomes tend to characterise boot camps across the United States, this has not served to dissuade politicians and others in other countries from advocating such initiatives as a way of dealing with youth crime. For instance, as Queensland Premier, Peter Beattie, glowingly announced in the wake of the introduction of a Federally-funded boot camp experiment in Australia: 'I think it ['Project Australia'] is a very worthy project. We will be keeping a very close eye on it.... This is about breaking that vicious cycle that could lead to jail'.

Queensland's Chief Justice, Paul De Jersey echoed these sentiments in stating that:

> One of the things that interests me is adding this [boot camp] to the list of options which are made available to judges when they have to impose penalties on youths (quoted in Smith, 2000).

With this there is no mention of concerns over possible abuses to the rights of young people (despite promising to keep a 'careful eye' on the project), or of the voluminous evidence which points to the general ineffectiveness of boot camps in curtailing crime. No mention either of the fact that boot camps may in fact exacerbate problems of crime and violence among detainees and/or do little or nothing to address the deep structural problems that confront tens of thousands of marginalised young people in neo-liberal states like Australia. As Atkinson (1995: 2) remarks:

> Many of these young people [who end up in boot camps] live at the margins, some of them will be substance abusers, and a disproportionate number of them will be members of minority groups. Boot camps provide a model of discipline, physical training and obedience, but there is no other path associated with it, and no attendant social welfare cocoon. Questions about the fundamental emphasis in boot camps on drill and rigour appear as a running thread through the literature.

Fundamentally, boot camps are based on a number of moral precepts concerning the possibility of redemptive change through the deliberate infliction of emotional and physical pain upon residents. In this sense boot camps reflect earlier (nineteenth century) manifestations of punishment in which pain to the body, along with intense moral regulation and coercive uniformity, were regarded as integral to strategies of crime control. That such practices currently operate in conjunction with other more 'humanitarian' approaches (for instance, 'reintegrative shaming') indicates the complex bifucatory nature of contemporary crime control practices across western countries. The fact also that the majority of boot camps in the United States are located not in exotic 'wilderness' locations or in lush suburban environments but rather are annexed to prisons, reveals their symbolic status in the culture of crime control (Atkinson 1995: 3).

Do Boot Camps 'Work'?

Inevitably, once the institutional practices of boot camps took hold in the United States, and then gradually (and somewhat more modestly) in other countries such as Australia and Canada, it became essential from an administrative point of view to know whether or not they 'worked'. Anecdotal evidence, 'feel good' boasts and dramatised TV representations could only go so far in demonstrating the benefits or otherwise of boot camps. At some point, politicians, correctional managers and administrators would call upon the services of accredited researchers to evaluate whether any of the broadly stated objectives of boot camps had been realised. These objectives included cost reduction, diversion from prison, lowering of the mainstream prison population and crime prevention/reduction. The picture that emerges from the literature is not entirely encouraging. As Atkinson (1995: 5) points out:

> ... the model's attraction at home [Australia] and abroad seems to lie more in its perceived public appeal, than in measurable effectiveness. This conclusion has been echoed in numerous other studies of boot camps, and it is difficult to find firm empirical evidence to support the view that boot camps are cheaper than their alternatives or that they significantly alter the behaviours of detainees (see also Travis, 1994; Parent, 2000; American Correctional Association, 1996).

Let us turn firstly to perhaps the main claim made by most boot camp administrators: that shock therapy has a beneficial affect in terms of reducing the rate of recidivism among discharged residents.

Recidivism

There is certainly no shortage in the number of empirical studies on rates of recidivism among former boot camp detainees (see Peters, Albright and Gimbel, 1996; Mackenzie, 1990; Polsky and Fast, 1993). Overall, it appears that when compared to ex-prison inmates, former boot camp residents tend to do no better or worse in terms of their propensity to commit further crime. An American study (Austin, 1993) of boot camp programs that operated in Los Angeles between 1990 and 1992 compared a total of 544 sentenced young offenders to 216 'Volunteers'. The purpose of the study was to compare both the rates of recidivism between the two groups and between boot camp inmates and those consigned to prisons. It was found that any differences between those sentenced to boot camps and volunteers were negligible and that the rate of recidivism among inmates of the so-called 'Regimented Inmate Diversion' program was on par with rates for ex-prisoners. In other words, the culture of tough discipline in the boot camp seemed to have little long-term affect on crime reduction when compared to traditional prison inmates. Similarly, in another US study of boot camp parolees in Louisiana (Mackenzie, Shaw and Gowdry, 1990) it was found that there was no evidence of reduced recidivism among inmates when compared to former prison inmates. Indeed, it was noted that prior incarceration, age, sex and other social characteristics correlated more closely to recidivism than the type of disciplinary regime experienced by the offender. A further US study focused on the outcomes of boot camps upon inmates in eight programs based in New York, Florida, Georgia, Illinois, Louisiana, Oklahoma, South California and Texas (Smykla and Selke, 1995). The study found that there was little or no evidence to suggest any significant or lasting changes to the rate of offender recidivism among former boot camp inmates, especially when compared to ex-prisoners in the same states. However, it is worth noting that in those camps where greater emphasis was placed on 'treatment' and education/training programs there was some evidence of a reduction in rates of re-offending (Mackenzie, 1994), although, again, the results were not overly significant and nor did they take account of long term trends. The evidence on boot camps appears to be quite conclusive: they do not serve to prevent further offending among former inmates. This suggests that while boot camps may appeal to the punitive instincts of some politicians, social commentators and law enforcement personnel, any claims to effectiveness in terms of crime reduction are unfounded.

Cost Reduction

Claims of cost reduction are an important source of justification for the use of boot camps. Thus boot camp placements are said to be less resource intensive than prisons. However, although some savings can be made in the short term this is often achieved through a range of operational decisions regarding the provision of 'treatment' facilities for inmates (Burns and Gennaro, 1995). The evidence suggests that while considerable resources are devoted to facilitate 'intensive training', cuts are often made to treatment programs. This is brought about because the 'in-your-face' nature of intensive training at boot camps requires a high ratio of interaction between officers and detainees. As Atkinson (1995) observes:

> A relatively high level of supervision, treatment and training applies at boot camps compared with regular prisons. Cost savings can therefore only occur providing capital costs are contained and the programs operate at or near to full capacity, thereby avoiding a substantial number of significantly longer prison sentences.

Additionally, as the enormous increase in the US prison population over recent years indicates, there is every likelihood that the proliferation of boot camps will merely contribute to a net-widening effect in which more and more inmates are absorbed into the prison-industrial complex. The evidence further suggests that rather than alleviating prison crowding, as claimed by advocates of boot camps, the end result is that vacancies in prisons are filled rapidly and that new, larger and more 'secure' institutions are built to house an ever-expanding prison population. As Parent (1994: 8) notes of the boot camp experiment in New York: '… even the best done boot camps cannot stop prison population growth if imprisonment rates are growing rapidly'.

The Needs Offenders

Can boot camps effectively address the many and varied needs of detainees? Given the tendency of such programs to concentrate of intensive training (often to the exclusion of much-needed welfare, education and other programs), the answer to this question is, probably not. Evidence from the United States shows that the overwhelming majority of those entering boot camps tend to come from the ranks of the urban poor and are disproportionately made up of young black men and others from 'ethnic' backgrounds (American Correctional Association, 1993). The social and personal circumstances of these inmates are invariably characterised by the brutalising conditions associated with cultures of crime and violence. Additionally, most of the personal records of these inmates reveal low levels of literacy, poor school records, patchy employment histories, repeat offending, violent backgrounds and conflict-ridden families. Given this, it is highly doubtful whether a brief experience at a military style boot camp can address the deep structural problems and personal circumstances to which most inmates inevitably return upon release.

The Failure of 'Redemptive Responsibility'

As noted, boot camps are underpinned by a highly individualistic view of crime causation that has its epistemological origins in classical criminological aetiology. In effect, the offender is abstracted from wider socio-economic, cultural and political contexts and regarded as an autonomous moral actor capable of making decisions that are both rational and calculating. The problem of offending is reduced to moral aberration rather than any reflection of the particular life chances, worldviews or cultural expressivities of offenders themselves. Additionally, little or no account is taken of the way in which certain sections of the youth population are rendered the 'targets' of police and welfare intervention, or indeed of how those deemed to be a 'threat' to social order are gradually absorbed into systems of regulation and control (Cunneen and White, 1996; Carrington, 1992).

Indeed, such matters would be regarded as meaningless digressions in the disciplinary context of boot camps where resources are devoted to the pursuit of cognitive and behavioural change at the individual level. The philosophical core of boot camps relies on what might be termed the goal of 'self responsibilisation'; that is, the proposition that irrespective of social and economic conditions the individual has the 'choice' to take charge of the general direction of his or her life. According to this view, poverty, disadvantage, exclusion, marginalisation, racism, sexism and so forth are insufficient 'excuses' or justifications for criminal behaviour. Indeed, such neutralising strategies are regarded by boot camp exponents as irritating justifications for actions that are premeditated in nature and self-rewarding in outcome. It is in this sense that boot camps constitute a strange mixture of antiquated ideas of punishment and contemporary notions of self-help and personal motivation. In relation to the former, boot camps rely on the infliction of physical and emotional pain to their inmates in order to send a message to others about the potential consequences of crime (general deterrence), and to deter the individual inmate from further engagement in criminal activity (individual deterrence). The instrumental nature of boot camp punishment is expressed through a simple but highly ritualised and purposeful process of training designed to bring about redemptive responsibility in its subjects. More often than not this results in a variety of outcomes ranging from short-term desistance from offending through to a continuation of the brutalisations that occurred prior to the offender entering the boot camp program.

The goals of self-reliance and personal motivation that are so central to the philosophy of boot camps have much in common with the self-directed individualism of contemporary culture. Specifically, the proposition that the exercise of 'individual moral choice' can determine the general direction of one's life (irrespective of any social constraints) tends to compliment popular ideas about 'self actualisation', 'self help', 'self motivation' and other derivatives of personal salvation. Thus, the enlightened subject can exercise 'choice' almost as if this were some free-floating and de-contextualised resource. Boot camps are designed to 'encourage' a particular brand of moral choice (law abiding, deferential, respectful), and to promote a strong sense of the responsibilised self in the redemptive subject. Pain to the body and mind is inflicted strategically so as to engage a process of redemptive change though which the subject finally submits to the cognitive possibilities of 'choice'. Like earlier projects designed to bring about 'normalisation' through regimentation and discipline (Tait, 2000), boot camps seek to address crime prevention/reduction through individual moral transformation rather than any appeal to social or institutional change.

The indications are that boot camps have not achieved their main goals. While there is evidence that such programs may have some marginal impact on reducing prison overcrowding – even though the probable long-term impact is net widening – the key objectives of crime prevention/reduction have not been realised. As with countless other crime control initiatives in western countries (see Cohen, 1985), boot camps have given rise to a wide range of unforeseen consequences that will eventually result in their reduction if not total demise. These consequences can be grouped under the following three headings: brutalisation, value reinforcement, and desensitisation.

Brutalisation

Most evaluations of boot camps have focused on their 'effectiveness' in terms of crime prevention/reduction. Less attention has been devoted to the routinised nature of degradation and humiliation inflicted in varying degrees upon inmates. The few studies to have focused on such matters paint a less than glowing picture of the way in which detainees are treated in boot camps and the impact of this upon their capacity to deal with many social and personal problems (Atkinson, 1995: 56). Indeed, as a number of psychologists have noted, the period of 'intensive training' characteristic of boot camp programs may actually work against the few educational and other 'treatment' programs operating in such places (Travis, 1996: 6). It is also worth remembering that boot camps, like other penal institutions, are often highly secretive and defensive, especially when subject to the attentions of researchers and government inspectors. What appears to be going on inside these programs via reports and academic papers may in fact be at variance with how inmates themselves experience the day-to-day realities of life therein. Indeed, there are few if any detailed accounts of such experiences in the official or academic literature.

Value Reinforcement

Perhaps the most glaringly obvious negative consequence of boot camps is their use of methods of regulation and control that legitimate the use of violence and intimidation as a means of bringing about individual change. As noted, given the fact that many boot camps have not been subject to rigorous empirical investigation, and therefore remain rather secretive places, it has hard to know what exactly goes on inside them. Nonetheless, enough is known to suggest that the verbal harassment, intimidation and confrontation are not a million miles away from the *modus operandii* of many of the violent young men who happen to enter these programs. At the very least, brutalising practices are likely to reinforce pre-existing orientations among detainees and may create militaristic 'role models' that reflect some of the most dubious of masculinist values.

Desensitisation

Desensitisation among inmates occurs at a number of different levels: from the legitimised use of violence and intimidation as a means of gaining control to the embellishment of a moralistic sense of self-responsibility. The later serves to deflect both detainees and their supervisors from viewing crime as connected to the world 'out there'. Instead, detainees are 'encouraged' to develop a consciousness of crime that locates it in the realm of moral aberration and personal deficit rather than in any other domain. This attempted removal of a social consciousness of crime turns the individual in on him/her self and promotes the idea that individual moral choice constitutes the basis of personal growth and development. Thus, in the pursuit of the responsibilised self, detainees are encouraged to negate the fact that they come from similar backgrounds with shared issues and concerns and instead to consider their own behaviours as the result of *personal* failure. The entire ethos of boot camps rests on the puerile assumption that if individuals remould themselves morally then crime reduction or desistence will follow. Like previous calls for conscription, the implicit message of shock incarceration programs is that what contemporary society cannot offer young people will be offset by enforced conformity to existing social arrangements. Boot camps desensitise in a profoundly social sense by instilling the view that crime is the result of individual failure and that the promise of secular moral redemption comes from within rather than from any transformation to the 'outside' world. Meanwhile, the contexts and conditions that have contributed to the criminalisation of offenders are conveniently forgotten or cast aside in favour of a tough and individualised approach to law and order.

What proponents of boot camps also choose to forget is that there already exists a wide range of well-established programs that have successfully engaged young people in constructive interventions that assist them in gaining a more meaningful place in the world. Programmes that assist with welfare issues, educational and social skills – and which rely on models of practice that encourage positive and non-violent approaches to conflict – are surely preferable to many of the implicit cultural messages running through boot camps and other such coercive regimes (Pitts, 1990). Additionally, it is important to remember that many of the factors propelling young people into the criminal justice system are linked to deep-seated structural and political inequalities, many of which have been generated through governmental neglect rather than any deficits in personal responsibility.

Conclusion

This chapter has focussed on the emergent contexts, application and use of boot camps in contemporary cultures of western crime control. It has been argued that such programs need to be viewed in light of various shifts and changes to law and order in late modernity. While boot camps exhibit a complex melange of antiquated and recycled approaches to punishment they nonetheless compliment a range of contemporary crime control techniques and practices that regard crime as resulting from moral aberration rather than from wider 'structural' and governmental conditions. The primary objectives of boot camps – crime prevention/reduction, cost savings, reduction in prison overcrowding – have generally not been achieved. Thus, boot camps cannot claim to have reformed inmates, or to have lessened the state's dependence on prisons. Indeed, high rates of recidivism among those released from boot camps (comparable to rates among ex-prisoners) indicate that the goal of self-responsibilisation remains something of a pipe dream. More worrying, however, is the fact that boot camps engage in practices which may well reinforce the capacity of inmates to brutalise others and to regard violence and intimidation as an appropriate means of conflict resolution. Additionally, boot camps cannot address the deep and enduring problems faced by inmates, most of who come from backgrounds characterised by poverty, disadvantage and deprivation. Despite the proliferation of boot camps in the United States and other western countries, their evident shortcomings are testament to the fact that such programs have little to do with whether they actually 'work' or not, and everything to do with the contemporary 'signs and symbols' of punishment. There is every likelihood that boot camps will join the long and depressing list of crime control projects that have failed to live up to their promises and which produce all manner of unintended consequence. Significantly, the reliance of boot camps on moralistic prescriptions of individual redemption through shock reflects a contemporary focus on law and order that is prepared to forgo some of the basic rights of young people in favour of the utilitarian goal of 'social order'. Perhaps the real story of boot camps begins with the socio-political and economic status of young people, many of whom find themselves increasingly on the margins of contemporary life and subject to a range of punitive state interventions. This is a story rarely to be found in the glut of empirical studies on boot camps.

References

American Correctional Association (1996), *Juvenile and Adult Boot Camps*, ACA, Lantham.

Atkinson, L. (1995), *Boot Camps and Justice: A Contradiction in Terms?'*, Australian Institute of Criminology: Canberra.

Austin, J. (1993), *The Growing Use of Jail Boot Camps*, National Institute of Justice, Washington.

Austin, J., Jones, M. and Bolyard, M. (1993), *Assessing the Impact of County Operated Boot Camps: Evaluation of the Los Angeles County Regimented Inmate Diversion Program*, National Council on Crime and Delinquency: San Francisco.

Bessant, J., Sercombe, H. and Watts, R. (1998), *Youth Studies: An Australian Perspective*, Longman: Melbourne.

Burns, J. and Gennaro, F. (1995), 'An Impact Assessment of the Alabama Boot Camp Programs', in *Federal Probation* Vol. 59, No. 1.

Carrington, K. (1992), 'Policing Families and Controlling the Young', in White, R. and Wilson, B. (eds.) 'For Your Own Good', *Journal of Australian Studies* (Special Issue).

Cohen, S. (1985), *Visions of Social Control*, Polity Press: Cambridge.

Coleman, C. and Moynihan, J. (1996), *Understanding Crime Data: Haunted by the Dark Figure*, Open University Press: Buckingham.

Crawford, A. (1999), *The Local Governance of Crime: Appeals to Community and Partnerships*, Clarendon: London.

Cunneen, C. and White, R. (1996), *Juvenile Justice: An Australian Perspective*, Cambridge University Press: Melbourne.

Enders, M. (2000), 'The Social Construction of Crime and Policing', in Enders, M. and Dupont, B. (eds.) *Policing the Lucky Country*, Hawkins Press: Sydney.

Foucault, M. (1977), *Discipline and Punish*, Penguin: Harmondsworth.

Garland, D. (1996), 'The Limits of the Sovereign State: Strategies of Crime Control in contemporary Society', in *British Journal of Criminology* Vol. 36, No. 4.

Garland, D. (2000), 'Cultures of High Crime Societies', in *British Journal of Criminology* Vol. 40, No. 3.

Garland, D. (2001), *The Culture of Control*, Oxford University Press: Oxford.

Garland, D. and Sparks, R. (2000), 'Criminology, Social Theory and the Challenge of Our Times', in *British Journal of Criminology* Vol. 40, No. 4.

Gowdy, V.B. (20000), *Boot Camps: Historical Perspective*, Koch Crime Institute: Topeka, Kansas.

Heyslip, D. (2000), *The Future of Boot Camps*, Koch Crime Institute: Topeka, Kansas.

Hil, R. (1998), 'The Call to Order: Young People, Crime and Family Responsibility', in *Journal of Australian Studies*, No. 59, pp. 101-14.

Hil, R. (1998), 'Cautionary Tales: Vigilantism, Crime and Social Order in Australia', *Just Policy* No. 14.

Hil, R. and McMahon, T. (2001), *Families, Crime and Juvenile Crime*, Peter Lang: New York.

Hil, R. and Moyle, P. (1992), 'A Day in Prison – A Solution to Reducing Juvenile Recidivism Rates or Not?' in *Alternative Law Journal*, Vol. 17, No. 15, pp. 224-26.

Hoffman. J. (1990), 'Shock Sisters', *Village Voice* Vol. 35, No. 21.

Hogg, R. and Brown, D. (1998), *Rethinking Law and Order*, Polity Press: Armadale.

Hogg, R. and Brown, D. (1998), *Rethinking Law and Order*, Polity Press: Armadale.

Hudson, B. (2000), 'Criminology, Difference and Justice: Issues for Critical Criminology', *Australian and New Zealand Journal of Criminology*, 2001.

Hunt, A. (1999), *Governing Moral: A Social History of Moral Regulation*, Cambridge University Press: Melbourne.

Johnson, L. (1996), 'What is Vigilantism?', in *British Journal of Criminology* Vol. 36, No. 2.

Mackarel, M. (1995), 'Putting the Boot into Young Offenders', *New Law Journal*, Vol. 12.

Mackenzie, D. (1990), *An Evaluation of Shock Incarceration in Louisiana*, Louisiana State University: Louisiana.

Mackenzie, D. (1994), 'Results from a Multisite Study of Boot Camp Prisons', *Federal Probation* Vol. 58.

Mackenzie, D., Shaw, J. and Gowdry, V. (1990), *An Evaluation of Shock Therapy in Louisiana*, Louisiana State University: Louisiana.

Mathieson, T. (1990), *Prison on Trial: A Critical Assessment*, Sage: London.

Mathius, R. and Mathews, J. (1991), 'The Boot Camp Program for Offenders; Does the Shoe Fit?' *International Journal of Offender Therapy and Comparative Criminology*, Vol. 35, No. 4.

Muncie, J. (1999), *Youth Crime: A Critical Introduction*, Sage: London.

Parent, D.G. (2000), *Boot Camps and Prison Crowding*, Koch Crime Institute: Topeka: Kansas.

Peters, M., Albright, K. and Gimbel, C. (1996), *Evaluation of the Boot Camp for Juvenile Offenders*, US Office of Juvenile Justice and Delinquency Prevention: Washington.

Pitts, J. (1990), *Working with Young Offenders*, MacMillan: Basingstoke.

Polsky, H. and Fast, J. (1993), *Boot Camps, Juvenile Offenders and Culture Shock, Child and Youth Care Forum* Vol 22, No 6.

Pratt, J. (2000), 'The Return of the Wheelbarrow Men: Or the Arrival of Post-modern Penalty', *British Journal of Criminology*, Vol. 40.

Ritter, L. (2001), 'Inventing Juvenile Delinquency and Determining its Cure', in Enders, M. and Dupont, B. (eds.) *Policing the Lucky Country*, Hawkins Press: Sydney.

Rock, P. (ed.) (1994), *Victimology*, Dartmouth: Aldershot.

Rose, D. (1994), *In the Name of the Law*, Vintage: London.

Seymour, J. (1988), *Dealing with Young Offenders*, Law Book Company: Sydney.

Silbey, D. (1996), *Geographies of Exclusion*, Routledge: London.

Simon, J. (1995), 'They Died with Their Boots On: Boot Camps and the Limits of Modern Penalty', *Social Justice*, Vol. 22, No. 2.

Smith, W. (2000), 'Youth Put Country Boot Camp on Trial', *Courier Mail* February 19, 2000.

Smykla, J. and Selke, W. (eds.) (1995), *In Intermediate Sanctions: Sentencing in the 1990s*, Anderson: Cincinnati.

Tait, G. (2000), *Sex, Youth and Government*, Peter Lang: New York.

Travis, J. (1996), 'Foreword', in Mackenzie, D. L. and Eugene, E. H. (eds.) *Correctional Boot Camps: A Tough Intermediate Sanction*, National Institute of Justice: Washington.

Walklate, S. (1998), *Understanding Criminology*, Open University Press: Buckingham.

Young, J. (1999), *The Exclusive Society: Social Exclusion, Crime and Difference in Late Modernity*, Sage: London.

Chapter 8

The Political Resonance of Crime Control Strategies: Zero Tolerance Policing

CHRIS CUNNEEN

What is Zero Tolerance Policing?

The principle underpinning zero tolerance policing is simply that a strong law enforcement approach to minor crime (in particular public order offences) will prevent more serious crime from occurring and will ultimately lead to falling crime rates. The approach relies on an analogy drawn by Wilson and Kelling (1982) regarding 'broken windows'. If one broken window is not repaired in a building, then others will be broken and the building vandalised, followed by other buildings, then the street, the neighbourhood, and so on. An unrepaired window is a sign that no-one cares and therefore more damage will occur. Similarly, according to Wilson and Kelling, if disorderly behaviour is not dealt with in a particular area, then more serious crime will be the result. Small 'incivilities' such as public drunkenness, vandalism, begging and so forth create an atmosphere where more serious crime can flourish.

In its original version the 'broken windows' thesis promoted the idea of greater use of 'beat' police who patrolled neighbourhoods on foot and negotiated acceptable public behaviour – constantly making distinctions between the respectable and the disreputable. Importantly, in the original thesis public order was improved and maintained through the informal rules which were worked out at the neighbourhood level (Wilson and Kelling, 1982: 30). More recently Kelling and Coles (1997) still stress the need for negotiation of a 'disorder threshold' and argue that 'crackdowns' and street 'sweeping' is far different from the ideas proposed in the broken windows thesis.

However, in the two decades since Wilson and Kelling wrote the 'broken windows' article, the 'zero tolerance' philosophy has developed towards a much more punitive approach to maintaining public order. Most discussions of zero tolerance policing today regard the strategy as directly aimed at increasing arrest rates for minor offences such as public drunkenness, offensive language and behaviour, loitering and other similar offences. References to negotiating acceptable public behaviour at the local level have been dropped from the equation. Indeed, beggars and vagrants are seen as legitimate police targets and the strategies have become popular among politicians of varying political shades, including Labour and Conservatives, Republicans and Democrats. In the crude model of zero tolerance policing, a partnership approach with the community and other agencies is forgotten (Morgan and Newburn, 1997). Kelling continues to argue that policing requires consent, cooperation and collaboration with the community. He has distanced himself from zero tolerance policing, arguing that it is not a credible policing philosophy (Howe, 1997).

The concept of zero tolerance is ambiguous. As one commentator noted it is 'a soundbite term regularly used by the media and politicians' (Burke, 1998: 12). It has been defined as a generic expression to cover a variety of 'proactive, confident, assertive policing strategies' (Burke, 1998: 12). Some of the advocates of what is referred to as a zero tolerance approach such as George Kelling and William Bratton have in fact disassociated themselves from the term 'zero tolerance' (Wadham, 1998: 49). Zero tolerance policing is no doubt favoured as a political slogan precisely because of its populist appeal and inherent ambiguity.

Although the notion of zero tolerance policing is largely associated with the broken windows thesis, it's derivation in fact lies in drug policies of the Reagan administration in the United States during the early 1980s. At this time it was associated with the 'war on drugs' which involved targeting users. The notion of 'zero tolerance' became applied in other areas of public policy. In the United States, the concept became associated with targeting drink driving among teenagers (Neimeier, 1995) and as an approach to violence and guns in schools (Lozada, 1998; Dykman, 1996). During the early and mid 1990s 'zero tolerance' was associated with campaigns against domestic violence, sexual assault and child abuse in various countries including the United States, Britain, Canada and Australia (Henderson and Reder, 1997; Hunt and Kitzinger, 1996; Hart, 1997; Canadian Panel on Violence Against Women, 1993; Mugford, 1996).

Leaving aside the definitional issues and the different policy uses to which the 'zero tolerance' concept has been applied, it is certainly most commonly associated with the New York Police Department's (NYPD) policy of strict law enforcement towards 'antisocial' behaviour and 'quality of life' offences during the 1990s under Police Commissioner William Bratton and Mayor Rudolph Guiliani. Guiliani was elected Mayor in 1993 and Bratton was appointed as Commissioner soon afterwards.

Guiliani's electoral campaign centred on 'reclaiming the streets' of New York. As Greene (1999) has noted 'reclaiming the streets' was only one of six crime strategies which Bratton developed. The others involved reducing youth violence, domestic violence, auto-related crime, drug dealing and the number of guns on the streets. However, 'cracking down hard on the most visible symbols of urban disorder proved to be a powerful political tool for bolstering Guiliani's image as a highly effective mayor' (Greene, 1999: 173). Reclaiming the streets through a focus on 'quality of life' offences became the hallmark of how zero tolerance policing was understood in New York.

The NYPD emphasised more minor 'quality of life' crimes, such as graffiti, vagrancy, begging, 'squeegee' windshield washing, subway turnstile-jumping, illegal vending, street-level drug dealing and street prostitution. These offences were pursued to demonstrate 'control' of the streets. Bratton had previously been Chief of the New York Transit Police and embarked on a 'quality of life' policing program which had seen large scale arrests of people for fare evasion. As Greene (1999) has noted, what Bratton embarked on as Police Commissioner was in some ways a traditional law enforcement 'crack down' on local crime: arrest and gaoling of low-level drug offenders, picking up school age youth for truanting, aggressive use of stop and search powers, warrant checks and arrest of those caught violating even minor public order laws.

Neo-Liberalism and Crime Control

The NYPD model became a beacon for police commissioners and politicians from around the world including other parts of the Americas, Britain, Australia, South Africa and Europe (Dixon, 1998; Cunneen, 1999;

Stenson, 2001). The populist appeal of zero tolerance itself raises questions: why is this approach to policing seen as having political reasonance at this particular historical juncture? Especially when the approach involves overturning much of the accepted wisdom about effective policing prior to the early 1990s (Dixon, 2001). A significant part of the answer to this lies in the extent to which the notion of zero tolerance can capture the political aspirations of neo-liberal approaches to crime control. Zero tolerance successfully bridges both conservative appeals to a social harmony of obligations and authority maintained through hard, uncompromising policing, as well as contemporary claims to managerialist and risk assessment approaches in policing. Zero tolerance distances itself from perceived permissive attitudes to crime; it distinguishes itself from welfarist explanations of offending behaviour and rehabilitative crime control strategies, and from notions of community-based policing. It has both a traditional conservative edge to it of maintaining the social through direct and unambiguous policing of the 'dangerous classes', as well as incorporating neo-liberalist approaches of risk assessment.

As a concept, zero tolerance tells us that we can control crime through 'in your face' policing styles which target low level offenders, which utilise pro-arrest strategies and which deny the need for the development of community-based negotiated approaches. This is indeed a powerful rhetoric which lays claim to a fundamental 'truth': tough policing can work if police are allowed unfettered power to do their job. Allowing police to do their job requires minimum oversight by external bodies and maximum legislative discretion to police the streets.

Zero tolerance also locks into another quite separate strand that is an important component of neo-liberal managerialism: the demand for performance indicators, targeted use of resources and measurable outcomes. Zero tolerance strategies are geared quintessentially to the type of performance indicators that are immediately measurable and perfectly understandable to government: zero tolerance is about arresting people for targeted offences. As will be discussed further below, risk assessment technologies form a core of zero tolerance approaches through the identification of 'hot spots', the statistical profiling of particular crimes and likely offenders, and the identification and surveillance of recidivists.

Zero tolerance is also conducive to governments that demand 'results' that can be easily represented in the public sphere. Zero tolerance is about highly visible policing, particularly through the use of crackdowns.

Well publicized operations against street level drug users, or against particular groups of (usually minority and young) people for anti-social behaviour, make great footage on the evening news. They show a police service and government in control. Being in control is also very much the domain of strong men. As Stenson (2001) has noted, there is a strong patriarchal flavour underpinning zero tolerance policing, particularly among its greatest proponents like Bratton and Guiliani in New York, and Mallon in the UK.

At a deeper level, zero tolerance is telling us that it is acceptable to heavily police the marginalised, the poor, and ethnic and racial minorities. Tough policing is not about repression or discrimination, it is the targeting of those we know who are most likely to offend – hence the apparent 'legitimacy' of racial profiling.

Similarly, the demand for increased police powers through new types of legislation is also conducive to governments keen to show the public they are serious about law and order issues. Zero tolerance allows police to be tough on the streets and politicians to be tough on the floor of parliament. There is no room for arguments about civil liberties or social justice within a crime control rhetoric that says police can be effective if they have the necessary legislative backing to enable them to do their job effectively. As Stenson (2001) has argued, most politicians no longer wish to be seen as 'liberal' when it comes to crime and policing. Thus, conceptually, zero tolerance can link into traditional arguments about the efficacy of 'old style' policing (as opposed to community-based policing) as well as being seen in distinctly efficient terms within the definitions imposed by a new managerialism.

Zero Tolerance and the New Public Managerialism: CompStat and OCR

McLaughlin and Murji (2001), in their discussion of policing and neo-liberalism, identify a number of characteristics of the nature of new public managerialism. Of particular concern to the current discussion are the following:

- The setting of clear measurable standards and targets.
- The explicit costing of all activities, choices and priorities.

- The development of performance indicators to enable measurement and evaluation of efficiency.
- The publication of league tables showing comparative performance against indicators.
- Increased emphasis on outputs and results rather than processes.
- Rationalization of the purpose, range and scope of organisations through the identification of core competencies (McLaughlin and Murji, 2001: 109).

As will become evident, the idea of zero tolerance policing and the practical police tasks developed within this approach coalesced with the demands of the new public managerialism.

There was also an intersection between zero tolerance as a popular, metaphorical descriptor of police work and various other intelligence-led or problem-oriented policing approaches. The introduction of these approaches rely on significant changes over the last decade in new information technologies available to police which allow for crime-mapping (and hence 'hot spot' analysis), repeat offender analysis and so forth.

In addition, the new information technologies have allowed for increased supervision of police work. Police conduct can itself be monitored, audited and subjected to management scrutiny in new ways (Ericson and Heggarty, 1997; Chan, Brereton, Legosz and Doran, 2001). The combination of new managerial imperatives and new information technologies support highly targeted police operations as well as enabling new forms of scrutiny. The combination of changing information technologies which enabled increased surveillance of both criminal activity and police activity, as well as the new managerial demands for efficiency and cost-effectiveness underpinned the extent to which zero tolerance policing came to be regarded as an effective and practical policing strategy.

The use of the CompStat process by the NYPD and its adoption by other police services provide a useful window on how the combination of new management demands and changes in information technologies altered police activities.

CompStat and the NYPD

It has been widely recognised that the use of a computerised managerial system, CompStat, was an important element in the development of zero tolerance policing in New York. According to Bratton, CompStat is based on four principles: accurate and timely intelligence; rapid deployment of personnel and resources; effective tactics and relentless follow-up and assessment. CompStat has been described as 'the engine that drives zero tolerance policing in New York City and it is the heart of the strategic organizational changes that Bratton introduced' (Greene, 1999: 172).

Police Commissioner Safir (who succeeded Bratton) described CompStat as a 'crime management tool which uses weekly crime statistics, computer mapping and intensive strategy sessions to direct the implementation of crime fighting strategies' (cited in Burke, 1998: 20). There is clearly considerable pressure placed on borough and precinct commanders to achieve reductions in crime within their areas.

> CompStat operates by the police commanders ... giving periodical briefings to the senior management of the NYPD. These take place in the central command room of the Department which is set out like a wartime operations centre. The management team sits around a horseshoe-shaped desk while the borough commander stands in the middle. The crime statistics for the borough are displayed on screens behind the commander whether they want them or not. The statistics... are selected by the management team ... . There is one CompStat meeting a week and the borough commanders do not know which of them are going to be called to give a briefing... . There is little doubt that these often 'brutal' periodical interrogations... by NYPD senior management in an environment that resembles a wartime operations centre have provided sufficient motivation to achieve success in the fight against crime (Burke, 1998: 20).

Nicholl (1997), a former senior officer with Thames Valley police, has noted however, that the performance by which commanders are judged is 'numbers': the number of street searches, the number of high rise searches (verticals), the number of summons, the number of arrests, the number of warrants executed, and so forth. Nicholl (1997) provides a selection of quotes from NYPD officers which reflect the distorting influence which CompStat has had on policing:

> CompStat is the tail wagging the dog. I am trying to build relationships with my community so my crime rates are increasing because there is more confidence in reporting crime to us. But I then get beaten over the head at CompStat.
>
> Robbery patrol hours and the number of verticals are more important than dealing with domestic violence and rape.
>
> You try reporting a crime to the station – they don't answer the phone, so their numbers are distorted because people just give up.
>
> I am not accepting this as an assault report – no-one gets their ribs cracked by a hairbrush. Get rid of it.
>
> We have to find more larceny reports – if we only have three this week, they will expect us only to have two next week.
>
> And from a lieutenant, 'I spend all my time counting crime reports and checking we are not recording too many. I don't get to go out on patrol with my officers anymore' (Nicholl, 1997: 5).

She adds,

> These are quotes from real cops in NYPD who have had to operate to CompStat and under the fear of being caught out with high crime figures. It strikes me this is wholly predictable – the consequence of a police department driven by fear of being embarrassed if they do not reduce the levels of crime. Crime statistics are notoriously unscientific. They are made even harder to make sense of if there is tomfoolery going on with the way crime figures are recorded (Nicholl, 1997: 5).

The New South Wales Police Service and OCR

In Australia, the New South Wales Police Service adopted the CompStat process and renamed it Operations and Crime Reviews (OCR). The format broadly follows the CompStat process of bringing in local police commanders to meetings where they are intensively questioned over performance and results within their local areas. Local Area Commanders appear before the Police Commissioner and Executive Team to report on crime reduction strategies and outcomes for the 'major' crime categories of assault, break and enter, motor vehicle theft, robbery and stealing.

Commanders also report on the use of specific powers such as 'move-on' and searches. According to the New South Wales Police Service:

> Intelligence led policing, such as crime density mapping, helped to target 'hot' crimes, times, locations and likely offenders. By noting patterns of what crimes are committed when and where, crime managers better allocate front line resources to get results and discourage potential repeat offenders. Every local area command is now identifying potential repeat offenders, crime areas and repeat victims (NSW Police Service, 1998: 12).

The Police Service describes the OCR as 'a key tool in driving down or stabilizing crime' which is 'moving the Service towards a performance based culture...'. The OCR process is 'one of the key drivers of reform and organizational success' (cited in Dixon, 2001: 208).

A number of recent reviews of various aspects of New South Wales policing have been critical of the OCR process (Chan and Cunneen, 2000; Dixon, 2001; Legislative Council, 2001). The report of the Qualitative and Strategic Audit of the Reform Process (QSARP) conducted by an external consultancy agency found that confrontational management styles characterised the OCR. 'The OCR highlights the potential for ambiguous leadership messages to be delivered to commanders. Commanders are being told to behave in an open consultative way; they are observing a 'management by fear' style on the part of some members of the Chief Executive' (cited in Dixon, 2001: 208). 'The experience of the OCR process by many personnel is one of "punishment" when standards are not met... The OCR reinforces the culture of "fear and punishment"' (cited in Dixon, 2001: 209).

The auditors were critical of the OCR's restricted focus of 'attention to 'hard' data only, and the exclusion of measures of effectiveness other than crime statistics'. The performance culture 'increases the potential for process corruption... we regard it as important that commanders be measured, not only against results (i.e. what is achieved) but also against the behaviours they demonstrate (i.e. how the results are achieved)' (cited in Dixon, 2001: 209).

The report of the Legislative Council's inquiry into policing in the Sydney suburb of Cabramatta was also critical of the OCR process. Cabramatta is an area where three out of five people were born outside Australia (27 per cent in Vietnam), and where three quarters of the population speak a language other than English. It is also a major centre for buying and selling heroin.

> The experience of Cabramatta Local Area Command ... shows how new style management tools ... were introduced on top of an unchanged authoritarian command and control culture. The result was a demoralized local command, a decline in effective policing and a breakdown in community trust and relationships which have yet to be recovered (Legislative Council, 2001: 167).

An evaluation of a police strategic plan introduced to improve relations with Aboriginal people also noted the contradictory pressures between the OCR process and the strategic plan to reduce arrests of a racial group severely over-represented in the criminal justice system (Chan and Cunneen, 2000). The performance indicators and enforcement strategies were centralised from the top down through the confrontational OCRs and were not developed in partnership with local Aboriginal communities.

The themes of pressure, embarrassment and fear of being pulled up with high crime figures were commented upon in interviews with police. One officer responded, 'I'm pretty cynical of the OCR, puts too much pressure on people. It pushes commanders too much into a competition'. Another response from a commander stated, 'I've been through the OCR process twice...we're here to talk about things and to prove the quality of what we do [but] there's also a feeling of inquisition' (Chan and Cunneen, 2000: 177).

Zero tolerance policing has relied on new information technologies which provide localised assessment of the nature and incidence of crime and provide for the targeting of police resources at the local level. They also provide the opportunity for police managers to place considerable pressure on local area police commanders to demonstrate results in reducing crime or increasing the number of arrests for particular offences. Both the experience in New York and Sydney show that the management processes can have a significant effect on policing which is far from either efficient or rational.

Has Zero Tolerance Policing Reduced Crime?

The proponents of zero tolerance policing point to the decline in the crime rate in New York as proof of the success of the strategy. However, there are doubts that the falling crime rate in the city during this period was simply attributable to zero tolerance policing given that many other large United States cities experienced similar declines, although using different policing strategies and with dramatically different levels of policing. Nationally the incidence of serious violent crime and property crime declined in the United States during the first half of the 1990s. National victimisation surveys show a decline in homicide, rape, robberies, aggravated assaults and property crime. Not all large cities or states recorded a fall. However, there appears to be no correlation between whether zero tolerance policing strategies were introduced, or indeed whether 'three strikes' legislation and mandatory minimum prison terms were introduced, and the decline in crime rates (Greene, 1999).

A range of demographic, social and economic factors, as well as some law enforcement strategies such as greater control on handguns, have likely contributed to the declining levels of particular types of violent crime. Economic growth, reduced levels of unemployment and greater community-based activities to reduce crime are likely to have had an effect on crime levels (Independent Budget Office (IBO), 1998; Greene, 1999). There have also been significant changes in the pattern of drug use including the decline in the use of 'crack' cocaine. An ongoing study by Hamid, Curtis, McCoy, McGuire, Conde, Bushell, Lindenmayer, Brimberg, Maia, Abdur-Rashid, and Settembrino (1997) of heroin use in New York has found that young African-Americans are avoiding both heroin and cocaine. Even licit drugs are viewed with disfavour. Others have argued that there is a direct connection between the drop in the murder rate in New York and the decline in the 'crack' cocaine epidemic (Dixon, 1998: 97).

Zero tolerance policing is a resource intensive policing strategy. It requires high staffing levels to achieve the necessary level of direct law enforcement on the streets. Does the increase in resources actually lead to a reduction in the crime rate?

The size of the NYPD increased dramatically during the 1990s. The city also experienced a forty six per cent reduction in the crime rate during the same period (1990-1996). San Diego is a city with a similar crime index rating as New York. During the same period it achieved over forty per cent reduction in the crime rate with a one per cent increase in its per capita police staffing levels (IBO, 1998). San Diego restructured its police department along a community policing model which stressed problem solving and police-community partnerships for reducing crime. In contrast to the New York experience the drop in crime rates in San Diego was achieved at the same time as the number of arrests between 1993 and 1996 actually declined by fifteen per cent. Complaints against police for misconduct also fell. San Diego police also made greater use of new information technologies in crime mapping and police intelligence in locating consistent areas of high crime. However, they were able to utilise the new technologies within a context of community policing (Greene, 1999).

The Independent Budget Office (IBO) for the City of New York provided comparative analysis to the City Council's Committee on Public Safety on differing rates of policing and crime rates in the twenty five largest United States cities. The IBO found that many other cities achieved significant reductions in the crime rate with either much smaller per capita police staff levels or with actual reductions in police staff levels. Two notable cases were San Diego, which achieved a forty per cent drop in the crime rate with a one per cent increase in per capita police staffing levels, and Dallas, which achieved a thirty nine per cent drop in the crime rate with a decline in the per capita police staffing levels of between two and three per cent. Other cities with significant drops in crime levels included Pittsburgh, El Paso, Miami and Seattle (IBO, 1998). Researchers have also argued that the crime control policies pursued in San Francisco have achieved significant reductions in crime. These approaches stressed community involvement in crime control and alternative sentences. 'Since 1992 San Francisco has outperformed New York City in violent crime rate declines and has received virtually no media attention' (Taqi-Eddin and Macallair, 1999: 4).

The Broader Consequences of Zero Tolerance Policing: Some Lessons from New York

Perhaps the insight that government is a constantly failing enterprise that requires perennial revision provides some clue to thinking about the broader impact and consequences of the introduction of zero tolerance policing. A further insight into the link between popularism and zero tolerance is the bond between the rhetoric of zero tolerance and the politics of intolerance and racism. What have been some of the identifiable consequences of zero tolerance policing?

The Suppression of Dissent

The introduction of zero tolerance policing in New York was accompanied by an attempt to control dissent, including the desire to ban a broad range of demonstrations including black rights activists, gay rights activists, groups highlighting police brutality, to demonstrations by taxi drivers and food vendors (Cunneen, 1999). Norman Siegel, the Director of the New York Civil Liberties Union, noted the following.

> I've been here 13 years and my legal director has been here even longer, and we've never filed as many cases involving one administration. The Mayor's vision of a new New York is a vision that is more authoritarian and repressive, a vision that it antithetical to our rich tradition of tolerance for protest and dissent (ACLU News, July, 1998).

Demonstrations and marches have occurred because of the intervention of the Federal court which has over-ruled the refusal of permits by the Police Commissioner. However, the policing strategies which have then been used to control marches and processions have reflected a hardline, non-negotiated approach, often leading to violence and large scale arrests. Similarly repressive attitudes to the use of public space has been evident in the use by police of city parks ordinances against groups as varied as the Socialist Worker's Party to members of the All Saints Lutheran Church who were distributing condoms as part of their HIV/AIDS education program in the South Bronx (Cunneen, 1999).

Police Brutality, Particularly Against Racial and Ethnic Minorities

Police corruption and the use of excessive force have long been recognised as a problem in the NYPD. The Mollen Commission of Inquiry into corruption in the NYPD in 1994 found police officers were involved in drug dealing, robberies, assaults, perjury and falsification of records. It also found a failure by the NYPD to discipline officers accused of brutality.

A 1996 Amnesty International investigation after the Mollen Commission found that some steps had been taken to tackle corruption within the NYPD. However, police brutality remained a serious problem. Importantly, Amnesty noted that local community and civil rights groups reported that aggressive zero tolerance policing policies 'had been accompanied by unacceptable levels of brutality, especially toward racial minorities'. There were many cases 'where police officers had used excessive force in response to minor incidents, including assaulting bystanders for taking photographs or criticising police treatment of others' (Amnesty International, 1996).

The Amnesty report noted that:

> The evidence suggests that the large majority of the victims of police abuses are racial minorities, particularly African-Americans and people of Latin American or Asian descent. Racial disparities appear to be especially marked in cases involving deaths in custody or questionable shootings, an issue Amnesty International believes should be the focus of particular inquiry (Amnesty International, 1996).

Certainly the police precincts with the highest number of reported complaints against police are in neighbourhoods with higher proportions of African-American and Latino residents (Greene, 1999). In the late 1990s, events like the police torture of Abner Louima and the shooting of Amadou Diallo increased perceptions of police force which was racist in its operations and without effective supervision.

Complaints Against Police and the Issue of Racism

Complaints against the police registered with the Civilian Complaint Review Board (CCRB) have risen sharply since 1993. During the specific period between 1993 and 1996 when Bratton was the Police Commissioner complaints concerning police misconduct rose by sixty five per cent. In the four years up to 1998 the filing of civil rights claims against police for abusive conduct had increased by seventy five per cent and they were continuing to increase (Greene, 1999).

There is little doubt that the increase in complaints is associated with the introduction of zero tolerance policing. According to Amnesty International, police have suggested that the sharp increase in complaints arose as a result of increased arrests and police activity. According to police, many complaints arose from more effective policing and an increase in arrests, rather than genuine abuses. However, the CCRB noted that most of the complaints arose from encounters with police that did not involve arrests or persons receiving summonses. Most complainants had no prior complaint history, so could not be characterised as 'chronic' complainers.

Statistics published in New York by the CCRB indicate that minorities are disproportionately the victims of police abuse, particularly African-Americans. For example, half the people who lodged complaints with the CCRB from January to June 1995 were African-American (fifty per cent), a quarter was Latino (twenty six per cent), while the remainder was either white (twenty one per cent) or 'other' (three per cent), including Asian. The CCRB semi-annual report for the first half of 1997 noted a similar trend where African-Americans and Latinos lodged seventy eight per cent of complaints against police. The 1996 investigation by Amnesty International also revealed that more than two-thirds of the cases of police brutality were African-American or Latino. Most of the police officers involved were white. Nearly all of the victims in the cases of deaths in custody (including shootings) reviewed by Amnesty were members of racial minorities.

Similarly, Human Rights Watch noted in a 1998 report that the cost of zero tolerance policing was revealed by

> citizen complaints against more aggressive NYPD officers during the past several years and continuing impunity for many officers who commit human rights violations despite the recent reorganization of both the civilian review board and the police department's internal affairs bureau ... . There is often a racial or ethnic component to police abuse cases in New York City, with many incidents also fuelled by language barriers and miscommunication in the culturally diverse city (Human Rights Watch, 1998, 268-69).

In November 1998 the New York City Council's Public Safety Committee issued a report arguing for stronger policies to control police brutality. The Committee's chairperson noted that

> The Department has perpetuated a police culture in which officers may be emboldened to conduct themselves in a manner that runs contrary to departmental policy, the law and public interest... It is not a stretch to suppose that officers – such as those implicated in the Louima incident – felt that they could get away with it (Cooper, 1998: B1).

The failure of the police department to deal with issues of brutality and corruption has been a constant source of criticism of the NYPD. It would be simplistic to argue that these issues simply arise as a result of zero tolerance policing. However, they are *indicative* of the types of problems which a strategy of zero tolerance policing has exacerbated: aggressive public order policing; the routine use of violence and, in extreme cases, torture; and the targeting of minority groups. Certainly the widespread use of violence against members of minority groups is a major issue. The New York City Public Advocate claimed that the police torture of Louima was part of a 'pattern of police abuse, brutality and misconduct' (Human Rights Watch, 1998: 282).

Conclusion

In many respects the concept of zero tolerance is ambiguous. It is a 'simple' crime control strategy: arrest more people to reduce crime. However, it also locks into a powerful populist truth about crime, law and order. It provides a justification for pro-arrest and punitive policing operations. Zero tolerance also provides a convenient bridge between old style police crackdowns on those groups defined as police 'property', with the demands of a managerialism besotted with easily measurable performance indicators. It makes a science of repressive policing strategies.

New information technologies have provided the opportunity for an intersection between zero tolerance policing and the new managerialism, through the increased ability for surveillance of both crime and police-work. The emphasis on rationalization of core goals and competencies ('reducing crime through arrests'), outputs and performance indicators (number of arrests, warrants executed, etc), and comparative performance between commanders have all been made possible through new computerised information systems.

Part of the appeal of zero tolerance policing is that it also legitimates heavy handed policing strategies against minorities. Zero tolerance fits closely with the growing xenophobia and racism in a range of countries. In parts of Europe, zero tolerance has been linked by both the far-Right and more moderates with strategies to control asylum-seekers and 'foreigners' (Stenson 2001). In Australia zero tolerance has been most attractive in jurisdictions with large indigenous populations such as the Northern Territory or in urban areas with racialised and criminalised minorities such as Arabic and Vietnamese people in Sydney (Cunneen, 1999; Dixon, 1998).

The international appeal of zero tolerance can be understood partly within the parameters of law and order populism, and the rising fear of 'outsiders' which is ruthlessly exploited by a range of political parties. Globalised media means that we are all aware of the New York 'miracle' in policing: the answer is not obscure, it is right there to be seen. The globalisation of crime control ideas like zero tolerance also needs to be understood as a function of the international dissemination of ideas about efficient public management and new information technologics. To argue against zero tolerance is to be seen as being opposed to efficiency, effectiveness and better management and control of police-work.

It would be misleading to view all senior police as favourably disposed to the idea of zero tolerance policing. Perhaps the most well-known police critic of zero tolerance has been the Thames Valley Chief Constable, Charles Pollard who claimed that zero tolerance policing was a 'short term fix and a long term liability'. He noted further,

> That part of zero tolerance policing characterised by the aggressive policing, confrontational management, opportunistic short-termism and undue emphasis on the 'numbers game' poses an enormous threat to the future. If this culture is not tackled, then, on the basis of the British experience, the risk of serious corruption and inner city disorder in the future is real (Pollard, 1997: 60).

References

ACLU News (1998) 'New York Mayor No Friend to First Amendment, NYCLU Says at Independence Day Rally', 4 July 1998. [http://www.aclu.org/news/n070498a.html].

Amnesty International (1996), *Police Brutality and Excessive Force in the New York City Police Department*. [http://www.web.amnesty.org/ai.nsf/index/AMR510361996].

Burke, R. H. (1998) 'A Contextualisation of Zero Tolerance Policing Strategies', in R.H. Burke (ed), *Zero Tolerance Policing*, Perpetuity Press: Leicester.

Canadian Panel on Violence Against Women (1993), *Changing the Landscape: Ending Violence – Achieving Equality*, Minister of Supply and Services: Canada.

Chan, C. and Cunneen, C. (2000), *Evaluation of the Implementation of the New South Wales Police Service Aboriginal Strategic Plan*, Institute of Criminology: Sydney.

Chan, J., Brereton, D., Legosz, M. and Doran, S. (2001), *E-Policing. The Impact of Information Technology on Police Practices*, Criminal Justice Commission: Brisbane.

Cooper, M. (1998), 'Stronger Policies Are Needed to Stem Police Brutality', *New York Times*, 10 November 1998, p.B1.

Cunneen, C. (1999), 'Zero Tolerance Policing and the Experience of New York City', *Current Issues in Criminal Justice*, Vol. 10, No. 3, pp. 299-313.

Dixon, D. (1998), 'Broken Windows, Zero Tolerance and the New York Miracle', *Current Issues in Criminal Justice*, Vol. 10 No. 1, pp. 96-106.

Dixon, D. (2001), 'A Transformed Organisation?' The NSW Police Service Since the Royal Commission, *Current Issues in Criminal Justice*, Vol. 13, No. 2, pp. 203-218.

Dykman, A. (1996), 'Hardship Duty', *Techniques*, Vol. 71, No. 6, September 1996, pp. 16-23.

Ericson, R. and Heggarty, K. (1997), *Policing The Risk Society*, University of Toronto Press: Toronto.

Greene, J. (1999), 'Zero Tolerance: A Case Study of Police Policies and Practices in New York City', *Crime and Delinquency*, Vol. 45, No. 2, April 1999, pp. 171-187.

Hamid, A., Curtis, R., McCoy, K., McGuire, J., Conde, A., Bushell, W., Lindenmayer, R., Brimberg, B., Maia, S., Abdur-Rashid, S., and Settembrino, B. (1997) 'The Heroin Epidemic in New York City: Current Status and Prognoses', *Journal of Psychoactive Drugs*, Vol. 29, No. 4, pp. 375-391.

Henderson, C. and Reder, R. (1997), 'Zero Tolerance Policing in Hillsborough County', *Police Chief*, Vol. 63, No. 2, February 1997, pp. 54-5.

Howe, S. (1997), 'Kelling's Law', *Policing Today*, Vol. 3 No. 4, pp. 17-19.

Human Rights Watch (1998), *Shielded From Justice. Police Brutality and Accountability in the United States*, Human Rights Watch: New York.

Hunt, K. and Kitzinger, J. (1996), 'Public Place, Private Issue? The Public's Reaction to the Zero Tolerance Campaign against Violence Against Women', in H. Bradby (ed), *Defining Violence*, Avebury: Aldershot.

Independent Budget Office (IBO) (1998), Correspondence with the New York City Council Committee on Public Safety, City of New York, 16 March 1998, 11 May 1998. On file with author.

Kelling, G. and Coles, C. (1997), *Fixing Broken Windows*, Touchstone: New York.

Legislative Council (2001), *Cabramatta Policing*, General Purpose Standing Committee No 3, Report No 8, New South Wales Parliament: Sydney.

Lozada, M. (1998), 'Ground Zero', *Techniques*, Vol. 73, No 3, March 1998, pp. 37-41.

McLaughlin, E. and Murji, K. (2001), 'Lost Connections and New Directions: Neo-Liberalism, New Public Managerialism and the 'Modernization' of the British Police', in K. Stenson and R. Sullivan (eds), *Crime, Risk and Justice. The Politics of Crime Control in Liberal Democracies*, Willan Publishing: Uffculme.

Morgan, R. and Newburn, T. (1997), 'Tough on Zero Tolerance', *New Statesman*, Vol. 126, No. 4336, 30 May 1997, p.14.

Mugford, K. (1996), *Zero Tolerance. Violence Against Women and Children*, South Australian Health Commission: Adelaide.

Neimeier, M. (1995), 'Zip, Zero, Zilch: The New Alcohol Tolerance Law for Underage Drivers in Michigan', *University of Detroit Mercy Law Review*, Vol. 73, No. 1, Fall 1995, pp. 45-71.

New South Wales Police Service (1998), *Annual Report 1997-98*, New South Wales Police Service: Sydney.

O'Malley, P. (2001), 'Risk, Crime and Prudentialism Revisited', in K. Stenson and R. Sullivan (eds), *Crime, Risk and Justice. The Politics of Crime Control in Liberal Democracies*, Willan Publishing: Uffculme.

Stenson, K. (2001), 'Some Day Our Prince Will Come', in T. Hope and R. Sparks (eds), *Crime, Risk and Insecurity*, Routledge: London.

Stenson, K. (2001), 'The New Politics of Crime Control', in K. Stenson and R. Sullivan (eds), *Crime, Risk and Justice. The Politics of Crime Control in Liberal Democracies*, Willan Publishing: Uffculme.

Taqi-Eddin, K. and Macallair, D. (1999), *Shattering 'Broken Windows': An Analysis of San Francisco's Alternative Crime Policies*, Justice Policy Institute: San Francisco.

Wadham, J. (1998), 'Zero Tolerance Policing: Striking the Balance, Rights and Liberties', in R.H. Burke (ed), *Zero Tolerance Policing*, Perpetuity Press: Leicester.

Wilson, J.Q. and Kelling, G.L. (1982) , 'Broken Windows', *The Atlantic Monthly*, Vol. 249, No. 3, March 1982, pp. 29-38.

Chapter 9

Good Prostitutes and Bad Prostitutes: Some Unintended Consequences of Governmental Regulation

BELINDA CARPENTER

We are determined to have the toughest prostitution laws in Australia, and we will. We're going to bring it out into the open, get rid of the scum. Get rid of the people who now are the parasites who are breeding on all this and have it out in the open for all the world to see (Queensland Premier Peter Beattie, 7.30 Report, ABC, 02/12/99).

One would have to be naïve to think that the mere institution of licensing arrangements would automatically eliminate all forms of illegal prostitution (Bill Carter, Chairman, Queensland Prostitution Licensing Authority, cited in Greber 2000:7).

Introduction

The history of prostitution in modernity is the history of the unintended consequences of government. While the express purpose of legislation has been motivated by what might be seen to be legitimate social concerns (disease control, public nuisance, police corruption, organised crime), the options available (criminalisation, decriminalisation, legalisation, regulation) and the process of governing such legal reform (police, politicians, local council, community groups) obscures the goals and makes the proposed outcomes unlikely. In order to examine these issues this chapter will firstly, briefly outline the historical and social context of prostitution. Secondly, discuss the reasons for governing prostitution and to outline the options available to government, and, finally, ruminate on why legal reform of prostitution tends to define and target problem populations and perpetuate dichotomous assumptions about men and women and the public and the private.

Knowing about Prostitution

In western nations like Canada, Australia, New Zealand, the United States and the United Kingdom, the majority of prostitutes are women between the ages of twenty one and thirty years. Most enter professional prostitution between the ages of sixteen and twenty-five, while five percent enter under the age of sixteen and a similar proportion enter over the age of thirty-five years (Lovejoy 1991). Between sixty and seventy percent of female prostitutes work in brothels, ten to fifteen percent work as escorts, ten to twenty percent work on the street, with the remaining ten percent working independently from their own premises.

Estimations of the number of prostitutes working at any one time vary. Official reports in Australia estimate there are 2,200 prostitutes in New South Wales (NSW), 4,000 in Victoria, 330 in Western Australia (WA), and 700 in Queensland (Qld). In Queensland in 2001 the standard rate charged was $180.00 for an hour visit, with each prostitute seeing on average fifteen to seventeen clients per week (Wynter 2000; Criminal Justice Commission 1991). It has been claimed that 14,000 men each week buy prostitutes' services in Birmingham, England and in north America each day there are 1,500,000 customers who spend $40 million (Pateman 1986). In Queensland, 9,975 men each week buy prostitutes' services spending an estimated $31,122,000.00 annually (CJC 1991). Recently the Queensland Police Service and the Queensland Crime Commission have estimated that the sex industry is an industry equivalent in economic significance to that of the sugar industry.

The primary motivation for entering prostitution is economic. Research suggests that in general sex workers have relatively low levels of educational attainment in comparison with the general population which does not equip them well for competition in the legal job market. Moreover, 'in a labour market, where women's wages are typically less than men's, prostitution appears to be an attractive alternative' (CJC 1991: 211). The flexibility of working hours and its relative autonomy is also attractive for women. Approximately fifty percent of female prostitutes are supporting school aged children and because of the widespread acceptance that women are primarily responsible for child care and domestic labour, women need to be able to combine a lucrative job with those tasks. Prostitution is one choice available (McLeod 1982:29).

Even when the industry is relatively depressed, the economic rewards offered to women by prostitution appear to be greater than any other accessible source of income. Earnings vary considerably, but in NSW in 1991 over half of the prostitutes in Perkins study of 128 prostitutes earned on average between $501.00 and $1000.00 a week, before tax (Perkins 1991:272).

In modern western nations, the criminalisation of prostitution is the dominant form of governmental intervention. Average prostitution arrests include seventy percent female prostitutes, twenty percent male prostitutes and ten percent customers. Eighty-five to ninety percent of prostitutes arrested work on the street, although, as noted above, street work accounts for no more than twenty percent of the total prostitute population (Alexander 1987; Flowers 1998). Thus it is women soliciting on the streets who bear the brunt of the law.

These demographics introduce a number of issues that will be discussed throughout this chapter. Of particular interest is the focus on the workers (predominantly women) as opposed to the clients (predominantly men) even though the latter outweigh the former in terms of the number of people involved; the criminal focus on street prostitution as opposed to brothel or escort work (the former generally attracting the most desperate and least marketable prostitute women) and the perpetuation of the problem of prostitution which focuses on the inappropriateness of sex in the public sphere. As McLeod (1982) notes, the criminal law places responsibility for the existence of prostitution and the burden of social invisibility onto the prostitute herself. 'She has to solve the dilemma between social necessity and social acceptability' (McLeod 1982: 23).

Criminalisation

Criminalising prostitution is justified on a variety of grounds. At its most extreme the purpose of criminalisation is to eradicate the industry. However, it is generally invoked to reduce the public nuisance element of soliciting. From about 1910 all Australian states introduced criminal laws on prostitution whereby the act of prostitution itself was not an offence but certain prostitution related activities were. These laws were based on the

English laws of soliciting, prohibiting under aged persons on premises used for prostitution, brothel keeping and leasing accommodation to prostitutes (Hancock 1992).

Recently, it has been argued that criminal sanctions are responsible for the creation of many problems in both the government sector charged with implementing the law and in the sex industry that must deal with its effects. These include police corruption and the discriminatory policing of workers, as well as the growth of organized crime, the removal of the autonomy of the workers and the difficulties inherent in implementing an effective health and welfare outreach scheme in an illegal industry (Egger and Harcourt 1991). Moreover, inconsistencies and gaps in prostitution related legislation expose the fact that the same behaviour might be permissible in one state or country but proscribed in another.

Since the late 1970s, Australian states have variously considered the issue of prostitution as a criminal activity and have made attempts to regulate it. Only once has soliciting been included in a package of law reform and moved outside the criminal law. As Hancock (1992: 167) states 'irrespective of legal reform, different Australian states are consistent in their efforts to control the more visible forms of prostitution and in particular street prostitution'. Increased arrests, and higher mandatory penalties to stop women convicted of prostitution from working in the same area, are examples of government efforts in this regard.

However, the logic of criminalising prostitution is inherently contradictory. If a woman is charged with an offence she may incur heavy fines, which forces her to work extra hours to earn money to pay the fine. More problematic still is that the role of intermediaries becomes more important for providing protection to the women and paying their bail. And as this chapter will attest, increasing criminal sanctions has little to no bearing on the supply or the demand for prostitute services. It has also been suggested that the main impact of criminalising prostitution is to drive women off the streets where they work independently, into the illegal brothels increasingly owned by organised crime (Perkins 1991).

Public Order

Traditionally the justification for legal prohibitions against prostitution, most specifically soliciting, has been in terms of public order. 'The conduct is regarded as offensive or indecent and a breach of community standards and taste as to what is acceptable in a public place' (Egger and Harcourt 1991: 147). The principle is thus not to eradicate prostitution but to deal with its nuisance value by keeping prostitution off the streets.

In 1979 the laws relating to prostitution in NSW, were reformed as part of a package of public order reforms. For the first time, an Australian state decriminalised offences prohibiting soliciting for the purposes of prostitution. It is argued by Egger and Harcourt (1991) that such decriminalisation had some obvious and perhaps predictable effects, including a dramatic increase in public order problems in the vice districts of Sydney and a corresponding increase in the number of complaints from citizens. However, there were other effects that were perhaps not as obvious or predictable. These included a dramatic decrease in police corruption (due to a decreased need to pay for police protection), and an increase in the number of independent women working in prostitution. Irrespective of these outcomes, the decriminalisation of soliciting lasted only four years and was amended in 1983 such that soliciting in a public street, near a dwelling, school, church or hospital became an offence. Further restrictions on street prostitution were introduced in amendments in 1988 and 1989. The central purpose of these increasingly restrictive amendments was to re-introduce criminal penalties and thus to contain prostitution so as to not cause annoyance to residents (Hancock 1992).

When legal reform packages are considered, they enable the sale and purchase of sex in the private sphere only. In all cases, the restrictions on public prostitution are increased and street prostitutes are dealt with even more harshly than in a wholly criminal system. In Queensland, for example, the Prostitution Act (1999) allowed for the establishment of legalised brothels for the first time, but also increased police powers to act against soliciting. 'The new legislation has allowed us to specifically target street prostitution and the statistics speak for themselves – 403 arrests in the year before the new legislation took effect, 170 in the first four months since its introduction' (Inspector Wilson cited in Doneman and O'Dwyer 2001). Increasing both the sentence and the arrest rate against street prostitutes concurs with public nuisance justifications but also directs attention to the establishment of a dichotomy of good legal prostitutes who deserve the protection of the law and bad illegal prostitutes who must be punished.

Moreover, increasing criminal sanctions against street prostitution does not eradicate it but simply displaces it to other parts of the city or town. For example, in Canada, the criminalising of soliciting in 1985 did not reduce the number of prostitutes or the visibility of street prostitution in many cities, but did lead to its displacement to other parts of the city (Hatty 1992). It is also suggested that increasing the criminal sanctions against soliciting, loitering and kerb crawling, in order to control the nuisance elements of the prostitution trade increases the risk of violence for the prostitutes. Because clients are fewer in number, prostitute women cannot reject as many customers as they had previously. This means that violence against street prostitutes escalates as a result of less time to negotiate and less choice in clientele. Moreover, while such legislation does decrease the number of men soliciting on the streets, (though not, it may be argued, the number of men buying prostitute services), most charges are laid against prostitute women by undercover police officers acting as decoy customers (Hatty 1992).

Such a focus on street prostitution, ostensibly to control the annoyance that prostitutes and their clients cause, masks concerns about the proper place of sex and women in society. The public nature of street prostitution displays the sexuality and activity of women through their soliciting, and this represents a challenge to the traditional role of women as passive and asexual. 'Legislation on prostitution is imbued with ideological support for the monogamous family, in as much as monogamy has traditionally meant a restriction of female non-marital sexual behaviour rather than male' (Smart 1981 cited in McLeod 1982: 92).

Clients

Clients are almost never prosecuted because they are generally not included in the criminal code. When they are, for example, within the public order offence of kerb crawling, policing is applied in a discriminatory fashion with the majority of prosecutions for soliciting against the women who sell, not the clients who buy. In fact, clients are often offered immunity if they will testify against the prostitute (Egger and Harcourt 1991). One explanation for this imbalance between prostitute and client arrests is based on the fact that many arrests are gained by undercover police officers posing as clients. However, as Lowman (1989: 209) states there is also a relevant attitudinal issue:

approaches to street prostitution are generally aimed at repeat offenders, that is, prostitutes. There is a tendency to treat the prostitute as the primary problem (it is mainly her visibility that stimulates resident complaints to police) and the criminal deserving of the greater attention (police usually refer to the customer as a square john or a citizen, not a criminal).

When legislation is brought in to criminalise the client, it is supposedly to bring equality to prostitute women by arresting clients and protecting 'innocent women' from harassment by kerb crawlers, as was the case in England and Wales in 1985 (West 1987). However, it has been found that criminalising the clients forces sex workers to work in more dangerous ways and places in order to protect their clients who are the source of income. For example, since 1993 in Ireland soliciting of both client and prostitute is an offence and the police may also force a person suspected of loitering in a street to leave. This has had the effect of reduced negotiating time with the client before joining him in his car which has increased the risk of assault. As Edwards (1997: 65) articulates, this is because:

> punters would be less willing to spend time in negotiations on the street or indeed in a stationary car, about price or place, and prostitute women would have less time to 'suss out' the punter, being forced under the pressure of this added surveillance to make a snap judgement and accept a client they might otherwise have refused (Edwards 1997: 65).

In fact, expanding criminal sanctions against prostitution related activities simply increases both the likelihood of prostitute arrest and the likelihood of violence against prostitute women irrespective of whether it is the prostitutes or the clients who are the target of the law. As Hancock (1992: 169) states 'laws on prostitution become a means of controlling women's sexuality and women's autonomous work, while at the same time, the industry is shaped by the prevailing conceptions of men's sexual needs'. This occurs partly through the discretion offered to police by the construction of the criminal law itself.

Policing

Prostitution, along with many other so-called victimless crimes has long been regarded as an activity that encourages police corruption. Police themselves have agreed that enforcing prostitution laws is difficult and expensive. As Egger and Harcourt (1991: 160) maintain:

> ... there are many facets of the industry which are believed to lead to corruption: the vast discretion exercised by the police when policing vaguely drafted soliciting and other public laws; the ambivalent community attitudes to prostitution; the existence of a thriving market prepared to pay for services despite any illegality; the large police discretion created by the gap between the formal prohibitions of the criminal law and the community tolerance and market demands on the other; the regular opportunities created by the squad style of policing.

In Queensland, the Fitzgerald Inquiry of 1987-1989 uncovered a thriving prostitution industry in which vice was largely unpoliced and in which politicians and police had a vested monetary interest in keeping alive. The Fitzgerald Report alleged that in mid-1981 'the first steps were taken to organize payments in relation to prostitution and by the end of 1984, police protection of prostitution was well established' (p. 7). Payments to police to reduce the risks of arrest, to ensure that business remains open, as protection from prosecution for living on the earnings and as a restrictive trade agreement where newcomers to an area are closed down are the most common. The industry generally regards such payments 'as the cost of doing business, not much more than a tax on earnings' (Egger and Harcourt 1991: 161).

Prostitutes do not necessarily support this view. McLeod (1982) suggests in her interviews with prostitutes, that there was not a heavy emphasis on police corruption (see also Perkins 1991). While this concept contradicts the literature and Australian governmental inquiries on the relationship between police activity and prostitution, (which presents a picture of bribery, blackmail and intimidation), discussions with prostitutes do bring out the propensity on the part of police to 'stretch the law' by elaborating certain practices in connection with it which undermine prostitute's civil liberties. These include, but are not limited to, arresting a known prostitute when she is not working, and 'verballing' the women –

'will you move on you dirty stinking prostitute' (Mcleod 1982: 107; Perkins 1991).

As Edwards (1996) discovered in her research, while police do not lack initiative or inventiveness in extending their powers in relation to female prostitute arrests, they appear reluctant to prosecute the clients whose only error, in their eyes, is to consort with a prostitute. Police forces prefer to use other methods of deterring prostitution and generally considered the exposure of men to prosecution and attendant publicity overly punitive. Instead they 'develop their own local methods of dealing with the problem ranging from informal warnings to cautions and thus only a few selected cases result in full blown prosecution' (Edwards 1996: 162). The outcome in prosecutions for loitering (which focus on the prostitute) and kerb crawling (which are used against the client) demonstrate this difference most clearly. In 1993 in England and Wales, 7,912 women were prosecuted for loitering and soliciting while 857 men were prosecuted for the offence of kerb crawling (Edwards 1996: 150). 'In practical terms if this reflects the reality of numbers on the streets, every 11 prostitutes would be fighting for every one punter' (Edwards 1996: 149). Clearly this is not the case and reflects instead the double standard within the law itself that prostitution is a 'female only' offence.

Legal Reform

> Legalisation has increased the middlemen (legally recognized pimps) and further isolated women from their families and society ... conditions in many brothels are squalid and rents are high (Sharpe 1998: 156-7).

Those who advocate alternatives to the punitive approach to prostitution often refer to the legalisation or decriminalisation of prostitution. These options may be encompassed within the regulatory approach to prostitution in which prostitution is permitted within the limits of a licensing or zoning system (Hatty 1992). Such control of prostitution has traditionally concentrated on efforts to ensure the enhanced sexual health of individual sex workers, and as a consequence, it is argued this enhances the sexual health of the clients and the wider community.

Interestingly, clients have always been excluded from such regulation of disease, which of course problematises any claims to social health. And, while it was in England in the 1800s that government began to get serious about 'cleaning up prostitutes', such policy soon found its way to Australia, the United States and Canada. Moreover, the rhetoric of prostitutes as carriers of disease continues in modern government and while prostitutes may no longer be pulled through the streets for compulsory internal medical examinations (as was the case in England in the 1800s), their sexual health is integral to any legal reform package.

Clean Women

In an attempt to control sexually transmitted disease in the British armed forces, *Contagious Diseases Acts* were initiated in 1864, 1866 and 1869, in eleven, thirteen and then eighteen garrison ports and towns in England and Ireland. The original Act provided that a woman identified as a diseased prostitute by a plainclothes member of the metropolitan police was to undergo an examination. If found diseased, she could be detained in a hospital for up to three months. The new clauses of 1866 'established a system of compulsory periodic fortnightly inspection or examination of all known prostitutes under a well organized system of medical police' (Walkowitz 1980: 78). Discovery of disease meant internment in a 'lock up' hospital for a period not exceeding six months, although this was increased to nine months in 1869. Apart from the infringement on working class women's civil liberties, the procedure excluded serviceman from examination. Thus any effect such legislation might have had in decreasing the incidence of disease, was rendered totally nugatory.

A similar Bill with similar outcomes was enacted in NSW in 1908. Tabled in NSW Parliament as the Contagious Diseases Bill in 1907, it was renamed The Prisoners Detention Bill in early 1908 and enacted by the end of that year. Originally conceived to detain any prostitute woman found to have a venereal disease, 'woman' was re-drafted as 'person' in the renamed Bill, ostensibly to include men. As was recognized by members of parliament at the time however, 'the bill means that every prostitute who is known to loiter or solicit will be made a prisoner at once. The bill will make healthy women for profligate men' (Allen 1990: 75). Forty years later, during the second World War, the Australian states of Queensland and WA enacted legislation to forcibly treat prostitutes (as opposed to clients) for venereal disease at 'lock' hospitals (Saunders 1992: 393).

For Zajdow (1992: 177) the fear of infection from prostitutes, in both a physical and moral sense, still pervades our society. However, she notes a shift in the discourse of responsibility from the criminal justice system to health and welfare services, especially since the onset of HIV/AIDS. While such a shift can be seen as positive, the effects of legal reform can be just as negative in stigmatising sex workers as police ever were. This is especially the case when any form of mandatory health testing is suggested.

> Immediately after the onset of the epidemic (in the USA) there was a hue and cry about the dangers of transmission of HIV from women who gave sex for pay, and in a number of jurisdictions there were implementations of the police power to test for HIV seropositivity or to otherwise constrain sex for pay, constraints imposed entirely on women. The initiatives were taken without any evidence at all to support them and in some cases the AIDS epidemic appeared to be used as an opportunity to impose moral values under the guise of disease control (Gagnon 1989: 61).

In the debate leading up to legal reform in Queensland, health workers argued that introducing licensed brothels would facilitate access to workers for the provision of peer support and education and the implementation of consistent safe sex policies. Licensed brothels it was argued would enable the effective regulation of health related practices occurring on the premises – with management encouraging staff to attend medical services and having greater control over client compliance with rules requiring the use of condoms and other safe sex practices.

In reality, this is not always what happens. In Greece, for example, which has the strictest health regulations regarding prostitutes in Europe, (mandatory medical screening twice a week), the requirement that all health care facilities and HIV/AIDS prevention activities be limited to those who are registered, renders such screening totally ineffective. This is because while 400 women are registered as prostitutes in Athens, estimates are that 5,000 more prostitutes operate unregistered. Similarly, in Germany 50,000 sex workers are registered and are regularly seen by the health services as required by laws to combat venereal disease. However, it is argued that up to 150,000 further people work in prostitution. As Mak (2001) argues, mandatory testing creates a two-tier system of registered and non-registered prostitutes with the latter having limited access to health care. It also supports increased criminal sanctions against those women who are not registered and perpetuates dichotomous understandings of good, clean responsible prostitutes and bad, dirty irresponsible prostitutes, the latter bearing the brunt of community concern.

Working Conditions

> The high cost of licenses would result in younger attractive and well dressed women being offered work in legal brothels while older poorer and less polished sex workers would be forced either to work alone or in illegal brothels (Sullivan in Griffith 2000: 3).

A further reason for legal reform of prostitution is in response to the poor working conditions and occupational health and safety standards that operate in the highly mobile, illegal industry. Often formulated with the stated rationale of protecting sex workers and ensuring a legal standard of health and safety, legal brothels are no less likely to operate in sub-standard conditions than illegal brothels and often operate in conditions that would not be tolerated in other legal businesses. Hancock (1991), Dobinson (1992) and Sharpe (1998) separately reported filthy work conditions, lack of regular cleaning, lack of clean bed linen and towels for each client and lack of separate toilet and shower facilities in many legal brothels.

West (1987) concludes that the legalisation of prostitution in Nevada, USA and Germany have basically created 'assembly lines for sex'. The women employed have no control over working conditions, hours worked, the number of clients they see, or tips they receive. Working women have to register with the police and therefore are known as prostitute women, subjected to health checks and restricted in their movements outside the brothels (English Collective of Prostitutes 1997). In Victoria, Australia, similar conditions apply. These include: brothel workers taking up to sixty percent of prostitute's earnings; brothel managers insisting on workers providing unsafe sex (sex without condoms) if clients demand it, on threat of dismissal; expecting workers to socialize with clients for no pay; arbitrary fines for laddered stockings, unpainted nails, unshaven legs; inflexibility of shifts that suit school days and school holidays; and auditioning workers (Hancock 1991).

The outcome is that prostitutes continually opt for illegal sex work. Illegal sex work is more profitable for comparable hours (as workers keep all their earnings). Illegal sex work also allows for choice in services provided, choice of clients and flexible working hours. 'Other sex workers – including male workers, transsexuals, workers on methadone programs, stereotypical drug users, non-competitive workers and old workers who cannot operate in the legal sector due to house rules – must also operate illegally' (Dobinson 1992: 117).

'Queensland Workers in the Sex Industry' president Jeff Mclaren concurs. New prostitution laws passed in 1999 allow for legalised brothels but 'many drug addicted prostitutes would not be permitted to work in legal brothels'. Moreover, 'the legislation failed to understand the motivation of streetwalkers. People have specific reasons for working on the streets. Some don't want to pay a brothel keeper a cut of their earnings, others do it to make quick dollars to buy food' (cited in Keim 2000). What this means is that the majority of sex workers work exactly the way they did before legal reform.

> Do I continue to break the law and make $2000 a week, do I go and work in a legal brothel and make far less or do I throw the whole lot in and go stack shelves at Coles? It's not a difficult choice for me to make (Anna, cited in Taylor 2000).

Moreover, given the reputed difficulties of proving the offence of illegally running a brothel, illegal brothels have increased with police estimates of around 150 to 200 illegal brothels in the city of Melbourne, in comparison to 80 legal brothels (Carter, cited in Taylor 2000). The choice between legal brothels and illegal forms of prostitution also forces sex workers into more hidden and dangerous sectors of the industry like escort work. This is because while escort work is illegal, it is not as dangerous or as regularly criminalised or policed as street work. It also offers the monetary, autonomous and flexible advantages of illegal work but does not contain the disadvantages of legal brothel work.

Unintended Consequences

The failure of government is thus its inability to manage many of the social and criminal problems associated with prostitution. Irrespective of the type of governmental intervention proffered, neither the demand nor the supply seems very much interrupted. It could in fact be argued however, that some issues do remain constant, irrespective of government policy – that prostitution is a necessary evil and that the women who sell rather than the men who buy are the focus for concern. This is evidenced by the target of governmental intervention: when criminalised, it is the sellers who are subject to policing and arrest, whether or not the clients are included in the criminal code; when legalised, it is the sellers who are the focus of mandatory health checks.

In fact, it is the invisibility of the client in the prostitution contract which demonstrates prostitution's inevitability. Such an acceptance assumes an immutable male sexual need, and female subordination to it. This excuses the male demand for paid sex and in fact requires his sexual servicing by prostitute women in order to protect 'innocent women and children' from his unrequited sexual needs (Carpenter 2000). Thus in the common imagination, prostitution, it is argued, decreases rapes and attacks on children. Police perpetuate this understanding in their reluctance to arrest men for buying sex.

Thus the unintended consequences of governmental intervention into prostitution is not only to fail to manage the sex industry but to perpetuate a series of dichotomies which do not challenge historically dominant ideas and assumptions about the rightful place of sexual activity (a private rather than public affair), the appropriate role of women (as sexually passive consumers), the transmission of disease (women as opposed to men are the carriers), or the problem population (women who sell rather than men who buy).

As has been argued in previous chapters, many of these unintended consequences are required for government to continually reinvent, respond and rewrite law such that criminal reform is possible. And, rather than the law affecting the extent or existence of prostitution, it can be seen that the law simply shapes the form in which it is pursued. Thus, increasing criminal sanctions against street prostitution, for example, simply displaces it to other areas of the town or city or establishes more venues for private prostitution in bars, saunas and hotels.

Central to this chapter has been the position, articulated by Simone de Beauvoir (1972: 569), that

> the prostitute is a scapegoat; man vents his turpitude upon her and he rejects her. Whether she is put legally under police supervision or works illegally in secret, she is in any case treated as a pariah.

This is not only reflected in the current policing practices of street prostitution, where women rather than men are the target, but also in all legal reform practices where prostitute women are held responsible for the sexual health of their clients and the community in general. Moreover, because the prostitute is defined primarily in terms of her difference from the feminine ideal, prostitution is seen as the negation of the respectable system of marriage and procreation. Hence the need for prostitution to occur behind closed doors.

Conclusion

> We can't stamp out prostitution what we have to do is regulate it and control it and that's what we're seeking to do (Qld. Premier Peter Beattie, *7.30 Report*, ABC TV, 02/12/99).

Queensland is the latest state in Australia to regulate prostitution through a two tiered legal/illegal reform package. While brothel prostitution is legal and regulated through a prostitution licensing authority, the penalties for street prostitution, and the policing of it, have substantially increased. The implications of this, it could be argued, are not that much different from the regulation of prostitution through criminal sanctions. When prostitution as a whole is criminalised, street prostitution, and street prostitutes more specifically, still command the majority of police attention, arrests, convictions and prison sentences, compared with other forms of prostitution. However, the legal model, which is being implemented slowly throughout the western world, also creates a two-tiered access to health care, as well as good legal prostitutes (who are generally, young, attractive and drug free) and bad illegal prostitutes. It also assumes that the good legal brothels are those that have the best work conditions, though evidence suggests that this is not necessarily the case. The outcome is that in most western nations where legal reforms have created a two-tiered system, the majority of prostitutes and their clients continue to choose to work illegally. This has few ramifications for the clients, who are generally ignored in both the criminal and legal models, but it has major ramifications for the prostitutes, who bear the brunt of community disapproval.

It has been suggested that most of the unintended consequences of government can be foreseen. Certainly, this is the case with prostitution where its regulation, underpinned by the assumptions outlined above, perpetuate an old fashioned moral crusade against the women who sell, while supporting and protecting the men who buy. What western governments need to consider is the ways in which prostitution can be managed without the creation of a two tiered system of good and bad prostitutes. This is the only outcome of current government control of prostitution, which continues to delineate between acceptable (private) prostitution and unacceptable (public) prostitution.

References

Alexander, P. (1987), 'Prostitution: A Difficult Issue for Feminists' in Delacoste and Alexander (eds) *Sex Work: Writings by Women in the Sex Industry*. Cleiss Press: Pittsburgh.

Allen, J.A. (1990), *Sex and Secrets*. Oxford University Press: Melbourne.

Carpenter, B. (2000), *Rethinking Prostitution: feminism, sex and the self*. Peter Lang: New York.

Criminal Justice Commission (1991), *Regulating Morality: An Inquiry into Prostitution in Queensland*. GoPrint: Brisbane.

De Beauvoir, S. (1972), *The Second Sex*. Penguin: Middlesex.

Dobinson, S. (1992), 'Victorian Situation with Legalisation', in Gerull, S. and Halstead, B. (eds) *Sex Industry and Public Policy*. AIC: Canberra.

Doneman, P. and O'Dwyer, E. (2000), 'Local councils attacked over brothel stance', in *The Courier Mail*, 21/09/2000, p. 3.

Doneman, P. and O'Dwyer, E (2001), 'Legal Sex Industry Rendered Impotent', in *The Courier Mail*, 17/3/2001, p.11.

Edwards, S. (1996), *Sex and Gender in the Legal Process*. Blackstone Press: London.

Edwards, S. (1997), 'The Legal Regulation of Prostitution: a human rights issue', in Scambler, G. and Scambler, D. (eds) *Rethinking Prostitution: purchasing sex in the 1990s*. Routledge: London.

Egger, S. and Harcourt, C. (1991), 'Prostitution in New South Wales', in *Regulating Morality: An Inquiry into Prostitution in Queensland*. GoPrint: Brisbane.

English Collective of Prostitutes (1997), 'Campaigning for Legal Change' in Scambler G. and Scambler D. (eds) *Rethinking Prostitution: Purchasing sex in the 1990s*. Routledge: London.

Flowers, B. (1998*)*, *The Prostitution of Women and Girls*. McFarland and Co: Jefferson.

Gagnon, J. (1989), 'Disease and Desire', *Daedalus*, Vol. 118, No. 3, pp: 47-77.

Greber, J. (2000), 'Brothel bid runs into a red light', in *The Courier Mail*, 3/5/2000, p. 7.

Griffith, C. (2000), 'No Applications for Legal Brothel Licences', in *The Courier Mail*, 15/7/2000, p. 13.

Hancock, L. (1991), 'Impact of Prostitution Related Laws in Victoria' in *Regulating Morality: An Inquiry into Prostitution in Queensland*. GoPrint: Brisbane.

Hancock, L. (1992), 'Legal Regulation of Prostitution: What or Who is being Controlled?', in Gerull, S. and Halstead, B. (eds) *Sex Industry and Public Policy*. AIC: Canberra.

Hatty, S. (1992), 'The Desired Object: prostitution in Canada, United States and Australia', in Gerull, S. and Halstead, B. (eds) *Sex Industry and Public Policy*. AIC: Canberra.

Keim, T. (2000), 'Prostitution laws fail to cut back illegal trade', in *The Courier Mail*, 18/12/2000, p. 8.

Lovejoy, F. etal (1991), *AIDS Preventative Practices Among Female Prostitutes and their Clients and Private Risk*, Part 1. University of New South Wales.

Lowman, J. (1989), *Street Prostitution: Assessing the Impact of the Law*. Department of Justice: Ottawa, Canada.

Mak, R. (2001), [http://allserv.rug.ac.be/~rmak/europap/summary/html].

McLeod, E. (1982), *Women Working: Prostitution Now*. Croom Helm: London.

O'Dwyer, E. (2001), 'Councils Divided on Prostitution Laws', in *The Courier Mail*, 24/2/2001, p. 11.

Pateman, C. (1988), *The Sexual Contract*. Polity Press: Oxford.

Perkins, R. (1991), *Working Girls: Prostitutes, their Life and Social Control*. AIC: Canberra.

Sharpe, K. (1998), *Red Light, Blue Light: prostitutes, punters and police*. Ashgate: Aldershot.

Taylor, C. (2000), 'Catch 22'. *The Sunday Mail*, 10/9/2000, p. 85.

Walkowitz, J. (1980*), Prostitution and Victorian Society: women, class and the state*. Cambridge University Press: Cambridge.

West, R. (1987), 'U.S. Prostitutes Collective', in Delacoste, F. and Alexander, P. (eds) *Sex Work: Writings by Women in the Sex Industry*. Cleiss Press: Pittsburgh.

Wynter, V. (2000), 'Love for Sale', in *The Courier Mail*, 30/7/2000, p. 8.

Zajdow, G. (1992), 'Sex Work and Regulation: Holding on to an image – a sociological reflection', in Gerull, S. and Halstead, B. (eds) *Sex Industry and Public Policy*. AIC: Canberra.

Chapter 10

Unintended Consequences or Deliberate Racial Hygiene Strategies: The Question of Child Removal Policies

JUDITH BESSANT

Removing 'neglected' and 'at risk' children from 'dyfunctional families', and placing them in church and state welfare institutions was a durable policy practice throughout the twentieth century. In Canada, the United States of America, the United Kingdom and Australia, tens of thousands of children and young people under the guise of child welfare policies, were taken from their families and relocated in institutions whose primary business was to protect and educate (Human Rights and Equal Opportunity Commission, 1997; Manne, 1998; van Kreiken, 1992, 1990; Read, 1983; Brett, 1997). This long history of systematic, state-sponsored removal of children from Aboriginal and 'poor white' parents was justified in terms of what was in the child's 'best interests' (Gorton, *SMH*, 1998; Jaggs, 1991, 1986; Gill, 1997, Carpenter, 1851).

Over the past few decades a raft of official enquiries, criminal and civil proceedings and investigative media reports initiated, has forced a major rewriting of this history (Human Rights and Equal Opportunity Commission, 1997; Royal Commission into Aboriginal Deaths in Custody, 1989; Wood Commission 1997; Commission of Inquiry into Abuse of Children in Queensland Institutions, 1999). What had once been located in an historical narrative of unequivocal benevolence and altruism, is now being rewritten to take account of well-documented evidence of systematic sexual, emotional and physical abuse of young people in state-run or state-sponsored institutions (Coldrey 1993; Bean and Melville 1990; Manne, 1998; Victorian Child Death Review Committee – VCDRC 1996; Human Services Victoria, 1997).

Given this revision many people are incline to the view the practice of taking children and young people from their homes and placing them in institutional 'care' where they were exposed to abuse and exploitation is a clear and obvious example of policy paradox or an 'unintended consequence'. In other words, it might be thought that outcomes like these constitute a terrible inversion of the original altruistic and benevolent impulses. In the simplest sense the notion of 'unintended consequences' might be thought to apply to policies where outcomes are antithetical to the primary intentions of the policy makers. In the instance of child welfare such a view can acknowledge the well established consequences of child-removal policies, including systemic abuse, physical violence, sexual exploitation and psychological mistreatment, while at the same time accepting that this pattern of abuse was unintended. This evaluation relies on the premise that the primary intention of statutory child welfare has been to secure the welfare and the interests of the child.

In this chapter I re-consider the idea of 'unintended consequences' as they relate to the removal of children and young people from their homes and their placement in welfare and education institutions. I question the apologist view that the abuse and neglect of young people while in care was an unfortunate and unintended consequence of policies directed towards securing the health and well-being of certain groups of young people.

I refer to child removal policies to illustrate the limitations of a rational action theory of policy that is relied on by apologists of those policies. From a cursory reading of official documents it might be argued that child removal policies were motivated by altruism with the intent of securing the well-being of disadvantaged children (Jaggs, 1991, 1986; Carpenter, 1851; Swain & Howe, 1995; Howson, 1999; Marsh, 1999; Maddock, 2000; Meagher, 2000; Bennett, 2000; Scott & Swain, 2002). As I demonstrate in this chapter, this has been a popular way of understanding policies, especially in light of the recent revelations of the abuse and mistreatment experienced by many children subject to these policies.

The continuing appeal of such explanations is apparent in the rhetoric of some Australian state governments who claim that protectionist policies which led to thousands of indigenous children removed from their families were policies informed by good intent:

> ... the intention of the British government was to treat the Aboriginal inhabitants with courtesy and respect and to extend to them the benefits of

western culture, Christianity and British law [but] ... that an unintended consequence of the segregation policy was invariably discrimination against and deprivation of the Aboriginal people? (South Australian Government, 1996: 7).

Theories of Policy: Rational Action Models

One way apologists justify child removal practices is by reading policy as rational action. In other words, there is a tendency to see policy as rationally informed action, in the case child of removal it was said to have been driven by altruistic intent. Such intent is identified in official documents and when compared to the unfortunate policy outcomes, it becomes 'apparent' that the abuse and exploitation was an unintended consequence.

At the turn of the twentieth century Max Weber (1868-1920) writing on the themes of bureaucratic organisation and the forms of action encompassed therein (i.e. rationality and causality) argued that modernity was a consequence of the spread of science, rational techniques and bureaucratic institutions (Weber, 1947). For Weber, science is an objective medium for accessing truth, and as such the work of social scientists, policy makers etc is value neutral (Weber, 1949).

Weber was interested in human action as the product of our consciousness, and saw human conduct as rational and goal directed. Moreover he believed the role of ideas, desires, the symbolic and cultural character of life as critical for understanding social action. Weber was particularly interested in large modern organisations like the Church and government bureaucracies and saw them as sites of social action in which particular norms, rules and other symbolic forms shaped the social action inside them. For Weberians discovering what is happening in such organisations was a simple task that required asking people what their intentions or goals are. Given that modern bureaucracies reflect the achievements of rationality, determining the outcomes of social actions simply involved the use of interpretative techniques to reveal the causal flow of rules, meanings and norms that informed human action. Once the intent is identified it is a simple process of following the funnel of causality to the outcome.

For liberal theorists committed to ideas of progress, policy and the state was fundamental for what they saw as an essential movement toward

                    Hard Lessons

progress (Beveridge, 1953; Marshall, 1951). This informed popular accounts of policy procedures as rational processes driven by evidence gathered systematically which in turn informed policy design. Central to this project was a process of evaluative research used to establish the extent a given policy had or had not delivered the anticipated outcomes. Dalton, Weeks, Draper and Wiseman (1996) point to Simon (1945) as an early proponent of policy as a rational process, describing it as a logical way of decision making:

> All the alternative strategies were listed, the consequences of each strategy were determined, and the different sets of consequences were evaluated. The policy that gave the preferred consequences was then selected (Dalton, et.al, 1996: 113).

Models of social policy have long been dominated by liberal-functionalist explanations that emphasize the rationality, functionality and benevolence of state interventions into the lives of 'disadvantaged and dysfunctional families' (see also, Polanyi, 1944: 73), and then in the 1960s by a newer styles of Marxist and feminist structuralism. (O'Connor, 1973; Habermas, 1974; Gough, 1979; Offe, 1983). Moreover, such readings of policy operated in a discourse of history-as-progress and professionals-as-altruistic and rational agents of progress. It is an approach embedded in a humanitarianism leading to inevitable outcomes of advancement and of upward movement.

According to both traditional liberal and radical-structuralist understandings of policy formulation, policy is rationally informed by the discovery of objective social problems (i.e. 'neglected children'). From such perspectives policy formulation is a 'funnel of causality' where Truth and knowledge are contested, slowly move on to the 'policy making processes', finishing up with specific policies. Following Weber, identification of problems and decisions about the solutions to any given social problem are said to be based on technical expert criteria, rational, proper co-ordination, planning and considered choice (Anderson, 1984; Rene, 1973; Emy, 1974). This model retains considerable appeal for many policy makers and researchers. Arguably however, it has little if any value in revealing the dynamic and contingent qualities of policy processes.

Policy Paradoxes

Returning to the focus of this chapter, the conventional approach to understanding policy assumes that establishing whether a contradiction or discrepancy exists between policy intent and outcomes is a simple matter of tracing the funnel of causality from intent and knowledge about a problem through the narrowing path to the outcome of a specific policy. This I suggest is naive and unrealistic.

The idea of policy as rational action ignores the creative or generative role of experts in discovering the problem, and it neglects the contingency of policy (i.e. the disorderly, variable, unexpected human character of policy making). Moreover, it overlooks the confusion and malevolence that can characterise policy making. It omits the possibility that policy makers sometimes operate in a delusional state about what is happening.

Indeed there are many well documented cases of policy making elites who have generated fictive accounts of what they are doing and why in order to veil their actual intent or actions. Typically this involves actions that, without the cover of secrecy or deceit, would otherwise invite criticism domestically or internationally. This is the case for example when military, diplomatic, intelligence gathering or financial (taxation/sensitive expenditures) activities are involved.

A further problem with the policy as rational action model is that the policy makers are sometimes misguided, ignorant or unaware either of their intentions/motives. This is to say nothing of them remaining ignorant, misguided or in a state of denial about the impact of their policies which take effect when the policies unfold. We need only consider the extensive history of abuse and neglect of young people in orphanages and other forms of 'welfare' to appreciate this point. National and institutional leaders have a vested interest in maintaining a 'problem free' public image particularly when the problems have the potential to undermine the credibility and legitimacy of their establishment or fraternity. Such a response characterised the decades leading to the 1980s and 1990s after which reports of the abusive conduct in welfare and educational institutions began surfacing in ways that could not be ignored.

Writing on state sponsored atrocities, the criminologist Stanley Cohen documents the various strategies of government in actively denying the horrific impact of their policies. As Cohen explains the typical response is: 'It doesn't happen here. If it does, "it" is something else. Even if it is what you say it is, it is justified' (Cohen, 1993: 103; 2001). Criminologists like Grabosky have also talked about the illegalities of organisations as 'wayward governance', observing similar refusals to admit what was happening (1989).

The Case of Child Welfare

There has been little hesitation in assuming that in the case of child removal policies through the twentieth century, a contradiction existed between the good intentions of policy makers (policies designed to secure the best interest of the child) and the actual horrific outcomes (Jaggs, 1986; Howson, 1999, Marsh, 1999, Meagher, 2000, McGuiness, 2000, Maddock, 2000, Bennett, 2000, Scott and Swain, 2002).   According to official documents the intent of practices that saw the removal of children from their indigenous families was to serve the interest of the child. In January 1912 the Commonwealth government (Australian Archives, 1993: 13) *An Ordinance Relating to Aboriginals (No 16 of 1911)* is indicative of declaration of good intent. That particular Act permitted:

> The Chief Protector ... to undertake the care, custody and protection or control of any aboriginal or half-caste, if in his opinion *it is necessary or desirable in the interests of the aboriginal or half-caste for him to do so.*

A few years later in 1918 the Aboriginals Ordinance (1918) (NT) repeated the original Ordinance, reinforcing a provision for the removal of 'aboriginal and half caste children':

> The Chief Protector shall be entitled at any time to undertake the care, custody and protection or control of any aboriginal or half-caste if in his opinion it is necessary or desirable *in the interests of the aboriginal or half-caste.*

For some contemporary Australian public figures like Prime Minister John Howard, policy makers responsible for the discriminate removal of children from their families and homes were well intended:

> ... the practices were meant, at the time, to be doing the right thing. They
> were thought at the time to be benefiting the people involved (Howard,
> interview with Alan Jones, 2UE radio, 30 May 1997).

Similarly, other politicians like the federal Liberal backbenchers Wilson
Tuckey, argue that not only were policies that saw the forcible removal of
children well intended, such policies remain worthy of defense despite the
revelations of systemic abuse and neglect. This, Tuckey suggested, was
because such policies prevented Aborigines from becoming 'semi-literate,
bush slum dwellers' (*Age*, 8 October 1996; see also comments by former
Australian Minister for Aboriginal Affairs, Senator John Herron, *Age*, 7,
October 1996, *Age*, 10 October 1996).

Many people holding such views operate from a structuralist
reading of those policies, and from the assumption that experts work
objectively in discovering the problem; that they were motivated by the
child's welfare, that policy formulation was a rational process connected
into a funnel of causality drawing from the intent to secure the welfare of
the child.

Identifying Motive

Determining motives that informed child removal policies is not as simple
as many people suggest. We can read the official reports to find 'evidence'
of the virtuous reasons for such policies, and on face value such statements
might appear convincing (Carpenter, 1851, reprinted; Gandevia, 1978). As
Markus observes for most of the twentieth century:

> ... the forcible removal of children was regarded as a matter of course and
> did not provoke controversy in the world of white Australians. Removal
> was said to be in the best interests of the children and of minor
> significance for the mothers (Markus 1989: 23).

However, a rationalist reading of child removalist policies overlooks the
complicating factors that obscure and confuse, which raise questions like
whether we can assume there was one simple motive (serving the child's
interests), or one simple unobstructed funnel of causality that flowed from
that intention.

Such structuralist readings of child removal policies which claim that an unfortunate discrepancy exists between the intention of the policy makers (i.e. child welfare) and the dire outcomes (abuse and mistreatment), ignore the discursive roots and irrational character of policy making and implementation.

When the mandatory removal of children is located in the liberal paradigm of social policy, it becomes an inevitable and benevolent response, albeit with unfortunate consequences, to the 'discovery' of a serious social problem (child neglect, racial fitness) (Baker, 1979). From this perspective such policies are understood as the rational reaction to an objective discovery of social problems (neglect, threat to social/national health etc) by reformers leading to state policy intervention.

More recent approaches to policy however downplay the apparent objectivity of the social problem and rationality of the process, stressing instead the creative role of stake-holders like reformers, professions and government in discovering and depicting social problems.

To understand more fully the policy of forcibly removing young people from their families through the twentieth century there is value in appreciating specific discourses that informed those processes. This requires attention to the historically specific character of the policies to help explain why the terms used to depict specific problems were adopted. Expressions like 'juvenile depravity', 'precocious lads', 'maladjusted youth', 'hopeless parents' (McCrae, 1934), 'half-castes' (McGregor, 1997) 'hooligans', 'delinquents' (Burt, 1938), 'the adolescent' (Hall, 1905) and so forth was part of a rich eugenicist discourse which underpinned the mandatory removalist policies.

Attention to the role of powerful networks reveals how specific discourses with their origins in psychologistic and eugenicist accounts of social health, vagrancy, criminality etc were key forces informing 'the intent' of removalist policies. 'Half-castes', 'neglected and wayward youth' were the object of 'admirable interventions' by eugenicists concerned about the 'need' to secure social and racial improvement. Many 'right minded people' felt obliged to prevent future degradation of the population by timely, scientific diagnosis and treatment of 'youth' 'in danger' of becoming a future problem.

A 'policy as discourse model' reveals that official accounts of the motives informing removal policies were critical to the overriding imperative to 'civilise' and enhance national and 'racial fitness'. I argue that this 'necessity' was popularly seen as complementing what was in the child's interests. In the eyes of many policy makers through the twentieth century, the ultimate objective – a racially healthy British nation – was fundamental to the child's interest.

The systemic removal of children and young people from their families was the product of perceptions of experts and many politicians about the incapacity of certain parents to adequately care for their children (Fernandez, 1996). Such claims however usually omit the fact that some families more than others are subject to intervention by the state (Carrington, 1993). Specifically, families from lower socio-economic backgrounds, single parent families and many Aboriginal families were, and still are, subject to the gaze of law enforcement and welfare agencies far more than most other families (Bersford and Croft, 1994, 75-96; Callahan and Lamb, 1995:715-809; MacKinnon, 1992).

The policy of removing children and young people from 'unsuitable homes' was also implemented immediately after the Second World War as thousands of British children found themselves to be participants in a mass child migration project. While the whereabouts of some children's parents was in doubt, all children shared a common background as 'urchins' of war-ravaged British working class cities. This was a eugenically inspired international program of forced child migration that saw thousands of British children transferred from their homeland and shipped across the globe to places like Australia, Canada, and America where they were 'taken into care' by various state sponsored church orphanages (Gill, 1997). The official intent of the British child migration policy was the child's best interest; it offered underprivileged children a fresh start in a 'young country'.

As mentioned earlier, whether the outcomes of such policies contradicted their declared intent, questions were raised after numerous revelations of institutionalised neglect and abuse. Those disclosures began emerging from the mid-1980s as courts and official inquiries confronted allegations of serious sexual, physical and emotional abuse and maltreatment of children and young people committed by workers in church, community and state-run organisations.[1] These inquiries and legal processes were central to the re-discovery of the child abuse problem in countries like Australia (see Anon, 1986; Bean and Melvill, 1989; Berry, 1992; Anon, 1993a; Anon, 1993b; Coldrey, 1993; Davies, 1994; Hughes,

1994; Stokes, 1994; Angus and Woodward, 1995; Briggs, 1996; Gill, 1997; Anon, 1997).

It would be reassuring to argue such policies were instances of well intended policies gone dreadfully wrong. And while this may have been so in some instances, I argue it was not the case generally and certainly not the case for policies directed toward the wholesale removal of indigenous children from their families. The removal of indigenous children from their families was a clear and deliberate strategy directed towards achieving cultural genocide, assimilation and land tenure. Removing children from their community denied them their cultural heritage and without a transferral of knowledge and practices across the generations the destruction of traditional indigenous life was assured. Child removal practices were directed towards making indigenous children, especially 'half-castes', as white as possible – assimilation. When examining these actions from a policy as discourse model it becomes evident how they were shaped by the pervading eugenicist discourses.

The Policy Making Community Model

Like the policy as discourse model, the notion of a 'policy making community' can also help understand child removal practices. It is a model that has become a dominant paradigm in the study of interest groups, partly because its proponents accept that policy making is a fragmented process and because it avoids grand macro-level theorisation (Brooks, 1994). This approach also acknowledges the confusion and irrationality that characterises policy making.

One important aspect of the policy community approach to policy (Heclo, Hall et al 1987) is its theorising of the professionally trained (Hall, 1990; Gagnon, 1989: 455-467). In this paradigm, intellectuals, and their work (in private and public sector agencies), in their roles as philanthropists, or as experts endeavouring to influence elites or public opinion, help shape communication and representations of policy problems (i.e. the 'delinquency' or 'half caste' problem), as well as the subsequent solutions (forced removal of children).

The constitutive role of networks, especially expert networks (i.e. advocates of national and racial hygiene), in ensuring that certain matters come to be seen as a social problem or public issue occurs on a number of levels. Kingdon argued that some things enter the public realm because of a combination of 'circumstances and politics' (Kingdon, 1984). By 'circumstances' Kingdon meant that particular issues impact on the state (i.e. 'the half-caste problem') and become so important that governments have to be seen to be responding effectively by taking action. This involves a major effort by certain individuals or groups who work towards making sure particular state interventions do happen; this is what Kingdon referred to as 'politics'. This way of understanding policy reveals how the policy process can often be highly unpredictable, thereby making the idea of a rational funnel narrowing from intent to outcome ridiculous.

Brooks argued that different interventions by experts ensured the selection of particular issues and guaranteed that they became the object of policy interventions (Brooks, 1994). He also suggested that discursive innovations are the prelude to major policy responses or shifts in debates. To illustrate this we can refer to discursive innovations like the 'discovery' of genetics and the development of psychology as a 'scientific' discipline, and the eugenic inspired imperative to address 'the race crisis'. Attention to these activities demonstrates how the work of the intellectually trained, philanthropic reformers etc was the prelude to campaigns for systemic child removal policies.

Children and Racial and National Hygiene

In the case of the post 1945 British Child migration program the question of whether a paradox exists between policy intent (i.e. the welfare of disadvantaged young people) and outcomes (re, the violation of many young people) may at first glance also seem unequivocal. To accept the official line that such policies were intended to safeguard the child's interest overlooks the influence of powerful eugenic and imperialist mindsets of progressive policy makers. In other words, it neglects the 'need' to 'seed the empire' and upgrade the racial hygiene of the British Empire. The policy as discourse approach and idea of a policy community reveal that a eugenic commitment meant making the most of every opportunity to inhabit the British Empire with uncorrupted British stock. The 'need' to secure social order was a further desirable outcome achieved by relocating potential trouble-makers to 'healthier environs'. It was an exercise that relieved the community of bad elements threatening social harmony (Gill, 1973; Jaggs, 1986).

In the case of non-indigenous young people, 'the problem of Aboriginality' did not apply and thus assimilation objectives were irrelevant. This being said however, national hygiene remained an important consideration for 'white children' and indeed children generally who all were seen to have a central role in the expansion of 'European civilisation'. For 'poor white' children the national hygiene objective ensured special attention was given to problems associated with the working class – namely, low intelligence, immorality, inherent criminality and comparable pathologies. As van Krieken notes:

> ... it is possible to chart the parallels and affinities between the racism of removing Aboriginal children for their Aboriginality and the class ideology underlying the removal of non-indigenous children for the immorality and viciousness of their impoverished surroundings. The significance of this is ... that it indicates a certain degree of isomorphism between 'race', 'class' and 'gender' ...(van Krieken, 1999: 304).

Appreciating the discursive qualities of policy and the role of experts in 'discovering' social problems suggests there were few contradictions between the overriding racial intent of child removal policies and the outcomes. From the very beginning, there was no inconsistency between the intent to remove children and the psychological and social effects of separating the child from family and culture. Australia's racial hygiene policies were intended to produce a terrible outcome – the obliteration of the Aboriginal people. That this program also exposed some children who were removed to additional abuse added insult to the basic injury.

The official discourse held that it was entirely congruent to pursue colonialist objectives of 'civilising the new world' while pursuing the 'best interests' of the child. Young half-castes and other 'problem youths', it was argued, were better off in 'nice white Christian homes'. Taking them from their own families was 'for their own good' and for the good of 'White Australia'. The mission to civilise superseded all other policy objectives.

Note

¹ See Anon, 1997; Anon, 1993 a and b; Wood Commission, 1997.

References

Alain-G. Gagnon, 1989, Social Scientists and Public Policies, *International Social Sciences Journal*, 122, no.4: 455-467.

Angus, G., and Woodward, S. 1995, *Child Abuse and neglect Australia 1993-1994*, Child Welfare Series, No 13, Canberra, Australian Institute of Health and Welfare, AGPS.

Anon. 1986, *Boys' Town to Keany College 1936-1986*, Congregation of Christian Brothers, WA Province.

Anon. 1993a, *My Heart is Breaking: A Joint Guide to Records about Aboriginal People in the Public Record Office of Victoria*, AGPS.

Anon. 1993b, *To Report or Not Report: A Study of Victim/Survivors of Sexual Assault and Their Experience of Making Initial Reports to the Police*, CASA House, Melbourne.

Australian Archives. 1993, *Between Two Worlds*, AGPS, Canberra.

Baker, J. 1979, 'Social Conscience and Social Policy', *Journal of Social Policy*, vol. 8, April.

Bean, P., and Melville, J. 1990, *Lost Children of the Empire: The Untold Story of Britain's child Migrants*, Unwin Hyman Limited, London.

Bennett, D. 2000, 'The Cubillo and Gunner Cases', *Quadrant*, vol. XLIV, no. 11, pp. 25-41.

Berry, J. 1992, *Lead Us Not Unto Temptation*, Doubleday, Sydney.

Bersford, P., and Croft, S. 1994, It's Our Problem Too! Challenging the Exclusion of Poor People from Poverty Discourse, *Critical Social Policy Issues*, 15 (2), pp: 75-96.

Beveridge W. 1953, *Power and Influence*, Hutchinson, London.

Brett, J. 1997, Every morning as the sun came up: the enduring pain of the stolen generation, *Times Literary Supplement*, 3 October: 4-5.

Briggs, F. 1996, *Child Sexual Abuse: Confronting the Problem*, Sydney, Allen and Unwin.

Briggs, F (ed.) 1995, *From Victim to Offender: How Child Sexual Abuse Victims Become Offenders*, Allen and Unwin, Sydney.

Brooks, S. 1994, 'Policy Communities and the Social Sciences', in S. Brooks and Alain G. Gagnon (eds), *The Political Influence of Ideas*, Praeger, Westport.

Burt, C. 1938, *The Young Delinquent*, University of London, London, 1938 (3rd edition).

Callahan, M. and Lamb, C. 1995, My Cheque and My Children: The Long Road to Empowerment in Child Welfare, *Child Welfare Journal of Policy, Practice and Program*, 74 (3): 715-809.

Carpenter, M. 1851 (facsimile reprint 1970) *Reformatory Schools for the Children of the Dangerous and Criminal Classes*, Montclair, New Jersey.

Carrington, K. 1993, *Offending Girls Sex Youth and Justice*, Allen and Unwin, Sydney.

Cohen, S. 1993, Human Rights and Crimes of the State: The Culture of Denial, *Australian New Zealand Journal of Criminology*, July, 26: 97-115.

Cohen, S. 2001, *States of Denial: Knowing about Atrocities and Suffering*, Polity Press, Cambridge.

Coldrey, B. M. 1993, *The Scheme: the Christian Brothers and Childcare in Western Australia*, Argyle-Pacific Publishing, Western Australia.

Commission of Inquiry into Abuse of Children in Queensland Institutions. 1999, May, QLD Government Printers.

Dalton, T., Weeks, W., Draper, M. and Wiseman, J. 1996, *Making Social Policy in Australia*, Allen and Unwin, Sydney.

Davies, K. 1994, *When Innocence Trembles*, Angus and Robertson, Sydney, Harper Collins.

Fernandez, E. 1996, *Significant Harm: Unraveling Child Protection Decisions and Substitute Care Careers of Children 1996*, Black Swan, London.

Fogarty, J. 1993, *Protective Services for Children In Victoria: A Report*, Community Service Victoria, Melbourne.

Gandevia, B. 1978, *Tears Often Shed: Child Health and Welfare in Australia from 1788*, Pergamon Press, Rushcutters Bay.

Gill, A. 1997, *Orphans of the Empire: The Shocking Story of Child Migration to Australia*, Vintage, Melbourne.

Gorton, J. 1998, *Sydney Morning Herald*, 30 May.

Gough, I. 1979, *Political Economy of the Welfare State*, Macmillan, London.

Grabosky, P. 1989, *Wayward Governance: Illegality and its Control in the Public Sector*, Australian Institute of Criminology, Canberra.

Habermas J. 1974, *Legitimation Crisis*, Beacon Press, Boston.

Hall, P. 1990, Policy Paradigms, Experts and the State: The Case of Macro Economic Policy Making in Britain in New York: 53-78.

Hall, S.G. 1905, 'Adolescence its Psychology and its relations to Physiology, Anthropology, Sociology, Sex, crime, Religion and Education', Vols 1 and 2, Appleton and Company, New York.

Heclo, H. and Masden, H. 1987, *Policy and Politics in Sweden: Principled Pragmatism*, Philadelphia.

Howson, P. 1999, 'Rescued from the Rabbit Burrow', *Quadrant*, June Vol XLIII, No 6, pp. 10-14.

Hughes, D. 1994, *Don't You Sing! Memories of a Catholic Boyhood*, Kangaroo Press, Kenthurst.

Human Rights and Equal Opportunity Commission. 1997, *Bringing Them Home: Report of the National Inquiry into the Separation of Aboriginal and Torres Strait Islander Children From Families*, Sterling, Sydney.

Human Service – Victorian Department of – 1997, *Overview of High Risk Adolescents in Placement and Support Services*, Victorian Government, Melbourne.

Human Service – Victorian Department of – 1997b, *Secure Welfare Services Review*, Victorian Government, Melbourne.

Jaggs, D. 1991, *Asylum to Action: Family Action 1851-1991: A history of services and policy development for families in times of vulnerability*, Family Action Advocacy Research, Oakleigh.

Jaggs, D. 1986, *Neglected and Criminal: Foundations of Child Welfare Legislation in Victoria*, Centre for Youth Community Studies, Philip Institute of Technology, Melbourne.

Kingdon, J. 1984, *Agendas, Alternatives, and Public Policies*, Little Brown Books, Boston.

MacKinnon, L. 1992, Child Abuse in Context: The Participants' View, Sydney: University of Sydney (Ph.D thesis).

Maddock, K. 2000, Genocide and the silence of the anthropologists, *Quadrant*, vol XLIV, no. 11, pp.11- 16.

Manne, R. 1998, The Stolen Generations, *Quadrant*, 42, 1-2: 53-63.

Markus, A. 1989, *Governing Savages*, Allen and Unwin, Sydney.

Marsh, R. 1999, 'Lost', 'stolen' or 'rescued', *Quadrant*, June, vol XLIII, no. 6, pp. 115-18.

Marshall, T.H. 1951, *Social Policy,* Allen and Unwin, London.

McCrae, C.R. 1934, *Psychology and Education*, Whitcombe and Tombs Limited, Sydney.

McGregor, R. 1997, *Imagined Destines: Aboriginal Australians and the Doomed Race Theory 1880-1939*, Melbourne University Press, Melbourne.

McGuiness, P. 2000, 'Aboriginal massacres and stolen children', *Quadrant*, vol XLIV, no. 11, pp. 2- 4.

Meagher, D. 2000, 'Not guilty?', *Quadrant*, vol XLIV, no. 11, pp. 11-16.

O'Connor, J. 1973, *The Fiscal Crisis of the State*, St. James Press, New York.

Offe, C. 1983, *Contradictions of the Welfare State*, Blackwell, Oxford.

Polanyi, K. 1944, *The Great Transformation*, Rinehart and Co., NY.

Read, P. 1983, *The Stolen Generations: The Removal of Aboriginal children in New South Wales, 1883 to 1969*, Ministry for Aboriginal Affairs, Sydney.

Royal Commission into Aboriginal Deaths in Custody 1989, Report of the Inquiry into the Death of Malcolm Charles Smith, by Commissioner J H Wootten, AGPS, Canberra.

Scott, D., and Swain, S. 2002, *Confronting Cruelty: Historical Perspectives on Child Protection in Australia*, Melbourne University Press, Melbourne.

Simon, H A. 1945, *Administrative Behaviour*, first edition, Free Press, Illinois.

South Australian Government, 1996, *Interim Submission to the National Inquiry into the Separation of Aboriginal Children and Torres Strait Islander Children from their Families.*

Stokes, E. 1994, *Innocence Abroad: The Story of Child Evacuees in Australia 1940-1945*, Allen and Unwin, Sydney.

Swaine, S. and Howe, R. 1995, *Single Mothers and their Children: Disposal Punishment and Survival in Australian*, Cambridge University Press, Oakleigh.

Thorpe, D. 1994, Evaluating Child Protection, Open University Press, London,

van Kreiken, R. 1990, *Children and the state*, Allen and Unwin, Sydney.

Victorian Child Death Review Committee – VCDRC, 1996, Human Services, Victoria.

Weber, M. 1947, *The Theory of Social and Economic Organisation*, trans, A M Henderson and T. Parsons (ed.), The Free Press, Glencoe.

Weber, M. 1949, *Methodology of the Social Sciences*, Trans and edited by E.A Shils and H.A Finch, Glencoe, The Free Press. *Wood Royal Commission into the New South Wales Police Service*, Final Report. 1997, NSW Government.

Postscript: Which Way is Up?

JOHN PITTS

...if you cannot bring good news then don't bring any

(Bob Dylan – The Wicked Messenger – 1968 Dwarf Music)

Which way is up?

This book not only offers ironic testimony to the unintended consequences of governmental crime control policies, it also suggests that the real purpose of these policies may be to control politically unpopular elements amongst the socially excluded rather than crime itself. Indeed, the book offers ample evidence that western governments in their pursuit of political popularity and electoral credibility have often demonised, and in so doing compounded, the exclusion of these populations (Feely & Simon 1992, Young 1999). This book also points, therefore, to the complexity of the task confronting those who would attempt to achieve progressive reform in the criminal justice system. Their problem is compounded by critical criminology's ambivalence about reform, too close an association with the state apparatus, and the fact that, in late- or post-modernity, or whenever it is we are supposed to be living, the very idea of progress has become problematised to the point where, quite literally, we are no longer sure which way is up.

Yet, as recent governments, in the UK at least, have taken ever greater political and fiscal power into their own hands, and as crime has become ever more central to their electoral credibility, the ability of both critical criminologists and system agents to influence policy and practice has been progressively eroded. Whereas in the not so distant past the impetus for change sometimes flowed upwards from the field to an occasionally receptive government, now the impetus for change flows down and prescription has taken the place of dialogue. This represents a significant re-configuration and concentration of power in the hands of a government which is using this power to pursue a strategy of penal populism. If criminological science has advanced, it has also fragmented, and criminologists now speak in a multiplicity of voices. In these circumstances governments have utilised science pragmatically, incorporating those scientific discourses which articulate most closely with their policy objectives, which come to serve as sources of both illumination and legitimation, as the slightly exaggerated depiction below indicates.

The Handmaiden's Tale

Britain's New Labour government, on the rare occasions it deigns to do so, castigates criminology's critiques as ideologically inspired anachronisms, being both pre-scientific and woefully inadequate to the problems of 'real-world' crime. We are living, New Labour argues, in a post-ideological era in which policy is formulated in accordance with the dictates of scientific rationality rather than redundant ideological posturing. And, indeed, behind the scenes a small army of uncritical criminologists, once dismissed as mere 'handmaidens of the status quo' (Taylor, Walton & Young 1973), are gleefully furnishing the state with the requisite 'non-ideological', 'scientific' and 'practical' prescriptions for action. Uncritical criminology (via the risk-factor paradigm and its derivatives) has, in recent years, achieved a level of political influence quite incommensurate with its explanatory power or intellectual bite (Farrington 2001). Nonetheless, it is the criminological perspective which gives substance to New Labour's claim that its criminal justice policies are 'evidence-led' and the practices of its agents are 'evidence-based'. (Tilley 2001) Meanwhile out in the real world, despite an unprecedented drop in the crime rate over the past eight years, unprecedented numbers of children and adults are being placed under penal control and surveillance.

The Curse of Wittgenstein

At the same time, back at the deteriorating campuses of the cash-strapped 'new universities', critical criminologists of a more relativistic bent, view these developments as a mere moment in the perennial struggle between a multiplicity of power-hungry political, professional and intellectual protagonists to totalise a set of socio-cultural practices into a single discursive formation. Thus the competing claims of 'welfarism', 'progressive minimalism', the 'justice model' or 'penal populism' represent neither a truth nor an untruth about a world out there (if indeed they feel able to speak of 'truth' or 'world' as anything other than tentatively held social constructs). They are merely 'truth claims', linguistic camouflage for political professional and intellectual power plays. The elegance of their arguments is matched only by their almost total irrelevance to the real problems encountered by both the perpetrators and the victims of crime, the bulk of whom are 'socially excluded', out there in the real world.

A Third Way?

We therefore face a dilemma, all too familiar to leftward-leaning criminologists, that while the present tome may offer a 'right riveting read' to the converted, it also testifies to the marginality of critical criminology to the politics, policy, and day-to-day practice within contemporary justice systems. Having thrown in our lot with the socially excluded, we risk being consigned to the ranks of the intellectually excluded because we fail to comply with what appears to be the fundamental injunction upon politically relevant intellectuals in the modern era, namely that if you cannot bring 'good news' you should not bring any. Yet, beyond the progressive triumphalism of the 'new youth justice' and the post-modern nihilism of the sociology department at the end of its tether, lies another possibly, one which I shall avoid describing as a 'Third Way' but with some apprehension will call 'critical engagement'. The issue of critical engagement took on particular urgency for me recently when my article about recent developments in youth justice in the UK, upon which the chapter in this book is based, first appeared (Pitts 2001).

Welcome Aboard?

The article was, apparently, very well received by workers, managers and others professionally involved with young people in the youth justice system. I think this was because some of the problems I pinpointed were those with which they were grappling. The article was not welcomed nearly so warmly by the Youth Justice Board of England and Wales (YJB), whose role in these matters I had criticised. Indeed, one or two members of the

Board objected that youth justice in Britain would be improved significantly if critical academics like myself would stop 'carping on the sidelines', and 'get on board'. A somewhat ironic turn of phrase this, since at the time, some YJB members were threatening to 'jump ship' in protest at Home Secretary David Blunkett's latest draconian youth justice proposal.

Tentatively up the Gangplank

Nonetheless, because the YJB numbers amongst its members recognised 'progressives' in youth justice, the suggestion that critical academics should 'get on board' governmental or quasi-governmental initiatives to improve youth justice systems, is not on the face of it an unreasonable one. More so perhaps, because one of the criticisms I had levelled at government, and by implication the YJB, was that they had been highly, indeed suspiciously, selective in terms of the experts to whom they were prepared to listen, the theories they chose to embrace and the interventions they endorsed.

However, critical criminologists must perforce be suspicious of such invitations because, all too often an apparent desire on the part of government to embrace its critics as 'partners in progress' may well mask a less creditable urge to marginalise, discredit or silence the critique. Moreover, I also divined that one of the implications of this ambiguous invitation was that vigorous public debate, of the type I was attempting to foster in the article, tended to inhibit progress. Regrettably, this desire to 'pull the plug' on critical debate of policy is no mere foible of the YJB, but a defining characteristic of the entire New Labour project.

Confronted with the all too familiar charge by government, or those close to government, that everything was proceeding very nicely until the critic 'stuck their oar in' (to continue the nautical leitmotif) the academic critic of public policy must reply that a defining characteristic of democratic societies is that vigorous public debate is a pre-requisite of progressive action and that the freedom to participate in such debate is a key element of citizenship. Edward Said (1994) has argued that academics have a particular responsibility in this regard, because their profession offers them both the opportunity and the means to gain privileged insights into pertinent public issues. Thus, Said enjoins them to put their analyses into the public domain and 'speak the truth to power', however politically uncomfortable this might be for the powerful. In this perspective, the citizens of a democratic society are best served if the academic, and for that matter the professional, resists the ever-present temptation to serve as an apologist for the ephemeral ambitions of governments and speaks out. This does not mean that academics cannot contribute to the development of improved policies, procedures and practices. It does mean, however, that in doing so they should honour their responsibility to maintain a critical dialogue with government rather than becoming what Taylor Walton and Young (1973) once described as a 'handmaiden of the status quo'. It is in this spirit that I accepted the invitation to clamber 'aboard' extended by members of the YJB. What such acceptance means will become evident to me as I pursue its implications. It will certainly entail a detailed and critical re-working of the evidence which currently informs policy and practice and a quest for fresh evidence with which to flesh out an alternative, realistic, and radically de-politicised, yet fully social, alternative perspective and active engagement with policy-makers and practitioners.

So, my postscript takes the form of a request. And it is that the follow-up tome to this excellent book, and there must surely be one, will embrace the idea of critical engagement so that, for once, critical criminology is not left standing on the sidelines being right but ineffective, but out there winning the arguments and effecting change.

References

Farrington D. (2000) *Explaining and Preventing Crime: The Globalisation of Knowledge, Criminology,* Vol.38 No.1 February 1-24.

Feeley M. & Simon J. (1992) *The New Penology: Notes on the Emerging Strategy of Corrections and its Implementation, Criminology,* 30(4) pp.452-74.

Pitts J. (2001) *The New Politics of Youth Crime: Discipline or Solidarity,* Basingstoke, Macmillan/Palgrave.

Said E. (1994) *Representations of the Intellectual,* London, Vintage.

Taylor I. Walton P. & Young J. (1973) *The New Criminology,* London, Routledge & Kegan Paul.

Tilley N. (2001) *Evaluation and Evidence-led Crime Reduction Policy,* Matthews R. & Pitts J. (eds.) Crime Disorder and Community Safety, London, Routledge.

Young J. (1999) *The Exclusive Society,* London, Sage Publications.